CW00797316

THE REAL PROBLEMS DESTROYING EDUCATION

AND EVERYONE IS TO BLAME

BRYAN THOMAS WETZEL

THE REAL PROBLEMS DESTROYING EDUCATION

AND EVERYONE IS TO BLAME

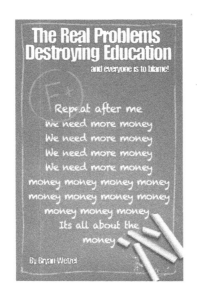

1

ACKNOWLEDGEMENT

If it weren't for the unwavering support and love of my children, wife, and the incredible upbringing I had with my loving mother, life would feel devoid and impersonal. To my beloved Carrie, words cannot fully capture the immense love I have for each of you, and it is your love that ignites my inner drive to continuously strive for self-improvement and be the best husband and father I can possibly be. To our kids, Ethan, Daniel, Sophia, and Olivia, your presence in my life brings warmth and meaning to every day.

2

PREFACE

In 2011, a group of passionate entrepreneurs and I embarked on a mission to establish an education company that would revolutionize the way students learn. Our vision was to create a comprehensive collection of educational videos tailored specifically for K-12 students, accompanied by quizzes that would reinforce their understanding of the content. Essentially, we aimed to develop a K-12 version of the highly successful Lynda.com platform.

At that time, the education landscape was undergoing significant changes with the impending implementation of the common core curriculum. Recognizing this opportunity, we were determined to be at the forefront of content creation, ensuring that our materials reached parents and schools before any other competitors.

Our primary objective was to expand Skubes.com beyond just videos, encompassing a wide range of K-12 educational resources such as assessments, interactive learning tools, and tutoring materials. To achieve this, we carefully selected experienced and highly recommended teachers to create the lessons for their respective grade levels. For example, a second-grade teacher with years of experience in the classroom would be the ideal candidate to develop video content for second-grade lessons. Their expertise allowed them to effectively communicate with students at their level, anticipate common questions, and address challenging concepts in a way that resonated with second graders.

By adopting this targeted approach, we firmly believed that our content surpassed that of our competitors. We initially focused on math and language arts before expanding into history and science, ensuring a well-rounded educational experience for students.

Despite our unwavering dedication, securing the necessary investments to develop an extensive content library and assemble a sales team, programmers, and other essential personnel proved to be a significant challenge. However, by the time we closed our operations in 2017, we had successfully created over 1,500 educational videos for K-12 education. These videos featured real teachers who brought their expertise and passion into the creation process. Additionally, we developed more than 2,000 short, interactive quizzes and assessments to complement each video, further enhancing the learning experience.

I take immense pride in the content we produced and the countless hours of hard work our teachers invested in crafting educational materials of the highest quality. Many of our videos can still be found on popular platforms like YouTube, continuing to benefit students to this day.

Throughout my journey with Skubes.com, I had the privilege of engaging with educators, administrators, and parents, gaining invaluable insights into the education system. These experiences, which I will share in this book, provided me with a unique perspective as an entrepreneur, husband, and a parent with children in the education system. It is my hope that this book will spark meaningful discussions and debates surrounding the challenges and opportunities within education.

Organizing the content of this book presented its own set of challenges. Some sections could have easily fit into multiple chapters. For instance, discussions about parents' interactions with teachers could have been placed in either the teacher or parent section. However, in most cases, I opted to place these discussions in the chapters that best reflected the individuals most affected by the outcomes, and some were split across more than one chapter.

INTRODUCTION

Much of this book is based on my personal experiences as a parent, the owner of an education technology company, and the husband of a teacher. Through these different perspectives, I have gained valuable insights into the public education system. However, it was my interactions with teachers and administrators that truly opened my eyes to the realities of education. In addition to drawing from my own observations, I have conducted extensive research and conducted interviews with 63 current and retired educators. Through this thorough process, I have gained valuable insights and formed some very strong opinions. The purpose of this book is to shed light on the hidden aspects of education that parents are often unaware of.

When we founded my education technology company in 2011, I, like many teachers, was driven by the enthusiasm to make a difference in children's education. We believed that our work had a meaningful purpose and set meaningful goals. However, as time went on, the system gradually eroded our optimism, leaving us feeling cynical and disillusioned. As an entrepreneur with over 25 years of experience, I expected that the inner workings of the education system would become more apparent as I gained a better understanding of the decision-making processes. Unfortunately, I was mistaken. Instead, I found myself even more perplexed, as you will soon discover in this book.

The term "education system" implies a well-functioning and efficient machine. However, the reality is that the American education system is dysfunctional in every aspect. There is a lack of smooth processes and logical decision-making. As you will see in this book, a comprehensive overhaul of the education system is necessary to address its deep-rooted issues. However, I am skeptical that such a transformation will occur, as there are numerous vested interests that prefer to maintain the status quo. The challenge of fixing education lies in the fact that it is not a matter of addressing one or two isolated problems. It requires tackling many areas of dysfunction, each with its own set of sub-issues.

Before delving further into the book, I want to issue a warning to those who are politically correct or easily offended. I have chosen not to adhere to political correctness in this book because I believe it is important to address the root causes of our problems honestly and openly. Many of our problems in this country never get solved because it's what people won't say or are afraid to say that is never a part of the open discussion. If any of my statements offend you, I apologize in advance. I stand by every word I have written. My intention is not to harm or offend anyone but rather to encourage critical thinking and provoke honest conversations. If you find yourself offended, I urge you to reflect on why that is. Is it because my words challenge what you have been told or what you already believe? It is crucial to recognize that there is no hidden agenda or wizard behind the curtain.

I began writing this book at the end of 2019, but due to the Covid crisis, I had to put it on hold. In a way, this pause may have been a blessing in disguise. The pandemic has brought many issues, including education, into the spotlight. It has exposed the abuses of power within many school systems and made parents in various states and counties realize that they have lost touch with their children's education. The focus of educators has shifted from teaching fundamental subjects like reading, writing, and math to social issues that may or may not align with the values of the parents in the community. The pandemic has revealed that many teachers see themselves not only as educators but also as influencers of their students' moral and social beliefs. This shift in priorities has resulted in less time being dedicated to essential subjects.

While some may argue that standardized test scores still hold importance, the continued decline in scores raises doubts about the seriousness with which these subjects are being taught. However, as you will discover in this book, the responsibility for the breakdown of education cannot be solely attributed to administrators or teachers; it is a shared responsibility.

I anticipate that some individuals will attempt to discredit this book by framing arguments along political lines. I make this prediction because today's discourse tends to be polarized along left or right ideologies. However, I want to assure you of two things: First, I have interviewed individuals from both ends of the political spectrum. Second, I did not conduct a survey to determine the political leanings of those I interviewed. Instead, I focused on their expertise and experiences, recognizing that valuable insights can come from individuals regardless of their political affiliations.

In the upcoming chapters, we will explore education from an insider's perspective and examine the external factors that contribute to its challenges. These external factors include parents, the home environment, and the influence of social media. The extent to which these factors impact education is a subject of debate, but they undoubtedly play a role in shaping student behavior and focus.

Let me reiterate: the breakdown of the education system is not solely the fault of the system itself or those in positions of authority. As we'll explore in this book, parents, students, and politicians also bear responsibility. From the federal level down to the smallest municipality, the education system is influenced by the demands and expectations of these stakeholders. However, each group has its own interests to serve, and their proposed solutions often diverge.

The issues surrounding education are vast and complex, and my initial outline for the chapters suggests that this book could easily exceed 1,000 pages. However, I am mindful of the limited attention span of many parents today, which is often mirrored by their children. My goal is for parents to read this book and reflect on how they can make informed decisions for their children's future and the future of our country.

Despite the numerous challenges we face, there is a glimmer of hope. The increasing number of parents choosing to withdraw their children from the public school system in recent years clearly indicates the growing awareness surrounding the issues plaguing public education. And maybe that will be the wake-up call administrators need to re-evaluate their policies and methods. Allow me to present some eye-opening statistics to further emphasize this point.

In the bustling metropolis of New York City alone, the NY Post reported that 3.4 percent of the 1 million students were withdrawn from public schools by their concerned parents as of November 2020[1]. This exodus demonstrates the gravity of the situation and the urgent need for change. Additionally, across the vast state of California, K-12 enrollment took a nosedive, with a staggering 160,000 students opting out of the public school system[2]. This represents a significant 3 percent decrease, marking the largest enrollment decline in two decades. The numbers speak volumes, even in the renowned Los Angeles Unified School District.. Enrollment plummeted by a staggering 27,000 students, constituting a nearly 6 percent decrease[3]. These figures not only exceeded the predictions of district planners but were also rather unusual considering the overall increase in population.

Furthermore, the power of social media platforms like YouTube has allowed concerned parents to voice their grievances and rally for change[4]. Countless videos depict passionate parents delivering impassioned speeches before their county's school board, demanding solutions and improvements to the current state of public education.

It is essential to acknowledge that public education in America is facing significant challenges. Ignoring these issues would be detrimental to the future of our children.

Lastly, if you are an educator reading this book, it is important to acknowledge that not all of the issues discussed may be present in every school. Some of the challenges addressed tend to be more prominent in specific districts or regions. The purpose of this book, however, is to prevent these problems from permeating the entire education system as a whole.

---

1. https://nypost.com/2020/11/14/thousands-of-families-yanking-kids-out-of-nyc-public-schools/
2. https://edsource.org/2021/projected-k-12-drops-in-enrollment-pose-immediate-upheaval-and-decade-long-challenge/662531
3. https://www.ocregister.com/2021/10/22/california-school-districts-see-plummeting-enrollment/
4. https://www.youtube.com/results?search_query=parents+speaking+out+at+school+board+meetings

4

SYSTEM ERROR..MORE MONEY
NEEDED

*"If money were the solution, the problems with education would
already be solved."*
Jay Greene

Education in this country is currently a broken system. I'm
not one to be overly dramatic, and I do not want to be later
lumped in with the people who us afraid of Y2K, but education, as a system, is broken! If parents were granted a firsthand glimpse into the inner workings of education, I believe
they would be genuinely concerned. The system, as a whole,
needs a top-down overhaul that I fear will never happen.
Because a top-down overhaul means that everyone at the
top has to agree that there's a problem, starting with people
at the top. And the people at the top have almost no incentive to make changes. For the most part, in my experience,
most education systems are fraught with rules, regulations,
embedded politics, and yearly policy decisions that make
very little sense. And much of it has little to do with making
education better for the students in the system. Of course,
everyone at the top would disagree and say that it has every-

thing to do with improving education for the students. Education, from the federal government to the state, county, & city, is a government bureaucracy, and it functions about as well as any other government bureaucracy. The only difference is that this is where our kids spend most of their non-sleeping time from kindergarten till they graduate high school.

The education system, as a whole, is a lot of government systems all trying to work together, from the federal system to the local systems, each trying to please the larger system above it. Satisfying the system above is necessary to collect the funds being passed down to each lower system in the chain. Non-compliance means losing money or some leader not climbing the ladder to a higher-paying job. Some people may believe that money is the root of all evil, but people at the top of the education system want you to think it's the root of all education failures. And they've done a great job selling this to the people. According to a PEPG survey (Performance Evaluation and Professional Growth), 51 percent of surveyed say that spending on public education should increase, and more money would fix education[1].

In an article on Wallethub.com about the best and worst school systems, the writer explains, "But the quality of public school systems varies widely from state to state and is often a question of funding.[2]" Does the writer honestly believe this? Did they write it because that's the popular opinion? If you line up a chart of states based on school spending and put it next to a chart of schools based on performance...guess what? The argument that more spending in schools simply doesn't hold up. I've searched for and never found any evidence that more school spending equals better education. It simply doesn't exist. Not even anecdotally. And it doesn't buy you better teachers, either. I've witnessed this firsthand, which we'll dive into later in greater detail. Most online articles about money helping education are merely pro-public school hacks stating this as if it were fact. At best, the idea that more money will fix this nation's educational woes is a guess because many of the people making such claims have no other ideas. However, when we compare private and public school teachers, certain trends emerge. On average, private school teachers make about 28 percent less and have fewer benefits than their counterparts in public schools[3]. Despite this, they seem to produce better education outcomes and are generally happier in their jobs. Indeed, most private schools do not allow students with disciplinary problems to remain in their schools, which makes for a less disruptive environment for the teachers. That alone probably leads to happier teachers. Dealing with problem students is the constant pushback that most public school administrators point to as a defense for why public schools do not reach the same quality as private schools. But if dealing with problem students is all it takes to fix the quality of public education, let us explore some options!

I started this chapter by talking about a top-down recon-struction of the education system... if you are one of the many convinced that reconstruction should start with addi-tional funding, then my assertions will disappoint you. The system is dysfunctional, and it's not for lack of money. Addi-tional funds will not fix what ails the education system and, especially, the biggest issue with student performance. But if we're going to argue for more money, let us use the funds already being wasted. In this book, I will go over the many ways money earmarked for education is wasted each year. If scores incrementally increased each time more money was put into the system, then we could assume that adding more money would continue to improve student scores. The chart showing the historical spending on education shows that education spending has increased dramatically, and yet student performance hasn't gone up; it's gone down[4].

The numbers vary by state, as you can see from the chart. There are 42 states where public schools spend more per student than it costs to send that same student to a private school[5]. And how do the test scores compare from private to public? By focusing on high school graduates in the year 2021, it is interesting to note that private school students attained higher scores on the ACT test. In fact, they outperformed their public school counterparts by an average of 4 points[67].

Average Cost of Private School by State	2021	These are the 42 States Where Private Schools Spend Less than Public
Alaska - $6,790	Kansas - $7,937	Ohio - $7,001
Alabama - $7,282	Kentucky - $7,159	Oklahoma - $6,514
Arkansas - $6,107	Louisiana - $6,925	Oregon - $9,775
Arizona - $10,508	Maryland - $13,054	Pennsylvania - $11,637
California - $14,975	Michigan - $7,191	South Carolina - $6,909
Colorado - $12,219	Minnesota - $6,994	South Dakota - $3,624
Delaware -$11,158	Missouri - $9,998	Tennessee - $10,185
Florida - $9,160	Mississippi - $5,542	Texas - $9,866
Georgia - $10,675	Montana - $8,771	Utah - $11,204
Hawaii - $13,206	North Carolina - $9,947	Virginia - $14,274
Iowa - $5,268	Nebraska - $3,797	Washington - $11,812
Idaho - $8,293	New Jersey - $13,936	Wisconsin - $4,591
Illinois - $8,273	New Mexico - $8,884	West Virginia - $6,239
Indiana - $7,120	Nevada - $10,561	Wyoming - $7,238

This discrepancy is supported by the National Center for Education Statistics (NCES), which also highlights a similar pattern for primary and middle schools. When comparing mathematics test results, private school eighth graders scored an impressive 18 points higher than their public school counterparts, while fourth graders achieved an 8-point advantage[8]. The trend continues in the field of reading, where private school students achieved a notable 18-point lead in the eighth grade and a 15-point lead in the fourth grade[9].

It is important to acknowledge that certain variables may contribute to this disparity. For example, it is widely recognized that parents who opt to invest in private education often exhibit a higher level of involvement in their children's academic journey. Consequently, these parents are more likely to motivate and encourage their children, fostering an environment that promotes dedication and high achievement. This aspect, alone, may account for the superior performance of private schools. In the subsequent chapter, we will delve deeper into the crucial role parents play in education. Jay Greene, the esteemed author of "Education Myths," astutely asserts, "If money were the solution, the problems with education would already be solved ... We've doubled per pupil spending, adjusting for inflation, over the last 30 years, and yet schools aren't better[10]."

What makes these statistics even more intriguing is the difficulty in obtaining them. Numerous sources, such as the teachers union and various pro-public school organizations, present vast amounts of contradictory data in an attempt to discredit these facts. Consequently, I had to personally collect and analyze the data from each state.

Many people hate it when business people or entrepreneurs compare running a government to running a business. It's a valid comparison from the eyes of someone who understands that a system that doesn't have to earn its income will always suffer from a lack of genuine desire to fix itself and improve. I can prove that the people running the system have no motivation to correct the problem.

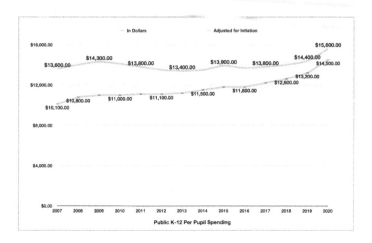

All you have to do is focus on how many people in any education system move up to bigger paychecks when their leadership at the lower levels made no difference or improvements in the locations they managed. Since education receives tax money, whether they perform well or not, they have no incentive to make changes for the better. They aren't expecting education to go out of business anytime soon as a new pile of taxpayer money will be coming down the pike to spend each year. However, a company must continue to perform well if it wants to continue receiving funds or increasing the money it makes. I can tell you first-hand that there's already more than enough money in education. The problem is not the amount but how it's used and how it is distributed. The funniest part is that the teacher's unions and the school districts both celebrate and brag about how much they spend and how much they've increased spending. However, you'll never find either bragging about the results of increased spending because more money doesn't equal better education. We care enough to spend is the virtual signal flare they continue to send out. They never tell us what we're getting for the additional spending. In many cases, it's just bigger salaries at the top. If you knew how many times people would reach out to my company because they needed to unload unspent money so they wouldn't lose it in the following year's budget...you might scratch your head and wonder why that money wasn't already marked to be spent on resources that were already needed.

According to a 2016 article from US News, the inflation-adjusted spending per student in American public schools has increased by 663 percent since World War II. This substantial increase in funding raises the question: where has all this money been allocated? One major area where the funds have been directed is the hiring of additional personnel. Between 1950 and 2009, the student population in American public schools grew by 96 percent. Remarkably, during that same period, schools increased their staff by a staggering 386 percent - four times the rate of student population growth. The number of teachers alone increased by 252 percent, which is more than 2.5 times the growth rate of students. Furthermore, the number of administrators and other staff members soared by over seven times the increase in students[11].

Public education by state rankings on a per-pupil spending basis as of 2021	List of public school Academic rankings 2021
Massachusetts: $19,776	1
New Jersey: $25,387	2
Connecticut: $21,658	3
Wisconsin: $16,543	4
Virginia: $12,303	5
Vermont: $20,276	6
Illinois: $18,215	7
Maryland: $16,121	8
Minnesota: $15,174	9
New Hampshire: $28,345	10
Utah: $8,830	11
Kentucky: $12,248	12
Colorado: $15,158	13
New York: $38,270	14
Pennsylvania: $15,665	15
Missouri: $10,855	16
Ohio: $13,237	17
Tennessee: $10,022	18
Iowa: $13,767	19
North Carolina: $9,637	20
Indiana: $11,226	21
Montana: $17,245	22
Nebraska: $17,818	23
Arkansas: $10,945	24
Delaware: $13,555	25
Kansas: $14,392	26
Florida: $14,989	27
Texas: $12,640	28
Maine: $14,954	29

Public education by state rankings on a per-pupil spending basis as of 2021	List of public school Academic rankings 2021
Rhode Island: $22,652	30
Georgia: $11,952	31
Michigan: $13,691	32
Wyoming: $25,795	33
California: $16,042	34
Washington: $17,238	35
Hawaii: $12,855	36
South Dakota: $15,244	37
District of Columbia: $29,115	38
Alabama: $10,820	39
North Dakota: $15,624	40
South Carolina: $10,767	41
Idaho: $9,214	42
Nevada: $15,650	43
Oregon: $13,171	44
Arizona: $10,827	45
West Virginia: $11,778	46
Oklahoma: $10,249	47
Louisiana: $12,079	48
Alaska: $25,710	49
Mississippi: $10,908	50
New Mexico: $14,983	51

Surprisingly, despite this significant surge in staffing, educational outcomes were actually better in 1950. This trend of a staffing surge in American public schools continues to persist to this day. For instance, from 1992 to 2014, there was a 19 percent increase in the student population, and yet the staffing levels saw a larger increase of 36 percent[12]. The decades-long surge in staffing has been an expensive endeavor for taxpayers, but it has not resulted in significant improvements in student achievement. This raises doubts about the assumption that increased funding directly leads to better educational outcomes. If this were the case, we would expect to see a correlation between high spending and high academic achievement scores. However, this is not always the reality. For example, states like New York and the District of Columbia, which spend substantial amounts on education, do not necessarily top the charts in academic achievement. On the other hand, states like Virginia and Utah, despite spending comparatively less per student, achieve higher academic results. These findings suggest that the relationship between funding and educational outcomes is not as straightforward as it may seem. Simply pouring more money into the system does not guarantee improved student achievement.

I have personally witnessed a striking disparity in school spending between Title One schools and non-Title One schools. Title One is a program to add additional funding to schools where more than 40 percent of students are from low-income families, as determined by free and reduced lunch programs[13]. When I visited Title One schools, I noticed that they had access to the latest technology and an abundance of resources for the entire student population. In stark contrast, non-Title One schools in 2015 typically had only one or two iPads or tablets per classroom. It was not uncommon for Title One schools to have such a surplus of tablet computers that they needed to repurpose an old library book cart as a tablet cart to transport them around the school.

I observed this stark contrast numerous times, particularly at the elementary and middle school levels. In every instance I am referencing, the Title One schools were underperforming in terms of academic achievement, while the non-Title One schools were either meeting or surpassing their academic scores.

It is important to note that the Title I program is a federal initiative established under the Elementary and Secondary Education Act (ESEA), as reauthorized by the No

Child Left Behind Act of 2001 (NCLB). This program sets forth the financial and programmatic requirements aimed at improving the academic achievement of students attending eligible Title I schools. The ultimate goal of Title I is to ensure that all children have an equitable and significant opportunity to receive a high-quality education and reach proficiency in challenging state academic standards and assessments.

Title I funds, as described by the Department of Education, are designed to provide additional academic support and learning opportunities for low-achieving children. These funds aim to help students master challenging curricula and meet state standards in core academic subjects. For instance, schools can use the funds to support extra instruction in reading and mathematics, as well as offer preschool, after-school, and summer programs that extend and reinforce the regular school curriculum[14].

On average, Title I grants exceed 16 billion dollars per year, and they are distributed across the country. As you might expect, this number continues to increase over time[15].

Contrary to what one might assume, the distribution of Title I funds is not test or score-based. Instead, schools can receive additional funding by ensuring that at least 40 percent of their student population is enrolled in Free and Reduced Lunch Programs[16]. The impact of this requirement is such that many schools actively work to maintain a high number of students on the Free and Reduced Lunch program. This is comparable to a welfare program that recipients do not want to see come to an end. I have had conversations with several principals who admitted that they make efforts to enroll enough students in the Free and Reduced Lunch program to secure additional funds each year. And it's understandable why they would do so.

A common complaint from non-Title I schools is that teachers often lack the necessary materials. In fact, many education companies, including mine, rarely conducted business in schools without Title I funds because those schools generally did not have the extra funds available.

Another interesting aspect of Title I funds, which is not uncommon in government spending, is that many schools end up with leftover money at the end of the year. In order to prevent a reduction in their funding for the following year, these schools would seek ways to spend their remaining funds. Although there were instances where they were not interested in our product or service, they still paid for it for multiple years just to meet the spending requirements and avoid a decrease in their budget.

Again, simply increasing funding will not fix the education system. In reality, it often results in financial gains for those who profit from education and larger paychecks for administrators at various levels of the education system (city, county, and state). Many administrators leverage the technologies they acquired as a resume booster to advance their careers and obtain higher-paying positions in education. Sadly, very few people inquire about the actual impact or outcomes of these expenditures. Administrators, much like politicians, tend to receive recognition for their efforts rather than the effectiveness of their actions.

Therefore, it is clear that more money alone cannot solve the challenges faced by the education system, and Title I funds serve as evidence of this fact. If increased funding truly improved the quality of education, then we would expect to see Title I schools consistently achieving higher test scores. However, this is not reflected in reality. Despite receiving significant additional funding over the years, these schools do not dominate the list of top-performing schools in their respective states.

Charter School Spending by Comparison

Massachusetts boasts one of the oldest charter school laws in the country and is home to some of the highest-performing charter schools in existence today. In particular, the charter schools in Boston have demonstrated remarkable success in fostering educational growth among low-income students. In February 2013, an analysis conducted by the Center for Research on Education Outcomes (CREDO) yielded compelling findings regarding the performance of students in Boston charter schools compared to their counterparts in traditional district schools. This study focused on matched student pairs and their MCAS (Massachusetts Comprehensive Assessment System) gains. The results of this analysis were remarkable, surpassing the findings of an earlier Harvard-MIT study. According to the CREDO report, students in Boston charter schools exhibited outstanding progress, equivalent to an additional 259 days of instruction in math and 245 days in reading when compared to their peers in traditional district schools. Put simply, the research unveiled that Boston charter school students are acquiring knowledge and skills at a rate that is more than twice the pace of their district-school counterparts[17]. However, not everyone shares the same enthusiasm. Certain groups, including the teachers' union, have expressed opposition to the state's Charter School Expansion Initiatives. Their argument centers around the concern that charter schools may not serve as many high-need students as their host districts,

creating a sense of inequality in educational opportunities[18]. Nonetheless, a comprehensive study conducted by
Stanford University in 2013 found that Boston charters were
actually doing more than any other group of public schools
nationwide to narrow the achievement gap[19].

Building upon this foundation, Professor Tom Kane of
Harvard led a research team that recently released a highly
publicized study. The study shows that charter schools in
Boston consistently outperform other public schools in the
city, including pilot schools. Professor Kane, who serves as
the faculty director of the Center for Education Policy
Research at the school, emphasizes that the charter school
movement in Massachusetts was initiated 15 years ago with
the goal of achieving gains in student achievement. The
results of this study undoubtedly indicate that charter
schools in Boston are making a significant difference in
fulfilling this objective[20].

Given the overwhelmingly positive outcomes of these
studies, one would expect individuals committed to the
well-being of our society and the next generation to
embrace and support any method or program that demonstrates such success. Unfortunately, the teacher's unions do
not share this sentiment.

A closer examination of the consistent positions taken
by the teacher's unions reveals a lack of interest in
promoting healthy competition or endorsing alternative
avenues that may surpass the current educational system.
Despite numerous studies and overwhelming evidence
supporting the benefits of charter schools, the teacher's
unions were able to successfully derail a significant ballot
initiative in Massachusetts.

In 2016, proponents of charter schools sought to include
a measure on the statewide ballot to allow for the establish-

ment of more charter schools in Massachusetts. However, this strategic move inadvertently played into the hands of the teacher's unions and other opponents of charter schools. These unions were able to mobilize their supporters and detractors of charter schools, creating a formidable force that actively campaigned against the initiative through phone calls and door-to-door canvassing[21].

As a result, the initiative suffered a resounding defeat, effectively subjecting these schools to years of political uncertainty and denying numerous families the opportunity to access high-quality educational alternatives for their children.

It is important to recognize that the success achieved by charter schools in Massachusetts is not an isolated phenomenon. It is a reflection of the broader trends observed throughout the entire country despite operating with lower per-child expenditures. A notable example of this can be found in a report conducted by the University of Arkansas' Department of Education Reform. The report concludes that, on average, charter schools receive approximately 29 percent less funding per student compared to traditional public schools. This finding is significant as it demonstrates that charter schools are able to deliver comparable outcomes with fewer resources at their disposal[22].

Despite the funding disparities, charter schools have demonstrated their ability to provide a quality education to their students. This serves as a testament to their innovative approach and their efficient utilization of resources. By operating with lower per-child expenditures, charter schools can allocate their funds more effectively, investing in targeted programs and initiatives that directly benefit their students. This personalized and tailored educational experience ultimately leads to improved academic performance and overall student success.

The report from the University of Arkansas' Department of Education Reform further challenges the notion that increased funding is the sole determinant of educational success. While adequate funding is undoubtedly important, it is not the sole factor contributing to student achievement. The report's findings underscore the fact that charter schools, despite receiving approximately 29 percent less funding per student compared to traditional public schools, have managed to deliver better educational outcomes.

If you were to talk to individuals affiliated with traditional public education or the Teachers Union, you would likely hear them disparage Charter Schools, considering them to be inferior to "real" education. However, a comprehensive examination of Charter Schools across different states reveals that their students achieve better educational outcomes. Take, for instance, the case of Indiana Charter Schools, where a report published in 2018 showcased superior performance compared to public schools. Upon learning of these results, the head of the Indiana State Teachers Association made the following comment:

"The accountability system is rigged in favor of many of the charter schools cited, as they are afforded the privilege by the Legislature of using only growth. If all schools were graded only on growth, traditional public schools would consistently outperform charters.[23]*"*

One cannot help but wonder what factors are considered in the evaluation of public education if student growth is not among the most important factors. In most states, student performance is measured using the same metrics for both public schools and charters. Moreover, it is worth questioning whether public schools would fare better if they were solely graded on student growth.

Based on my personal experience, the Charter Schools we collaborated with demonstrated meticulousness in reviewing our educational materials and extending invitations to observe the teachers in action before reaching a decision. Due to budget constraints, Charter Schools are highly conscious of not acquiring unnecessary or redundant materials. Every Charter School that purchased our product would request multiple visits from us to provide the teachers with thorough guidance on utilizing our resource. It was absolutely crucial for us to receive the teachers' endorsement each year, as this determined whether we would be welcomed back to the school. Although seemingly trivial, as you will later discover, this process holds significant importance.

This is not to imply that public schools universally invested the same level of effort in reviewing our product. For some, the evaluation process lasted only a few minutes, while others dedicated extensive time to it. Some schools or districts simply require the completion of a budget form. Although certain schools or districts occasionally requested monthly user data, the majority of Charter Schools employing our resource expressed a strong desire for regular reports to monitor in-school and at-home usage by both students and teachers.

Selling the Money Myth

The teacher's unions have devoted a considerable amount of time and resources to persuade the public that there is a lack of funding for a quality education. They utilize various tactics, such as quotes, press releases, and endorsements from experts, to effectively convey their message. One contributing factor to their success is that the majority of television and print news media outlets consistently turn to teacher's unions for comments or reactions on any education-related news. Consequently, the media often portrays the teacher's unions as the primary authority on education, disregarding the fact that their primary objective is to increase the funds they receive by enlisting more public school teachers. It must be noted, however, that not all states have active teachers' unions.

For instance, consider the case of Robert Pianta, the dean of the Curry School of Education at the University of Virginia. In an article he wrote for the Washington Post, he erroneously claimed that "public funding for schools has decreased since the late 1980s." Although the Washington Post eventually issued a correction, it took a full eight days for the misinformation to be rectified, leaving readers misinformed during that period. The teacher's unions capitalized on Pianta's quotes to bolster their calls for increased funding and even continued to use them after the correction was published[2425].

An example illustrating the teacher's unions' ability to undermine better educational options can be found in the charter school story from Massachusetts. They possess the power to dismiss superior educational alternatives as insignificant. Whenever studies indicate that private or charter schools outperform public schools, the teacher's unions launch aggressive campaigns aimed at convincing the public that the studies and their findings are biased or rigged. Don't take my word for it, simply search for private or charter school scores in your state, and you will undoubtedly come across quotes and follow-up interviews from local public school associations or teacher union representatives.

As I mentioned earlier, I have yet to come across any evidence supporting the notion that increased funding directly translates to improved education. In fact, data from the U.S. Census Bureau shows that approximately one-third of all state budget allocations are already dedicated to education. This makes it challenging to argue that K-12 education is insufficiency funded[26].

Eric Hanushek, an economist from Stanford University, conducted an extensive analysis of nearly 400 studies on this subject. His research concluded that there is no consistent or significant relationship between student performance and the amount of resources provided to schools. Consequently, it comes as no surprise that merely pouring more money into the same flawed system will not address the underlying issues plaguing public education. One possible reason why allocating more funds to education fails to yield positive results is that the majority of the money does not reach individual schools or classrooms. Instead, it tends to accumulate at the top, creating a top-heavy system[27].

The Why's

This chapter would go on for another 30 pages if we try to analyze why more money doesn't necessarily lead to better educational outcomes. Throughout the later chapters, you'll find numerous examples that support this fact. However, for now, let's delve into the three primary reasons behind this phenomenon.

First and foremost, as highlighted in the previous section, the allocation of funds often fails to address the areas that truly need improvement. As mentioned at the beginning of this chapter, the public education system has transformed into a political system rather than an educational one. At the highest level, the priority is to ensure political alignment and maintain strong lobbying support from unions. At the state level, individuals who ascend to positions of power often do so through political maneuvering or personal connections. Unfortunately, this sometimes results in individuals with questionable qualifications taking up influential positions. A common observation made by teachers is that many department heads and their subordinates are often friends who secure their positions through personal connections. Additionally, new positions are frequently created and filled by individuals with close ties to the district administration. Consequently, county administrations tend to have inflated budgets at the top, while the budgets at the lower levels experience only marginal growth[28]. In terms of teacher salaries, progression is typically based on experience and educational qualifications. However, there is a limitation to how much a teacher's salary can increase before reaching a cap, which often occurs long before retirement. The third possibility for a salary increase is if the state or county grants a pay raise. When teachers consider pursuing further education to improve their qualifications, they often find that the increase in salary barely covers the student loan debt they acquire. Finally, another way to increase pay is to transition into leadership roles within the administration.

The second major reason why increased funding does

not necessarily lead to better educational outcomes lies in the fact that pouring millions of dollars into a school or education system cannot fix the issues that students face within their home environments. We will delve deeper into this topic in later discussions, but it is crucial to acknowledge that the environment in which a child lives plays a significant role in their education. Some districts have a higher concentration of dysfunctional homes compared to others, often corresponding to the income levels of the parents, although this is not always the case.

The third reason can be attributed to the influence of political correctness and the emphasis on social justice within the education system. Fundamentally, education revolves around presenting facts as they are, rather than as some might wish them to be. However, once education begins to apply different grading scales to certain groups or areas, the system becomes imbalanced. Two plus two equals four, and there is no room for interpretation in this equation. Yet, if one were to search for discussions on whether two plus two must always equal four, they might be surprised to find educators advocating for equity. This begs the question: equity in terms of right and wrong answers? This type of thinking comes along with (SEL) Social & Emotional Learning initiatives. This focus on subjects that were traditionally not part of the curriculum consumes resources that could otherwise be allocated to more effective use within schools and districts. Introducing Social and Emotional Learning or social justice into educational institutions increases spending not only in terms of finances but also in time and teacher resources.

Historically, the education curriculum has centered around subjects such as math, science, reading/writing, and history. However, parents may not be aware that education has gradually incorporated social justice and teaching social issues, which are largely unrelated to education as a whole. Proponents argue that this inclusive approach molds a more well-rounded understanding of the world, suggesting that education should encompass more than just basic facts. Nevertheless, this is a contentious issue, with varying opinions on how far public education should go in shaping young minds to become better individuals. While teaching children to be kind and understanding is essential, it appears that the goal has shifted toward transforming children into activists. Most parents I have spoken to express a desire for their children to acquire a solid foundation of knowledge, secure a good education, find meaningful employment, and lead happy and productive lives as adults. What upsets many parents is the concealment of the social curriculum and the content being taught[29]. Parents often teach their young children that hiding or lying about something indicates wrongdoing. The secrecy surrounding certain aspects of the curriculum raises concerns among parents and should motivate them to explore further the nature of their children's education.

It should be noted that the extent to which these issues manifest varies significantly depending on one's geographical location, whether residing in a major city or suburban area. While teachers in the suburbs may have initially believed that such issues would never affect their schools, this assumption is increasingly proving to be false. The influence of social engineering on our children is undoubtedly more prevalent in certain regions, but its reach has extended into many suburbs without parental awareness.

———————————————

1. https://www.educationnext.org/what-americans-think-about-their-schools/
2. https://wallethub.com/edu/e/states-with-the-best-schools/5335
3. https://theenterprisingeducator.com/teaching-in-a-public-vs-private-school/
4. https://educationdata.org/public-education-spending-statistics
5. https://www.gobankingrates.com/saving-money/education/private-school-cost-vs-public-school/
6. https://www.lcs.education/private-school-students-perform-better-on-act/
7. https://www.privateschoolreview.com/average-act-score-stats/national-data
8. https://nces.ed.gov/nationsreportcard/pubs/studies/2006461.aspx
9. https://www.nationsreportcard.gov/dashboards/schools_dashboard.aspx
10. https://www.acton.org/pub/commentary/2012/07/25/moral-formation-and-school-choice-movement
11. https://www.usnews.com/opinion/articles/2016-09-20/more-money-wont-fix-failing-public-schools
12. https://files.eric.ed.gov/fulltext/ED583004.pdf
13. https://www.positiveaction.net/blog/title-1-school-funding
14. https://www.cde.ca.gov/sp/sw/
15. https://www.brookings.edu/articles/expanding-title-i-could-eliminate-k-12-spending-gaps-if-the-funds-are-well-targeted/
16. https://nces.ed.gov/blogs/nces/post/free-or-reduced-price-lunch-a-proxy-for-poverty
17. https://www.educationnext.org/boston-and-the-charter-school-cap/
18. https://www.bostonglobe.com/opinion/2019/06/05/the-teachers-union-sad-anti-charter-zealotry/1ePvit5sGoiAwhRCWaLakL/story.html
19. https://www.bostonglobe.com/opinion/2013/03/07/charter-schools-results-too-good-ignore/tJXHyX3Ri34KQClg68NadI/story.html
20. https://www.gse.harvard.edu/ideas/news/09/01/new-study-boston-charter-and-pilot-schools-finds-charter-schools-have-positive
21. https://inthesetimes.com/article/teachers-defeat-charter-school-expansion-in-massachusetts
22. https://news.uark.edu/articles/38765/study-finds-large-funding-gap-between-charter-schools-traditional-schools
23.
24. https://www.heritage.org/education/commentary/washington-post-concedes-government-spending-education-has-increased-not
25. https://www.dailysignal.com/2019/12/18/washington-post-concedes-that-government-spending-on-education-has-increased-not-decreased/
26. https://www.washingtonexaminer.com/how-much-of-each-states-budget-goes-to-education

27. http://hanushek.stanford.edu/publications/assessing-effects-school-resources-student-performance-update

28. https://www.edweek.org/teaching-learning/staff-benefits-are-eating-up-bigger-shares-of-district-budgets-report-finds/2018/08

29. https://defendinged.org/incidents/rockwood-school-district-teachers-receive-email-telling-them-to-hide-lesson-materials-assignments-from-parents/

5

THE ECONOMICS OF (FAILING) SCHOOLS

"What we are teaches the child far more than what we say, so we must be what we want our children to become."

Joseph Chilton Pearce

In 2015, in the state of Georgia, then Governor Nathan Deal proposed having the state take over failing schools. I have nothing against Governor Deal, but this plan made no sense. What will the state do that the county or city could not do? Most likely, the state of Georgia would have thrown more money at the failing schools! Unfortunately, we won't know because the Governor wasn't very forthcoming with a plan that listed what the state would do differently. The plan was dead on arrival as most counties argued it was an over-reach of authority[1]. The first thing I want all parents to know is that a failing school is failing because of a lack of income, but it's not the school income that matters the most. It is the households that feed into the school. Yes, despite what TV shows and movies tell us, more money in the schools makes less of a difference than the district's economic development. It is the parent's dedication to their children's education that matters most. Unfortunately, many low-income communities have fewer parents who are putting educating their children as the highest priority This is politically incorrect to say...but it's true!

Low-income districts often come with higher-than-average community problems. All school districts have kids who go home to homes with drugs, missing parents, parents in jail, no food, etc., but these problems exceed the norm in low-income areas. Almost every teacher and principal I've talked to will tell you that what the students go home to impacts their schooling more than the teachers. This is not a popular opinion among some circles who believe that teachers should be able to overcome it. That's a very naive statement, and it makes me cringe whenever someone uses it in a sentence. How will a teacher adequately teach a student who comes to school without supervision at home or clothes, hasn't bathed, doesn't know where they will eat that night, or witnessed a parent being arrested, or has one already in jail or missing? These problems weigh more heavily on a student than whether or not they finished their math homework. Of course, there are outliers in every situational data, and those students who rise above their home situations must fight even harder to succeed. Lower-income areas have more significant problems at home and often the community where the homes reside, which makes it difficult to focus on whether or not the kids have good grades or how they did on tests. Not every parent who lives in a lower-income location is absent from their kids' schooling. Still, the percentage is higher. Often, parents with lower income or no income didn't complete their schooling or move on to higher education and cannot help their kids now. You can see anecdotal evidence of this in most middle-class neighborhoods, where the students who fare better on average come from more stable homes, and the kids who perform worse, on average, come from the poorest parts of the community. This is slightly less noticeable at the elementary school level. Still, it quickly becomes a reality in middle and high school.

It is likely that I may receive criticism for suggesting that parents in lower-income areas are less invested in their children compared to higher-income parents. In these areas, the percentage is higher for children who live in situations where day-to-day struggles consume their lives. The conditions they are exposed to are not conducive to growing up with a positive life direction. Argue what you will, but whether a parent is black, white, or yellow, and they are successful in life, work, or business, they would most likely have higher expectations for their children than the parent who is still working fast food for minimum wage or who have no job, or is selling drugs. Plus, kids learn how to deal with life and challenges from their parent's philosophies, actions, and behaviors. The amount of effort a child sees their parents give towards life and succeeding is a more significant influence long-term than any schooling could ever achieve. The needed positive force that would push a child towards success in school and, ultimately, life starts at home.

For people who still want to argue, most of the failing schools are in low-income areas. The others are in lower-middle-class areas. Some people will tell you it's because the more affluent areas have more money, which is their argument for needing more money to fix a failing school in a lower-income neighborhood. But this is an incorrect association. The higher income areas have more money in the home, and the children often live in stable situations.

They are not worried about eating or staying warm without utilities or more traumatic life events such as seeing their parents arrested or abused. No teacher can overcome this, nor can the state by taking over the school. Simply stated, what the students go home to affects them more than what a teacher does during the limited time they see the student. And most every teacher you know has seen this demonstrated firsthand. Another point to consider is that higher-income areas rarely have schools that receive Title One funds; thus, the schools in higher-income zones have less funding than the schools in lower-income zones.

Some will still write this off as a money issue. They will say that parents in low-income communities would love to send their kids to tutors and do more to help them in school but can not because the lack of affordable assistance confines them. However, most schools offer after or before-school programs for students needing extra help. I have met families living below the poverty line who do what they can to take advantage of the available free help. In those instances, the parents are trying their best, and that fact alone is positive for their kids. The struggles those parents go through to keep their kids safe, off the streets, and away from drugs should be celebrated. And I'm willing to bet, if we followed the kids from those families, they would fare better than the average student in their neighborhood.

Let me make it clear that it has nothing to do with intelligence. Teachers will tell you that students at the elementary level, before they've given up on school, are intellectually all on par, no matter their home economic situation. Of course, some students are lower and higher learners, but that is distributed evenly no matter where the student comes from or their ethnic background. It's following these students as they move up in grade levels where the difference starts to appear.

I've often heard teachers describe their elementary-age students in this way: "They're very smart, but with their home life, they just don't stand a chance," or "It is going to be so hard for them to get through the challenges they face at home."

British comedian Francis Foster, who was a teacher for 12 years, tells this story: *"I was teaching at a school in a tough area. There was a kid, we'll call him Darren, who was always getting kicked out of class. One of the jobs you do as a teacher is to walk around and gather up the kids who've been kicked out of their class. I taught Darren chess, and in about two days, he could beat me at chess. He was super bright, one of the brightest kids I ever encountered. But because he came from a family of criminals, he was never gonna make it through school. His family felt no value for education as he was a product of the culture in which he grew up. The values that were instilled in him were not conducive to a successful life"*[2].

To be clear, people with habits that bring them economic prosperity usually apply and teach those habits and attitudes to their children. People in lower-income areas often have reverse life habits and attitudes, which are also taught to their children and become a cycle or a loop that repeats itself generation after generation. Suppose you dismiss this argument by standing on a racial platform. In that case, you should know that in my experience and what I've heard from black, Hispanic, Asian, and white teachers simply contain no racial component. Sure, there are more minorities in many low-income areas of the country. We're not going to solve that in this book. Still, teachers overall will tell you that how the parents handle their children's education shapes out to be the outcome by the time they graduate. Parents with disciplinary action attached to not doing school work, studying and doing well on tests, or just trying their best to pass every subject and grade typically, at the very least, have kids who graduate high school and go on to college or a skilled career. These parents are usually concerned about the kids doing poorly on tests or not performing well overall and want to discuss this with their kid's teachers. We'll discuss that more in the chapter on parents. In short, parents absent from the school's day-to-day activities rarely show up for conferences, seldom clean out their child's school folder and read what's going on in the class, and will have students in many cases that treat education with the same regard. It's quite likely that's also the kind of attention the child gets at home. This behavior or lack of awareness of the child does translate to other areas of the child's home life.

If you think that most parents care enough to attend parent-teacher conferences and respond to correspondence from their child's teachers, then you are naive. It might also surprise you that parents who won't participate in conferences, except to fight about their child being disciplined, often have children underperforming in school, possibly because their focus is on the wrong problem.

Let's illustrate this by looking at elementary school children. By the time most kids have made it through the 8th grade, they understand the challenges of their situation. And so do their peers, which begins to show up in teasing or other embarrassing ways. They have either embraced it by heading down the path of "I don't care about school", or a smaller percent have buckled down to get out of their situation. But at the elementary level, the children are still young, and they reveal their fears and insecurities openly. I could fill a chapter with stories that elementary teachers have told me about children not wanting to go home, even crying, because the school environment feels safer for them. There's no fighting or abuse; they have food to eat, and the people at school, mainly the teachers, pay attention to them. How would a governor or any other state bureaucrat fix that?

Once, when I was in a lower-middle-class area school in Florida, I asked all the teachers in the room I was presenting in, just by average, how many of your parents show up for their child conferences? Most agreed it was about 40 percent, or less than half. I asked the same question in a presentation in a Georgia school where the parents were upper middle to high-income families, and the answer was about 85 percent. I relayed this fact at a conference in Savannah, Georgia, where I was speaking, and afterward, several administrators wanted me to know that wasn't fair because the lower middle-class families probably couldn't get off work or they didn't know about the parent-teacher conferences or a slew of other excuses. I was somewhat appalled. Anyone who has had school-age children knows that the conferences are scheduled with the parents beforehand, and the parents pick the time. The parents either forgot or attending the conference wasn't a priority. They also argued that middle-class parents often have one parent at home who doesn't work. Statistically, that's not true. According to the Bureau of Labor Statistics, in 2019, 64.2 percent of American families with children had both parents working[3]. From my experience, working with my wife, we coordinated with each other on who was taking the kids.. But as most conference times are flexible, we tried to make it so that both of us were at the conference.

It's important to recognize that the majority of teachers genuinely care about their students and are committed to their success. However, it's crucial to understand that both teachers and administrators have limitations and cannot work miracles. They often have to suppress their emotions when confronted with the challenging situations that some students face at home. Teachers approach their work with a similar mindset as that of a police officer or social worker. They do their best to support their students within their capacity while also acknowledging that they cannot single-handedly solve all the problems. It's important for them to strike a balance between providing necessary support and maintaining a level of professional detachment to avoid becoming too emotionally invested.

Teachers I've spoken to who've worked in low and high-economic areas and can compare their experiences will have much the same opinion as the beginning of this chapter.

It Shows in the Behavior

During my interactions with schools and teachers to promote our educational products, the topic of behavior was rarely discussed. However, I eagerly anticipated my interviews with teachers and administrators to delve into this important issue. These individuals had a wealth of experience in the education field, with many having worked for over ten years and some recently retired. The alarming increase in disruptive student behavior transcends economic groups, but the nature of the misbehavior in upper middle-income areas and above tends to lean more towards entitlement rather than simply being categorically poor or disrespectful. Nonetheless, the impact of both types of behavior on the learning environment is equally disruptive and disrespectful, and the problem continues to worsen.

Behavior is inherently linked to the success or failure of schools. This is because disruptive behavior hampers the teaching and learning process, often intertwining with issues such as bullying and violence. Every school grapples with disruptive students, but in certain regions of the country, the prevalence of problematic behavior surpasses the capacity of teachers and administrators to effectively manage it. Consequently, this gives rise to more significant challenges, as many teachers come to the realization that their efforts to establish control in the classroom and educate their students are in vain. It was disheartening to hear from a teacher with eight years of experience in an inner-city school who shared that some of her colleagues resorted to reading books during class sessions, conceding their inability to capture the attention and engagement of their students. As a result, these same students were often allowed to progress to the next grade without acquiring foundational skills in subjects like mathematics, reading, or writing.

In these troubled schools, it is necessary to implement drastic disciplinary measures or consider the possibility of expelling disruptive students. Some may consider such actions harsh, but we must recognize that we are dealing with students who are already failing to learn and are impeding the progress of those few who are motivated to break free from their circumstances. Which explains why safety emerges as the primary concern for parents when surveyed about their desire to enroll their children in better schools through school choice programs. If you do not believe it matters, consider the fact that the teachers unions often proclaim that private schools have more success because they can get rid of disruptive students or not allow them in the school at all. Are they saying that removing disruptive students from public education would bring the level of success up to near private school levels? They are never going to answer that question but its important to understand the cause and affect that behavior has on a school overall when it exceeds the level that is no longer manageable.

Pass Them On

According to testing data for 2017, Project Baltimore found that 13 out of 39 high schools in the city had zero students that were proficient in math[4]. Another six schools only had 1 percent of their student body who tested proficient in math. "It's not a funding issue," responded Jason Rodriguez, the deputy director of People Empowered by the Struggle, a nonprofit organization based in Baltimore. When questioned about the failure of Baltimore Schools, Rodriguez emphasized that they are receiving an adequate amount of funding. He firmly stated, "I don't think money is the issue. I believe that accountability is the root of the problem.[5]"

In plain numbers, out of the 3,804 students who took the state test, a mere 14 were proficient in math[6]. The funny thing is, the teachers union disputed this by boasting that about 70 percent of students in the Baltimore area graduated high school[7]. Not a good percentage by any stretch of the imagination, but even more puzzling...if only about 1 percent of the students are proficient in math, how did they graduate 70 percent? The answer is simple; the schools chose to pass them on each year, even though they couldn't perform the work of the previous school grade level. Those graduation rates haven't gotten much better[8]. Makes you wonder what the union is bragging about.

It is truly puzzling to see the stark contrast in educational statistics. Take Chicago, for instance. As of December 2022, approximately 80 percent of students attending Chicago Public Schools are struggling to read at their grade level. Additionally, the proficiency rate in math stands at a mere 15 percent. Despite these concerning figures, Chicago Public Schools achieved its highest four-year graduation rate in at least a decade. In 2022, 83 percent of students graduated on time[9]. How can this be? This discrepancy has raised serious concerns, and Illinois state Sen. Willie Preston, a father of six, sounded the alarm in February 2023. An alarming report revealed that 55 Chicago schools claim not a single student is proficient in math or reading, despite the billions of dollars poured into education by both state and federal government[10]. Once again making the argument that more money will not make a difference.

Unfortunately, this issue is not unique to Chicago. The LA Weekly boldly proclaimed in 2011 that California has the highest number of failing schools in the nation[11]. Parents have begun to take notice, resulting in declining enrollment in many areas. They are seeking alternative options for their children's education. But here's the twist: News in California boasted a graduation rate of 76.30 percent. Not bad for having the highest number of failing schools in the nation[12].

As a logical person, you can't help but wonder how these two headlines can coexist. The truth is, these examples are just the tip of the iceberg. Statistics like these can be found in major cities across the country. It's clear that something is amiss in our education system.

It is evident that in many districts, the practice of simply passing students along is commonplace. During a conversation with a teacher from New York, it was revealed that due to an influx of incoming students, it is not feasible to retain all of them until they willingly engage in learning. Although this may sound cynical, there are those who would concur. Even within schools where the majority of students are meeting the required standards, those who consistently struggle academically are not typically retained unless specifically requested by their parents. The existence of data in support of both approaches makes it impossible to exclusively adopt one method. In certain cases, it may be in the best interest of an elementary student to be granted an additional year to develop and mature[13]. However, repeatedly holding the same student back for multiple years does not contribute to their long-term educational success.

It is rather disingenuous to boast about high graduation rates when a significant number of students are being graduated despite their inability to pass fundamental courses required for high school completion. It is important to recognize that political leaders, including those serving on local school boards, often manipulate data to conceal their shortcomings.

Breaking down the failures of a low graduation rate or proficiency rate is tough and reveals an entanglement of factions. Most students who are not proficient by the time they are in high school haven't been proficient for many years or as they've made their way through the prior grade levels. These days there is a multitude of levels and tiers for intervention programs aimed at helping a student who needs special attention or extra services to help them be on par with their age group. These services go by many acronyms, but the framework supports students in grades K – 5 who are at risk of not reaching or maintaining academic grade levels. These interventions (EIP, RIT) provide additional instructional resources to help students who are performing below grade level obtain the necessary academic skills to reach grade level performance in the shortest possible time.

Is that the fault of the teacher, the parents, or the school? In my opinion, it is the collective responsibility of all parties involved. However, I believe that ultimately, the parents should take a more proactive role in addressing the issues their child is facing in school. I will delve deeper into the roles of parents, teachers, and administrations in later chapters, but for now, let's skim the surface of this argument.

Imagine this scenario: your child has been struggling in school for years, and the teachers are well aware of their lack of proficiency. The administration has access to the test scores and other relevant data. Each year, the teachers diligently send home progress reports, report cards, emails, and provide updates on homework grades and test scores, expecting the parents to review them.

Now, let's assume that the teachers have also made efforts to offer additional assistance or services along the way. In this case, they have done everything within the system's capabilities to support the student. As a parent, if you are actively following your child's progress throughout their school years, how could you possibly overlook these facts? Unless the teachers are deliberately lying about your child's performance in class and on assignments, you would expect the parents to be fully aware. Have you seen the grades on their homework? But this raises the question: did the parents of these struggling students ever attend a parent-teacher conference or take the initiative to discuss the situation with their child's teachers?

In this chapter discussing schools, it is important to

acknowledge that schools are not just comprised of students and teachers, but rather an entire community. It is crucial for the community to prioritize and invest in the education of their children. It is common for parents of students attending struggling schools to place the burden of responsibility on teachers and the school itself, neglecting their own role in their children's educational failures. However, it is essential to recognize that this is not a realistic expectation for any local school, whether it be high-achieving or underperforming.

The Other Economic Drivers

We started this chapter with the economics of the community as it relates to the success of the schools and students attending. But another economic consideration is to be studied: school grants and Title I funding.

Title One Funding

In the first chapter, we discussed Title I as one of the federal grant streams that supplements state funding for schools. However, it's worth noting that there are other "Title" funds, known as Title II to Title VII, which also aim to support students facing various barriers to education. These barriers include poverty, homelessness, living in state-run institutions, residing in isolated rural areas, and English language learners. It's important to mention that students with disabilities have a separate funding stream dedicated to their needs.

While federal Title One funds cannot replace local and

state school funding, they provide additional financial support to schools that qualify. The allocation of Title funds to schools is done through school districts, and the formulas used for distribution may vary from state to state. On a national average, schools receive an additional $1,489 per child through Title I funding. However, some states may receive more or less funding per student living below the poverty line[14].

School districts have the flexibility to utilize Title I funds in various ways. Examples include providing extra training for teachers, supplying one-on-one devices to eligible students, implementing new literacy programs, and strengthening community engagement initiatives.

In the context of the targeted assistance program, a school that is receiving Title I money is specifically allocated these additional funds to support low-income students. These funds are designed to provide resources and assistance to improve the educational outcomes of students from economically disadvantaged backgrounds. By focusing on the needs of these students, schools can implement targeted interventions and support programs that directly address their unique challenges and help them succeed academically.

On the other hand, when a school receives Title I money for the entire school, it has the flexibility to use these funds more broadly to reform and enhance the overall educational program of the institution. This allows the school to allocate resources towards improving curriculum, instructional techniques, professional development for staff, and other initiatives that can benefit all students, regardless of their socioeconomic status.

It's important to note that the distribution of Title I funds is based on the number of low-income students reported by each public school within a school district. This means that schools with a higher concentration of economically disadvantaged students will receive a larger amount of funding to address the specific needs of these individuals.

While the federal law states that students must be "identified" as eligible, my personal observations and conversations with educators and administrators reveal that the application process serves as the main determining factor. In other words, parents only need to submit an application, and there is no requirement for income or poverty level verification. This has led to instances where even in affluent neighborhoods, the number of students benefiting from the free lunch program surpasses 40 percent.

The school or district administration has no incentive to say no or verify income; they are getting extra money based on the lie. It's a welfare program that is often abused. Get into a conversation about the abuses, politicians, or anyone involved with education and you will find a deaf ear. Their position is simple "Why do you want to take away education funds from schools?" As I stated in the first chapter, there is more than enough money for education, but like every federal and state government funds, they are wasted or misappropriated for the wrong causes or the wrong groups with little or no accountability. Almost no auditing goes on with Title 1. The school simply needs to provide invoices or receipts for what the money was spent on, and if it fits the guidelines, then it's approved. I tried finding out how many schools come off of the Title 1 list, but no list seems to exist. In my experience, I have observed that schools often lose their Title 1 funding due to changes in eligibility rules or a failure to enroll a sufficient number of students in the free and reduced lunch program. It is rare to see a school's funding revoked solely because it has demonstrated improvement in its academic performance. Especially since that is no a determining factor is receiving Title One funds.

Changes in eligibility rules can occur as a result of modifications implemented by the government or educational authorities. These changes may include adjustments to the criteria for determining which schools qualify for Title 1 funding. Thus, even if a school previously met the requirements, it is possible for its eligibility status to change due to these alterations.

During a visit to a local school, I had the opportunity to discuss training their teachers on our resources with the principal. Arriving in the morning, I noticed the parents dropping off their elementary students. Despite knowing that this was a Title 1 school, I couldn't help but notice the luxury cars that were present. The neighborhoods I passed through before reaching the school were clearly middle-class or higher in terms of affordability. Of course, it would be unfair to make assumptions about the school's overall economic makeup based solely on this limited observation. However, when I spoke with the principal, I was taken aback by what she shared. She informed me that an astonishing 70 percent of the student population was receiving free and reduced lunch. Additionally, she mentioned that the majority of the parents in the school district were minorities, comprising over 70 percent of the total population. Interestingly, she also expressed that some of these parents believed they were entitled to these benefits. It's important to note that this sense of entitlement is not exclusive to districts with a higher minority population; it's a phenomenon observed across the board. Nevertheless, it does highlight a broader issue within our society, which is how many people believe they are owed more. This illustrates the way in which tax dollars are allocated to schools, regardless of the actual level of need.

If there were any doubts regarding the importance of the home environment in a student's success, it is worth noting that the federal government designates Title 1 for children from low-income households. This recognition acknowledges that students from lower-income homes face more challenges in achieving academic success. An even more compelling confirmation is that Title 1 schools, despite receiving additional funding, still underperform in terms of student success and learning. I personally witnessed this stark contrast between two schools located just 9 miles apart. One school qualified for Title 1, while the other did not. Over the years that I observed them, the non-Title 1 school consistently outperformed its counterpart. Despite the Title 1 school receiving an extra $100,000 per year in funding, it struggled to overcome the social and community issues prevalent in the students' home environments. In my experience, Title 1 schools often have more abundant resources compared to non-Title 1 schools, yet they still fall short in terms of academic performance. It becomes evident that pouring additional funds into a school does not bring about significant changes to the economic and social health of students' home environments. Moreover, increasing financial resources alone does not automatically lead to improved student achievement.   And once again we've proven that more money does not equal successful schools.

Experimental Grants

When you visit grants.gov, you will discover a vast array of grants that are available to schools and districts. These grants offer substantial funding, ranging from hundreds of thousands to millions of dollars, to school districts that agree to abide by the predetermined requirements for implementing specific educational resources or techniques. Some of these grants are specifically targeted towards assisting marginalized groups, such as Native Americans or students with disabilities[15].

In the realm of education, there is a significant emphasis on grants that aim to revolutionize teaching methods. These grants are typically developed by education professionals, including professors with advanced degrees in education. However, it is important to note that not all of these program creators have direct experience in K-12 classrooms.

Based on my personal observations, I have noticed that many of these programs face challenges when it comes to garnering widespread participation from teachers. When I engage in conversations with K-12 educators, they often express doubts about whether the individuals behind these programs truly understand the realities of the classroom or if the programs have been thoroughly tested on actual students. Despite these concerns, the prevailing term associated with these programs is "research-based." Unfortunately, this term is used broadly and does not necessarily guarantee efficacy.

Proponents of these programs argue that securing these grants is intended to facilitate implementation and assessment on a larger scale. Additionally, these programs are often marketed as being grounded in research. However, having been involved in similar research-based projects, I can confirm that, in many cases, the research and testing environment are carefully controlled to yield favorable outcomes. This practice mirrors the selective omission of outlier data and the omission of results that do not align with desired outcomes, commonly seen in the pharmaceutical industry. It is important to acknowledge that our resource was only considered "research-based" after a substantial amount of funding was funneled into it for a teaching college.

When assessing new programs in the field of education, teachers frequently raise concerns about whether the creators of these methodologies possess firsthand teaching experience in real-world K-12 settings. While some may perceive this question as cynical, it is a valid inquiry. Many grants that require teachers to adopt new methods often impose additional time requirements. In a controlled environment singularly focused on implementing these program methodologies, achieving success may be more attainable. However, these new methods often overlook the time constraints that teachers face when juggling multiple subjects. While this may seem obvious, my experience has shown that it is a significant barrier hindering broader teacher involvement in such programs. One common complaint voiced by teachers when school districts propose new programs is that these initiatives demand too much time and fail to consider the fact that teachers have strict schedules to adhere to. Let's consider the example of an elementary school teacher who must teach multiple subjects consecutively. They are expected to stay on track with each subject, making it nearly impossible to allocate an additional 10 minutes per day to address a specific topic solely to fulfill a district grant requirement. Furthermore, districts rely on comprehensive adoption and accurate reporting of results to secure the full funding promised by the grant. Unfortunately, this becomes even more challenging when teachers are expected to use a mandated teaching program throughout the entire academic year, especially when it does not align with the format of county or state testing. This misalignment often leads to frustration among teachers. To make sure the funds aren't withheld, some resort to fudging the data they provide to the grantor.

Furthermore, teachers are often introduced to these new methods or programs just a week before the start of a new school year. They are expected to quickly become proficient in implementing these new approaches, which can be quite challenging considering the extensive list of tasks teachers must complete in that final week before the academic year commences.

It is important to note that I am not opposed to the idea of experimenting with new teaching methods on a larger scale. However, shouldn't parents be informed and given the choice to opt-out if they wish? Unfortunately, this would create complications, and no school district wants to raise awareness among parents. Nonetheless, they are eager to receive the grant funding, which means that your children have likely been unwitting participants in unproven teaching methods and applications without parental knowledge.

Finally

Several years ago, my wife and I were watching a movie called "Won't Back Down." A 2012 movie directed by Daniel Barnz starring Maggie Gyllenhaal, Viola Davis, and Holly Hunter. The film is loosely based on the events surrounding the use of the parent trigger law in Sunland-Tujunga, Los Angeles, California, in 2010, where several groups of parents attempted to take over several failing public schools. The Parent Trigger law, which was passed in California and other states in 2010, allowed parents to enforce administrative overhaul and overrule administrators in underperforming public schools if petitioned. It's a feel-good story, and overall it's a good movie. However, there's a line in the film that Maggie Gyllenhaal's character delivers that made my wife, a teacher, laugh out loud. "If we clean up this school and make it better for the kids, we make the whole community better[16]." Not exactly!

Interestingly enough, most mainstream media and websites associated with education attacked and ripped the movie. The crux of their complaints, if we boil them down to their common denominator, is that it's ridiculous to believe that parents in the community can take over or fix a failing school.

I realize the story is loosely based on a true story. But we should be inspired by a group of parents who cared enough to get involved and try to improve a school. The fact is that schools, unions, and administrators do not want parents meddling in their work. As we have seen throughout the pandemic and beyond, there's too much secrecy about what goes on behind the closed doors of many schools, which has to change. Schools should want open participation from parents. That's how you'll get better students who are more engaged. If parents actively participate in the school community and stay informed about school activities and events, they are more likely to pass on this enthusiasm to their children. By doing so, parents can contribute to raising children who enjoy school and are actively engaged in their education. This involvement has the potential to yield positive outcomes within our education system.

1. https://www.ajc.com/news/local-education/school-boards-defy-gov-nathan-deal-state-schools-takeover/VFduIlBpAULefTfD8uIsON/
2. https://www.battleofideas.org.uk/2018/speaker/francis-foster/
3. https://gitnux.org/two-working-parents-statistics/
4. https://foxbaltimore.com/news/project-baltimore/at-13-baltimore-city-high-schools-zero-students-tested-proficient-on-2023-state-math-exam
5. https://foxbaltimore.com/news/project-baltimore/at-13-baltimore-city-high-schools-zero-students-tested-proficient-on-2023-state-math-exam
6. https://www.theburningplatform.com/2017/11/10/13-baltimore-high-schools-have-zero-students-that-are-proficient-in-math/
7. https://thehill.com/opinion/education/350315-baltimores-failing-schools-are-a-tragedy-of-criminal-proportions/
8. https://foxbaltimore.com/news/project-baltimore/graduation-concerns-10-baltimore-high-schools-have-four-year-graduation-rates-below-50
9. https://www.illinoispolicy.org/chicago-public-schools-hit-record-graduation-rate-as-math-reading-scores-drop/
10. https://www.fox32chicago.com/news/chicago-lawmaker-schools-report-no-proficiency-math-reading-very-serious
11. https://www.laweekly.com/california-has-most-failing-schools-in-nation/
12. https://www.csba.org/GovernanceAndPolicyResources/~/media/CSBA/Files/GovernanceResources/GovernanceBriefs/201305FactSheetHSGradRates.ashx
13. https://www.gse.harvard.edu/ideas/usable-knowledge/17/07/when-kids-are-held-back-gains-can-follow
14. https://journalistsresource.org/economics/2020-census-title-i-maps/
15. https://grants.gov/
16. https://www.imdb.com/title/tt1870529/

6

EDUCATORS

Dear Society,

Teachers want to stay in teaching, but many are being forced to choose between their mental health, happiness, and financial stability, or stay in teaching. And this is not a teacher problem, it's a societal view and treatment of teachers problem.

Nicholas Ferroni

When reflecting on my school days, I realize there were certain teachers who had a profound impact on me. Their names are etched in my memory, and I am grateful for the positive influence they had on my life, no matter how seemingly small or subtle. Extensive research supports the notion that teachers can have long-term effects on their students, both in positive and negative ways. It's easy to see why someone who loves to teach or mentor would go into the profession of education. From the outside, people think that teachers have an easy job. I hear this often, because the general public has no idea what goes on inside the schools they send their kids to attend. It's easy to see why someone who loves to teach or mentor would go into the profession of education. From the outside, people may think that teachers have an easy job. However, as someone who spent several years working with teachers, I can attest that being a teacher is far from easy.

Unfortunately, there is a common misconception among the general public regarding the challenges and demands of the teaching profession. Many parents and community members have no idea what goes on inside the schools they send their children to attend. They often fail to realize the tremendous amount of time, effort, and dedication that teachers put into educating and shaping the minds of their students.

Inside the classroom, teachers face a multitude of responsibilities on a daily basis. They not only need to facilitate a positive learning environment, but also develop and implement lesson plans, assess student progress, provide individualized support, and manage classroom behavior. Beyond the classroom, teachers are often involved in extracurricular activities, meetings, and professional development, further adding to their workload.

Moreover, teachers are faced with diverse students, each with their own unique learning needs and abilities. They must find creative ways to engage and motivate students, adapting their teaching methods to ensure that every student has the opportunity to succeed. This requires a deep understanding of educational pedagogy, as well as the ability to differentiate instruction to meet the needs of a diverse classroom population. When it comes to teaching, there is a lot more that goes on behind the scenes than meets the eye.

The teaching profession is not without its share of challenges and stress, which has only intensified in recent years. Throughout their tenure, teachers will encounter moments of sadness, such as when they are unable to save a student from a difficult home environment characterized by abuse, sexual assault, or neglect. Teachers often have a front-row seat to the various struggles their students face, as well as the numerous problems that plague the communities they serve. It should come as no surprise that many seasoned teachers, who have spent a considerable amount of time in the profession, can become jaded and less inclined to hold back their opinions. Similar to law enforcement officers and first responders, teachers witness both the best and worst aspects of their communities and humanity, leading to a sense of cynicism.

Currently, there are over 3,842,796 teachers employed in the United States, with approximately 74.3 percent of them being female[1]. The high representation of women in the teaching profession can be attributed to two primary factors. First of all, teaching offers an excellent job opportunity for individuals with young children who still want to work. Elementary school teachers, for instance, have the unique advantage of being able to bring their own kids to work and return home with them. It is rare to find a work situation that is more accommodating for individuals planning to start or who are already raising a family. Secondly, women, in general, possess more nurturing qualities and greater patience when working with younger children men.

There tends to be a higher percentage of male teachers at the middle and high school levels as compared to male teachers at the elementary level.

However, despite the advantages and fulfillment offered by the teaching profession, it is far from being stress-free, as we will explore in detail in this chapter, which is why a significant number of teachers leave the profession before completing their fifth year of teaching.

Blame the Teachers

Ever since my kids entered kindergarten and officially became students of the public education system, I noticed that any discussion about the problems with education began and ended with teachers. No one ever pointed the finger at the school administration or the people making the decisions above the administration. It's been twenty years, and it doesn't seem like the debate has changed much. Teachers are always at the center of what ails the education system. I used to go along with this notion because I didn't have enough information to tell me otherwise. However, my perspective has shifted. I must disclose that I am married to a teacher and once ran an education company. While some may assume that I am biased, I now have a more informed point of view. I have seen the inner workings of the education system, which allows me to compare what I hear and read with what I've witnessed.

While teachers do bear some blame, the problems with education are primarily not their fault. Teachers are simply doing what they are told and are often constrained by policies and rules that are not of their choosing and often do not work in their favor. It's not difficult to understand why so many have reached the opposite conclusion. Teachers are the face of education. They are the people parents see and interact with most of the time. Another reason why they have shouldered the blame is that political leaders and sometimes administrators at the top have thrown teachers to the wolves in an effort to divert attention away from their decisions and failings, making teachers the patsies.

So why should we not blame teachers? First, let's understand that teachers are at the bottom of the bureaucratic ladder. They do not make the rules or policies, nor do they have any say in what's taught. If we compare education to a corporate structure, teachers are the worker bees at the bottom, carrying out all the tasks they are instructed to do while facing criticism from their customers due to company policies. In essence, focusing our ire on teachers is misplaced. Teachers face immense pressure these days, from the administration above them to the parents of the children they teach. The teaching profession is one of the few that still offers a pension plan and full benefits. Even with the benefits, more and more teachers are finding that the indifference they feel from parents, administrators, and society in general is not worth the time needed to earn their pension. On average, 19 to 30 percent of new teachers do not continue in the profession for more than five years. However, some estimates suggest that this figure is closer to 44 percent. This statistic does not paint a favorable picture of the teaching profession[2]. Even worse, 50 percent of the teachers who make it past five years will leave before their 12th year. It is alarming that we are losing good teachers because they have simply decided it's not worth it. I have witnessed this time and time again as I visited schools - teachers who are burned out, stressed out, and unsure if they can continue teaching. A common question I would be asked about our education products when visiting a school was, "Do we have any job openings?" Overall, most teachers I know or have met are proud of the job they do and are very proud when they make a difference in a student's life. Yet, teachers are often blamed for situations that are entirely out of their control. Although teachers have a couple of months off during the summer and several other breaks during the year, most teachers will be working after the students leave and on weekends for several hours to catch up. If you are reading this chapter and you believe that teachers have it easy, you would be wrong. You don't have an attrition rate mentioned in the last paragraph for an easy workload. By the way, some counties have moved away from lifelong pensions and have replaced them with standard IRA's or something similar[3].

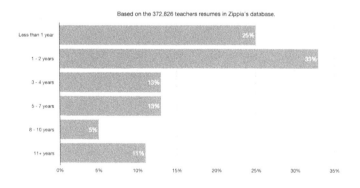

Based on the 372,826 teachers resumes in Zippia's database.

Let's take a closer look at some of the situations that create a work environment that is counterproductive to the expectations we have for teachers.

A mountain of paperwork is now a day-to-day necessity for working teachers, and the amount depends on the type of class or grade level they teach. According to the teachers I have spoken with, the amount of documentation and forms a teacher must keep up with for disciplinary actions, interventions, and meetings has more than doubled in the past 20 years. Documentation is needed to refer students for special services or any number of school programs. Speaking with a teacher who is the head of the RTI program (Response to Intervention) for her school, she told me that she has almost become a part-time paralegal. She has to keep the minutes of any meeting, paperwork, and official documentation before and after any meeting with parents. She does this in addition to her regular teaching responsibilities, without any additional pay. This is just one example among many academic or disciplinary programs in schools. One reason for the increased paperwork for teachers is budget cuts, which have eliminated some jobs specific to handling school programs. A teacher with an inclusion class must now do the paperwork that the special education teacher once handled. The increase in paperwork is also a result of documenting everything to preempt increasing parental complaints and sometimes lawsuits. Many teachers I have spoken with tell me that they just want to teach and be effective in the classroom, but they continually have more to manage outside the classroom.

A common complaint from many teachers is that some teachers have stopped referring kids for additional help or services because they do not want to have to keep up with the paperwork. Some documentation of behavior and poor grades is definitely necessary. If you are going to have an after-school meeting with parents about their child's bad behavior, which might lead to expulsion, or if you are going to meet with parents about getting their child tested for learning disabilities, then you most definitely want to have your ducks in a row and be able to point to specific data and learning outcomes that support the school's concerns. Most parents, we assume, know that their child is not well-behaved. By the time you get to an after-school conference for behavior issues, you should already have had several incidents that required the school to contact the parents. We will discuss how today's parents handle this in the parent chapter.

Another common issue that arises in the education system is the dissatisfaction of parents with teachers who implement stricter grading standards. If you happen to be a parent who dismisses this concern as solely the teacher's responsibility, it may be worth considering the findings of the influential study conducted by David N. Figlio and Maurice E. Lucas called "Do High Grading Standards Affect Student Performance?" This comprehensive report, published in 2000, focused on elementary school report cards in Florida and included a survey where parents were asked to evaluate their children's teachers. Interestingly, the results revealed that while two-thirds of parents gave their children's teachers A's, nearly half of them were more inclined to assign a grade of B or lower to a teacher who had stricter grading standards compared to a teacher with rela-tively easier standards. This suggests that there is a direct correlation between the perception of grading difficulty and parental evaluation[4].

Consequently, teachers who are inclined to avoid conflict or prioritize pleasing others might be more inclined to soften their grading standards in order to avoid difficult conversations with upset parents. Suppose you are the teacher who follows a teacher who passes on students without informing parents about their lack of proficiency in the curriculum. In that case, you may find yourself in a posi-tion of defending your grading standards. This is especially true when parents believe that their child performed well in the previous teacher's class. It can be a challenging situation as you strive to maintain consistency and fairness in your teaching practices.

If it Aint Broke...

I once heard a teacher in a school ask out loud, "What's this year's teaching strategy going to be?" The question was asked sarcastically.

Every year, teachers are told that the next great idea for how to teach has come along. In most professions, a veteran in the field would be asked to share their knowledge with newcomers about what works best and how they have succeeded year after year. Unfortunately, this is not the case in the teaching profession. The new way of teaching is something that changes every other year and is a great frustration to many teachers. Since teachers are reviewed and observed, they must implement the latest teaching strategy that their county or state has decided will improve student grades and test scores.

To be fair, most teachers I talk to are interested in learning new strategies. However, it becomes problematic when the strategies are forced upon them as if there is one teaching method that works for all students in every situation, especially for a teacher with years of experience who knows what works and has seen what gets the best results.

A seasoned teacher knows their class and can typically adjust their methods to fit the needs of the students. This is how it works in most private schools. Instead of helping struggling teachers become better, successful teachers are routinely asked to change their methods to fit the new way of doing things. This makes no sense.

Have you ever heard the phrase, "If it ain't broke, don't fix it"? Apparently, administrators in education have not. Teachers who have a high rate of success should be asked to help other teachers by sharing what they do and how they do it. Teachers need the freedom to use whatever method is bringing results. The teaching strategy of choice should be tailored to the students or, at the very least, their class.

As this chapter has covered, experience in teaching goes a long way, and good teachers can use their expertise and knowledge to be more effective.

For instance, I know of a teacher who was praised during a school meeting at the beginning of the year for successfully leading a class of struggling students to surpass expectations in their state tests. However, just 30 minutes later, in the same meeting, county officials announced that the teaching strategies used in the previous year would no longer be deployed as new strategies would be implemented. This contradictory approach is a glaring example of why the education system is faltering. Whenever a successful method is working, it is immediately discarded in favor of conforming to the district administration's preferences. This constant shift in teaching methods can also confuse students who are still mastering previous approaches while being introduced to new ones.

In the business world, when an employee consistently delivers exceptional results, they are often asked to share their strategies for success. Companies seek to replicate those same strategies across their workforce. Unfortunately, in the education system, teaching strategies and curricula change so frequently that there is no opportunity to determine what truly works in the long run. How can we evaluate the effectiveness of a teaching method if it is constantly altered every 2 or 4 years? For example, in Georgia and numerous other states, schools implemented Common Core for four years before abruptly changing the curriculum due to backlash. To be fair, many states claimed to have eliminated Common Core, but they merely made superficial changes by altering the names, removing some identifiable Common Core elements, and adjusting the grade levels at which certain lessons were taught. It is the constant reshuffling of curriculum requirements that causes the most challenges and student failures.

So why is this cycle of constant change occurring in school systems across the country? There are several fundamental reasons for this phenomenon. Firstly, administrators, in general, strive to climb the ladder in the education system and leave their mark on the department or system they manage. Progressing in their careers involves being able to boast, "Look at what I have achieved." This pattern is prevalent in most school districts. In the business world, changes are also made within companies or departments, but if those changes fail to yield positive results, individuals are often demoted, reassigned, or even terminated. In the education system, I have witnessed administrators receiving credit for introducing new programs without being held accountable for the outcomes. This is a grave error; as the renowned economist Milton Friedman once stated, "The biggest error we make is judging politicians for the virtues of the policies they make, but not the outcomes." This problem is mirrored in the education system, where good intentions are praised, but the results are ignored.

Secondly, it is not widely known that some of these changes are driven by grant money. Teachers are being asked to modify their teaching methods and experiment with new ideas that are funded through grants. Consequently, our children are unwittingly turned into guinea pigs, subjected to these new ideas, often championed by individuals with PhDs who persuade state or county school systems to implement their methodologies. They seek to use the results to validate their theories and boost their professional reputation. The majority of research grant money comes from state or federal sources. If these new ideas prove successful, that's fantastic! However, if they fail, parents should have been alerted to the fact that their child's education was being disrupted by what essentially amounts to a research project.

The third reason is that the districts simply don't know what works. It's evident that the powers that run the districts are constantly implementing various strategies and making changes in an attempt to find workable solutions. This ongoing experimentation demonstrates a lack of true expertise in fixing the education systems in their districts.

Let me reiterate that I am not opposed to the exploration of new ideas. However, when we do not afford teachers the autonomy to make decisions based on what is best for their students at the classroom level, we are failing our children. This should be common sense for those in higher positions within the education system, many of whom began their careers as classroom teachers but now believe they know what is best for all. Unfortunately, most school districts are burdened with top-heavy administrative offices, where everyone must justify their positions by tinkering with rules, policies, and methodologies.

As mentioned earlier, we are currently facing a teacher shortage. It is high time that downsizing becomes a practiced reality within district administrations. It would be beneficial for administrators to experience teaching once every 3 to 5 years, allowing them to witness firsthand how their policies affect teachers, students, and classrooms. Many individuals in top-level positions could return to schools and fulfill teaching roles, helping to bridge the teacher gap. However, this decision would have to be made by the very individuals I am referring to, and they likely would not vote to relinquish their administrative positions and return to teaching in a school.

Where are the Resources?

Teachers in this country face the challenge of managing a constantly changing curriculum with limited resources to adequately prepare students for these changes. In the past, school systems provided textbooks and accompanying teacher versions, as well as workbooks with homework sheets that aligned with the curriculum. This ensured that everything was in sync and harmonized. However, the landscape has changed significantly. Many schools now expect teachers to find resources online, create their own materials, or even purchase resources themselves. This has led to the rise of websites like teacherspayteachers.com, where teachers can share resources they have created for a fee. As a result, textbooks are no longer the norm, and the worksheets available may not always align perfectly with the content students will be tested on.

Don't believe that last paragraph. More than 85 percent of K-12 teachers in the U.S. use the platform to find teacher-created resources. Founded in 2006, Teachers Pay Teacher's sales exceed $60 million a year. That is because the vast majority of teachers have to pay for resources that were once provided by the school systems where they teach[5].

Teaching:
The only profession where you steal supplies from home

and bring them to work.

Today's teachers find themselves with fewer resources than ever before. While some argue that the internet offers a wealth of educational resources, these resources may not always meet the specific needs of each teacher and are not always reliable. Additionally, the cost of accessing reliable online resources is almost never covered by the school. In a survey of teachers with ten or more years of experience, 100 percent reported having fewer resources now compared to when they first started teaching. While technology has improved, the provision of resources has not kept pace.

One of the reasons for this resource shortage is the frequent changes in curriculum. As a result, investing in expensive textbooks or teaching workbooks that quickly become obsolete is not a viable option. Instead, schools have turned to online resources. For example, I spoke with an administrator in one county who laughed when asked about ordering new textbooks for the transition to Common Core. He revealed that they had approximately $3 million worth of textbooks sitting in storage from the past ten years. With curriculum changes occurring so often, it made no sense to invest in books that would soon be outdated.

It appears that school districts are increasingly relying on digital resources. However, most schools have not fully embraced digital resources and instead choose which digital learning sites to invest in. Teachers often request memberships to various online educational resources that they prefer. As a result, there is a lack of cohesion among schools and even among teachers within the same school. Most teachers view online educational sites, including the one we created, as supplemental rather than primary teaching tools. These resources are used to reinforce lessons that have already been taught. It would be difficult for most schools to use online only since most schools do not have enough working computers or tablets for every student to use.

It may come as a surprise to those outside the field of education, but teachers often have to dig into their own pockets to fund their classrooms. This is especially true for elementary school teachers, but middle and high school teachers also face the same issue of not being compensated for the resources and teaching aids they purchase themselves. According to a 2022 survey conducted by Savings.com, the average teacher spends $560 out of their own pocket each year. This figure has seen a steady increase compared to the previous year's average spending of $511[6]. Some of the teachers I interviewed, said they spends around $250 in the first ten days of planning and at the beginning of the school year and an additional $150 throughout the year. Unfortunately, these expenses have been increasing year after year.

If teachers were working for a corporation or a private business, these expenses would typically be reimbursed. However, this is not the case in the field of education. While teachers can write off these expenses, it doesn't truly cover the financial burden they face in preparing their classrooms for their students. The county or school district does not provide any reimbursement for these expenses. Case in point. Many schools give each teacher an allotment of paper to use for copies each year. In one school, the teachers were told to find online worksheets for classroom exercises and homework and were told they would have to pay for the paper if they went over the allotted inventory of paper they were given. The school district complained that the teachers were using too much paper. But they were told to find online resources and make copies each day/week for their students! This is another example of the disconnect between district administration and the teachers. Or maybe it's more an example of the illogical edicts heaped upon the teachers by the administration. You be the judge.

The good news is that there are options available for support. Through platforms like Amazon and several other websites, parents can contribute by purchasing supplies for the classrooms to assist the teachers. Without the help of parents in providing school supplies, the average expenses for teachers would exceed $900 per year. It's important to reiterate that none of these expenses are covered by the county or state where the teacher teaches.

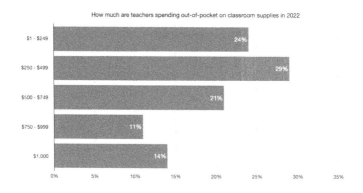

How much are teachers spending out-of-pocket on classroom supplies in 2022

Speaking of resources, the in-school support that teachers require seems to be lacking. Between 2011 and 2016, many schools I visited had several paraprofessionals, special education teachers, and other support staff available to assist in the classrooms as needed. However, due to budget cuts, many schools now have fewer special education teachers and rely heavily on paraprofessionals.

Under the Every Student Succeeds Act (ESSA), paraprofessionals serving in an instructional capacity in schools receiving federal Title I funding must meet specific qualifications. These include having an associate degree, completing two years of college, or demonstrating proficiency in reading, writing, and math through a state or local academic assessment. For paraeducators in schools without Title I funding, a high school diploma or GED is the minimum requirement, along with a demonstration of skills in assisting in classroom instruction through a state or local test. It is important to note that paraprofessionals cannot serve as substitutes in the absence of primary teachers or provide full instruction without direct supervision from teachers.

Special education teachers play a crucial role in supporting students with various learning disabilities, developmental delays, or physical disabilities. They are trained to create individualized education plans (IEPs) for each student, addressing their unique needs and facilitating progress in academic and social-emotional development. In the past, these teachers often worked with a team of professionals, such as speech therapists and occupational therapists, to provide comprehensive support. However, to cut costs, speech and occupational therapists are now assigned to multiple schools, resulting in less day-to-day assistance and allowing the district to save money by not having one in each school.

The reduction in classroom support adds additional stress to teachers. It is important to clarify that this is not a criticism of paraprofessionals, as they play a vital role.

However, teachers who have students with limited English proficiency require the support of an ESOL teacher in the school. Similarly, teachers with special education students in their classes need the expertise of a special education teacher to provide targeted assistance. These services need to be fully reinstated to alleviate some of the responsibilities placed on teachers. It is worth noting that under the ESSA requirements if your child has special needs, you have the right to demand that the school provide a special education teacher to support them in their classes. But you didn't hear that from me[7].

Behavior

I conducted a series of standardized questions during my interviews with educators and administrators to gather insights. Interestingly, the one topic that both administrators and educators unanimously agreed on was the decline in student behavior. It is a matter of concern that student behavior has worsened over time, and this sentiment is shared by experienced educators who have been in the field for more than two decades.

Today's children are growing up with a sense of entitlement, narcissism, disrespect, and laziness, unlike any other time in history. While this assessment is based on personal anecdotes, the evidence is clearly visible in classrooms across the country. I could compile a book filled with the stories that have been shared with me. If you doubt the severity of the situation, I encourage you to search for videos on YouTube of students fighting teachers. In certain school districts, being a high school teacher means facing threats of violence or having to defend oneself against physical attacks. As I write this, there are reports of students at West-field High School in Texas allegedly forming a mob and brutally assaulting an assistant principal, leaving her unable to speak[8]. In California, one of our content creators returned from lunch to find a note stuck into the white-board with a knife, warning him to watch his back.

Even as early as first grade, I have witnessed and heard numerous stories of elementary students using profanity and disrespectful language toward their teachers. In one second-grade class, a student in the midst of a meltdown openly declared, "Fuck all of you, including you," singling out the teacher. And that's just in

Student: Why am I failing your class?
Teacher: You haven't turned in any assignments.
Student: It's because you don't like me, isn't it?
Teacher: No, it's definitely the assignments.
Email from parent: Why are you bullying my child?
Welcome to teaching in 2019...

elementary school. The stories from middle and high school are even more distressing. Depending on the community and location, the threat of violence can become a chilling reality, extending beyond mere verbal threats from angry students. Teachers who have worked in high-crime districts have shared accounts of finding knives stuck in their desks, being followed by students outside of school, and even having students waiting for them at their cars. It's important to note that these incidents are not limited to high-crime areas; teachers in middle-class suburbs are also reporting an increase in threats from both parents and students. I won't delve into further stories at this point, as we will revisit the topic of behavior in the chapter dedicated to students. However, it is evident to everyone in the education field that while violent and disrespectful behavior is not the norm, there has been a noticeable increase in both the frequency and severity of incidents.

The crux of the issue is that many parents are failing to instill respect for authority in their children. Instead, they are teaching them to view authority figures as oppressors or obstacles. Those parents who march up to the school immediately to fight to get their child out of trouble. This poses a significant problem for teachers, as maintaining control of the classroom is crucial for effectively delivering lessons and activities each day. I have personally experienced how a disruptive student can disrupt the entire class, causing the curriculum to fall behind schedule and negatively impacting all students who are eager to learn. Now, imagine the challenges that arise when there are not just one or two but multiple students causing disruptions in a class.

New behavior issues have emerged in recent years. In some schools, as early as second grade, students are hacking into student accounts or teacher logins and causing problems. I know of a school near my location where a second-grade student hacked into another student's account and posted a vulgar message about the teacher. A quick internet search will reveal how frequently kids as young as 13 are hacking school computers to alter grades. During a visit to a school in Alabama, I learned that a fifth-grade student had hacked into several teachers' computers, using other teachers' email addresses to send vulgar messages to other teachers and administrators[9].

Teachers have had their disciplinary options severely limited. Today, teachers are left with only timeout or sending the student to the office as disciplinary measures. However, many schools have instructed teachers not to send students to the office unless they are physically out of control. I have visited schools where more than a dozen students were in the front office for disciplinary issues. It's important to note that school front offices are not designed to accommodate such a large number of students, which places additional burden and stress on the school staff, who are now expected to handle these problems themselves, taking away valuable class time from other students.

Furthermore, some elementary administrators have resorted to literally bribing students with candy or other incentives to behave and return to the classroom. Unfortunately, this approach only creates bigger problems, as students and their peers witness the rewards that come with disruptive behavior. This undermines the authority of teachers and adds additional stress to their already challenging role. Teachers send students to the office for disciplinary action, only to have them receive a lecture and a treat before being sent back to the classroom. While this example may pertain to elementary school, it sets a precedent that students have the power to manipulate the system.

Dealing with Parents

Student and parent behavior has increasingly become a problem. It's a trend that has been highlighted by a popular meme that has been circulating for several years. The meme humorously points out the shift in parental attitudes towards school discipline. In the past, when a child got in trouble at school, parents would want to know what the child did. But nowadays, when a child gets in trouble, parents often want to know what the teacher did wrong. This meme reflects a larger truth about the changing dynamics between parents, students, and teachers.

The rise of helicopter parenting, which has now evolved into what some call "lawnmower parenting," has created a situation where tension and confrontation are more common in schools[10]. The level of disrespect that many students and parents bring to school these days is alarming. Teachers often find themselves powerless in the face of the abuses they endure from students and parents. Speaking their mind would lead to reprimand. They must remain professional.

Unfortunately, the prevalence of both helicopter and lawnmower parents has become a common issue in educational settings. Teachers often find themselves navigating the delicate balance between supporting parents' concerns and promoting their students' independence and growth. The presence of overbearing parents can create challenges, as they may question and contest decisions made by the teacher, intervene excessively in their child's academic journey or even try to influence the grading process.

Teachers are no longer able to use meaningful forms of punishment, and students are well aware of this. They know that if a teacher crosses a line, it can result in a legal battle and financial compensation. As a result, teachers are often advised to take the high road and avoid engaging in confrontations that could jeop-

DEAR PARENTS:
YOUR EXPECTATIONS
OF TEACHERS
SHOULD MATCH
YOUR COMMITMENT
AS A PARENT

ardize their careers. It's not uncommon to hear elementary students using language towards their teachers that would have led to expulsion in the past. However, today, teachers who discipline a student or send a note home are more likely than in the past, to face pushback from parents who believe their child can do no wrong. It's important to acknowledge that many children lie. They lie to avoid trouble, to get out of work, or to escape any situation that may pose a problem for them.

And by the way, teachers want you to know that your kid is not failing because he's bored and the curriculum or lessons aren't challenging enough for your Mensa student. About 99percent of the time, the student isn't paying attention, and the parents aren't paying attention to what's being sent home either. Parents who parrot this nonsense look foolish to the teacher who spends hours a week with their child.

Teachers would like parents to work with them, not against them, in addressing behavioral or academic problems. But a partnership between parents and teachers would greatly benefit the students. Both parties should be on the same side when it comes to the educational goals of the student. In my experience, the majority of parents are responsive and willing to assist teachers when they request help in resolving behavioral issues.

However, there has been a noticeable increase in instances where parents become upset with teachers and request to have their children moved to another classroom. These parents hold the belief that a specific teacher has unfairly targeted their children, hindering their academic progress.

The Race Card

This is a sensitive topic that needs to be addressed, both within the context of education and society as a whole. It is important to have these discussions without succumbing to the pressures of political correctness. My intention in addressing this matter is not to diminish or discriminate against any particular groups, but rather to highlight a significant issue that impacts a wide range of individuals, both in educational institutions and various professional environments.

Over the years, I have heard countless stories from former teachers about instances where the race card was used against them. I have personally witnessed a few of these situations as well. It is worth noting that my purpose in discussing this matter is not to provoke accusations of racism, as I firmly believe in equality and reject any notion of racial superiority. If you happen to disagree with the sentiments expressed in this section, or if you believe that I, as a middle-aged white man, am not qualified to touch upon this subject, I want to assure you that I sought feedback from a diverse group of individuals, including black friends, who read this section before it was published. To my surprise, they all confirmed the prevalence of such incidents and expressed their concern.

That being said, it is undeniable that the race card is often used as a convenient trump card in situations where individuals are dissatisfied with the outcomes or circumstances they find themselves in. It is difficult to gauge whether these individuals genuinely believe that their child was treated unfairly due to their race or if it is merely a tactic to assert pressure and get their way.

Before we delve back into the topic of education, allow

me to provide some background on my own experience. I was the owner of two small businesses: a gym and a restaurant. In February 2021, I found myself in an ironic situation where a young black man took offense when I asked him not to park in the handicapped spaces. He proceeded to label me as a racist on social media and a local app, though he conveniently omitted important details from his version of the story. For three days, people from out of state who had never set foot in or visited my establishment joined in the chorus of accusations, branding me and my gym as racist. Interestingly, on that very same day, I had to remove an older man from my restaurant for repeatedly using racial slurs. This incident illustrates a few things: firstly, racism still exists, and some individuals continue to exhibit racist behavior; secondly, people are quick to label others as racist without truly knowing them, often driven by personal dislike or anger. Such accusations can be used as a tool for bullying. I want to emphasize that being called a racist is a deeply unpleasant experience, particularly when you make a conscious effort to treat everyone with the respect and fairness prescribed by the golden rule: "Do unto others as you would have them do unto you."

The race card is not only played against teachers, but it can also have a profound impact on them. Teachers, especially those who work with young children, generally have a genuine affection for their students and feel a deep sense of responsibility towards them. Therefore, being accused of racism can be emotionally devastating. As I mentioned earlier, being labeled a racist is just as hurtful as experiencing racism firsthand. For teachers, this accusation can ruin an entire year, as it is often accompanied by a complete disregard for the underlying problems their child may be facing in the classroom. In some cases, individuals make these racist claims in the hope of pressuring the district into a settlement, making it impossible to determine the true motivations behind such allegations.

During my discussions with various teachers, including black educators, I came across instances where the race card was unfairly invoked. For example, one black teacher shared her experience of being told by a black family during a conference that they expected more from her as a black teacher after she had discussed the discipline issues she faced with their child. In another case, a teacher in Mississippi recounted how a parent accused her colleague of racism because they were unhappy with their child's grades. The parent was unaware that the accused teacher was married to a black man and was herself of mixed race.

It is essential to clarify that I am not claiming that racism has been eradicated from schools or society in general. However, it is crucial to approach situations where a teacher is said to be singling out a particular child with caution, especially when that teacher is responsible for a classroom of 15 to 20 students. It is all too common for parents these days to believe everything their child says without considering the possibility that their child may be at fault.

What many people fail to realize is that an accusation of racism results in an investigation, which becomes part of a teacher's permanent record. This investigation often involves interviewing students and colleagues who closely work with the teacher and sometimes even goes as far as involving the district or school board. It is not uncommon for parents making such claims to threaten to involve the media. Imagine having a camera shoved in your face while someone questions whether you are indeed a racist and whether you mistreated minority students. Such situations can be emotionally and professionally damaging.

We must put an end to the use of the race card, as it only serves to exacerbate racial tensions. I had a conversation with a Hispanic tutor, who is a retired teacher, and she expressed her hesitation to take jobs from certain minority parents due to the traumatic experience she had endured when falsely accused of racism in her previous teaching position. Before passing judgment on her, consider the lasting damage such an accusation can have on a person's reputation. Unless someone proudly identifies as a racist and disregards the consequences, being a teacher accused of racism is like wearing a scarlet letter, causing significant harm to the individual being attacked.

In our current society, the media has extensively focused on the issue of racism, often amplifying it to an extreme level of discussion. This has created a situation where nearly everything is labeled as racism or white supremacy, even when it may not necessarily be the case. However, it is important to recognize that this narrative is not always accurate or fair.

The Sad Part of the Job

One of the recurring issues that teachers often encounter, even without direct inquiries, is the observation of students coming from unfortunate backgrounds or challenging home environments. This holds true whether at the high school or elementary level, where teachers bear witness to both the best and worst aspects of their pupils' home lives. It is not uncommon for these observations to be heart-wrenching. We have previously touched upon the difficulties teachers face in helping their students overcome the challenges brought about by their home environments. However, it is an intricate labyrinth of problems.

One prevalent issue teachers face is parents who neglect their children, failing to provide basic care such as washing their clothes, ensuring they are well-fed, or maintaining their personal hygiene. This sad reality is more common than most people would imagine and is not solely due to financial constraints but also stems from sheer neglect. Nowadays, teachers frequently encounter parents who have children but demonstrate little interest in spending time with them, treating them more like a burden or a hindrance. Many teachers I've spoken to have shared stories about parents who are absent during nighttime, preferring to leave their children at home while they go out on dates or socialize at bars with friends. Surprisingly, such scenarios are not limited to high school-age children but also occur distressingly often among elementary school students.

Furthermore, physical abuse and sexual assault are issues that teachers inevitably come face to face with. I have yet to meet a teacher who hasn't had to refer or report cases to counselors or the Department of Family Services for investigation. It is disheartening to witness children with sores, bruises, and poor hygiene being subjected to mockery by their peers. There have been instances where young children draw pictures depicting sexual acts they have either witnessed or tragically experienced themselves.

The spectrum of parenting quality spans from poor to exemplary, and it is not always easy to discern. One may come across a financially strained parent who is genuinely doing their best but still struggles to adequately care for their child. Conversely, there are cases of affluent or middle-class parents engaging in unthinkable acts towards their own children. Teachers sometimes hesitate to report these incidents because the signs can be subtle and seldom glaringly obvious. Nevertheless, they remain profoundly distressing. I recall speaking with a teacher who hesitated to report signs that could have indicated sexual abuse, only to discover the parents two years later being arrested for precisely that. Such stories can haunt teachers, leaving them to question their decisions and harbor a sense of responsibility for not intervening sooner.

If you are inclined to think that teachers, as mandated reporters, should simply report any suspicions, regardless of substantiation, it becomes a delicate matter. State departments of family and children services are often overwhelmed with cases and may choose not to investigate if the presented evidence is not sufficiently compelling. Additionally, teachers are wary of reporting something that may result in a temporary separation of a family, only to later discover that no abuse had occurred. The situation is far from clear-cut. I should point out that teachers do not report directly, they report to their school administrators or to the school counselors.

We have yet to touch upon the issues surrounding drug abuse and drug-infested homes. In bygone years, teachers did not have to be overly concerned about a child smelling like cat urine because they hadn't been washed or had their clothes laundered since their family cat urinated on them. However, today, such an odor could be an indication of the presence of methamphetamine in the household or the house serving as a meth lab[11].

In some of the most impoverished districts, where drug use and dealing are alarmingly prevalent, teachers recount instances of elementary students drawing pictures portraying people using drugs with needles or pipes. Unfortunately, this is something they frequently witness in their daily lives. Some children even depict the violence they witness in their neighborhoods or within their own homes. The extent of these occurrences far surpasses what most well-intentioned and decent parents would ever want their child to be exposed to.

In the chapter on failing schools, we discussed the insurmountable challenges that teachers face in trying to help their students navigate circumstances that are far from conducive to a normal life. If you believe that these issues are confined solely to the poorest neighborhoods, you would be mistaken. However, it is undeniably more prevalent in those areas. Regrettably, it is often better concealed in more affluent neighborhoods, likely because it seems less believable.

We are Losing Good Teachers

If there's one statement from this chapter that I want you to remember, it's this: "We are losing good experienced teachers at an alarming rate." This has a direct impact on the quality of education your children receive. As a result, class sizes are increasing, leaving less time for individual attention and putting more strain on teachers to maintain order and control. This, in turn, adds to their stress levels. Additionally, the shortage of experienced teachers means that there are more inexperienced teachers in the workforce. This is already becoming a problem, with three-quarters of U.S. states reporting teacher shortages[12]. These are not people simply walking away from an hourly pay job.

These are teachers who went through college, got their degree, interned, passed the PRAXIS or GACE Core Academic Skills test to be certified, and then started a career. Only to find that the job is not worth the stress and frustration. When a system loses its best employees, the quality of its output inevitably suffers. This is precisely what we are witnessing in education today.

In January 2022, the National Center for Education Statistics conducted a survey that found that 44percent of public schools have full or part-time teacher vacancies[13]. Unfortunately, this problem is only expected to worsen in the future.

In our current news culture, it has become common-place to bash teachers both politically and publicly. I have personally witnessed people with little to no education experience tearing down the hard work that teachers do. Calls for more teacher accountability and oversight, imply that teachers cannot be trusted to do their jobs effectively. In the past, teachers were held in high esteem by the public. They chose a profession that may not pay as much as others with similar demands, but they were dedicated to their work. However, nowadays, teachers are sometimes regarded as slackers who don't know what they're doing and only take the job to have summers off.

Given the challenges mentioned above, it's understand-able to question why anyone would want to become a teacher today. More importantly, why should we blame the teachers? They are simply navigating a minefield of distrac-tions that take away from their primary job of teaching. The teachers I know care deeply about the success of their students. They want them to thrive and take pride in seeing their former students years later and witnessing their accomplishments. Many teachers choose this profession for the same reasons someone would become a nurse or a social worker - to help people. There is an altruistic side to being a teacher, although not all teachers enter the profes-sion for those reasons. For others, it's the best way to start a career and raise a family since you can literally bring your kids to work and bring them home.

I personally know many exceptional teachers who not only do a great job but also know how to teach effectively, consistently achieving positive results from their students. It's important to acknowledge that not all teachers are equal, and we'll discuss ineffective teachers later in this chapter. Teachers with years of experience have honed their teaching methods and should be allowed to teach in the way they know best. They understand that students have different personalities and learning styles, and one teaching style may not work for all students. For example, some students thrive in group settings, while others prefer to work independently. Some students require more praise, while others do not.

However, year after year, teachers are told that their teaching methods are not good enough and that better results would be achieved if everyone followed a specific approach. These approaches often change based on curriculum programs or grant funding. Teachers are often presented with new teaching programs designed by academics who have conducted research in controlled environment, rather than real-world classrooms. Speaking with teachers who have been teaching for over 20 years, they will tell you that these methods rarely stick around for an extended period of time.

As we discussed in the chapter "System Error," much of the spending on education remains at the top level, resulting in bloated administrative positions. These positions often micromanage every aspect of education or create new positions for friends within the district. District-level administrators, who may have started as educators themselves, add more responsibilities to teachers' plates. They forget what it's like to be in the classroom and how the additional procedures have reduced the time teachers have to teach. Districts justify the increased spending and positions by claiming the need for better outcomes on state testing and overall grades. However, the results have been declining for more than two decades. Clearly, the micromanaging isn't working and appears to be making things worse. Micromanagement of teachers' work adds to their stress levels. Like

most government agencies, the focus is on following procedures rather than achieving results. Districts and schools
want better outcomes, but teachers must first adhere to
procedures set by individuals who have little understanding
of the current realities in schools. While these administrators receive reports, it's not the same as being in the trenches
as a teacher. The more procedures, paperwork, stress, and
disruptive behavior that teachers have to deal with, the
fewer good teachers we will have.

The demand for teachers is rapidly increasing, creating
a significant gap between the need for educators in the
classroom and the available professionals. This surge in
demand is primarily driven by changes in student enrollment, shifts in pupil-teacher ratios, and a considerable level
of teacher attrition, as highlighted in a report by the
Learning Policy Institute. According to the Learning Policy
Institute report, new teachers are leaving the profession at
higher rates compared to those leaving due to retirement.
Additionally, the report reveals that within their first five
years of teaching, new educators are leaving the profession
at rates ranging from 19 percent to 30 percent. This growing
demand for teachers and the concerning attrition rates
emphasize the pressing need for strategies and initiatives to
address this issue.

The importance of experienced teachers cannot be over-
stated. When creating our educational videos, we made sure
to select teachers who had taught the same lessons for
several years. Repetition is key to effective learning. A
teacher who has taught a particular lesson multiple times
has refined their approach to address the specific needs and
questions of their students. Experience allows them to
anticipate areas where students may struggle to understand
and predict the questions that are likely to arise. The value

of experience in teaching a lesson cannot be emphasized enough. For example, when I needed a video on "right angles," I asked a high school teacher who had been teaching videos for us on "solving right angles" instead of waiting for a 4th-grade teacher to create the lesson. However, when I shared the video with 4th and 5th grade teachers for peer review, the feedback was not positive. The information in the video was accurate, but it lacked explanations that were appropriate for 4th and 5th graders. A 4th-grade student does not understand why it's called a "right angle" or whether angles that turn the other way are called "left angles." A teacher with experience at that grade level would include answers to these questions in their lesson because they understand the age group and their level of knowledge. Their understanding comes from their experience.

In January 2023, Business Insider published a story about a teacher who left the profession to work at Costco. The article highlighted how much happier and less exhausted this former teacher is now that she's no longer working in education. Her statement speaks volumes: "I do not miss it at all. My work-life balance is so much better, and I am no longer sick or exhausted like I used to be when I was a teacher[14]." This sentiment resonates with many people who would find it challenging to work as a teacher in the public school system. Teachers are expected to teach a class of students while their ability to discipline them has been stripped away. Teachers must also navigate the varying levels of parental involvement, from barely present to overbearing. They cannot express their true thoughts and feelings to administrators, students, or parents, so they often have to bite their tongues. On top of all this, teachers are constantly told to change their teaching methods, restrict their speech, and abandon previously effective approaches. Many teachers have to purchase their own resources due to limited funding. Furthermore, parents often blame them for their students' failures. It's no wonder that unofficial estimates suggest that over 50 percent of teachers rely on anxiety and depression medication to cope or sleep.

When I interviewed numerous educators, the numbers were shocking, with estimates ranging from 50percent to 65 percent of their colleagues being on medication.

All these factors contribute to severe teacher shortages. A survey conducted in November 2021 found that 48 percent of teachers had considered changing jobs in the past month, up from 32 percent in June 2021[15]. The Economic Policy Institute estimates that there are currently about 118,000 unfilled teaching positions nationwide. By 2025, this shortfall is projected to reach 200,000[16]. The nationwide teacher shortage is a significant and growing issue that surpasses previous estimates. It is a real concern that needs to be addressed. However, teaching colleges have seen a significant drop in enrollment since 2015[17]. I reached out to four colleges that offer teaching degrees in early childhood education, and all of them confirmed that they do not have full classes. The problem of teacher shortages has been a concern since 2011 and has only worsened over time.

In December 2022, Governor Phil Murphy of New Jersey signed a bill that has significant implications for prospective teachers in the state. The bill eliminates the Education Teacher Performance Assessment (edTPA) requirement, which was previously mandatory for individuals seeking a permanent standard teaching certificate. Starting in the spring of 2024, teacher candidates who have completed the necessary steps to become educators will no longer be obligated to take this test[18].

This legislative move has received mixed reactions. Sean Spiller, the President of the New Jersey Education Association, which represents the largest teachers union in the state, applauded the decision, deeming the test requirement unnecessary. In his statement, Spiller expressed that Governor Murphy's action is a victory for both students and educators in New Jersey. Not sure I'd call this a win-win. Many critics are also questioning whether this change will truly benefit the students in the long run.

One concern that arises from states lowering the requirements to become a teacher is the failure to address the underlying issues that have pushed many current teachers to leave the profession. While these new laws may offer a temporary solution, they do not tackle the root causes of the exodus. It raises the question of how long these newly minted teachers will endure the same challenging working conditions before they, too, realize that they may have made a career mistake. In essence, these laws may be seen as mere band-aids that temporarily alleviate the problem rather than providing a comprehensive and sustainable solution.

How About Teacher Pay

Some would argue that we need to spend more on teachers. I'm not opposed to giving teachers pay raises. So, why do I advocate for better teacher pay after arguing that more money won't fix education? It's because we need to incentivize the brightest among us to share their knowledge with students who are eager to learn. After all, there are experts in every subject, and we want to ensure that students have access to the best possible education.

To be clear, I believe that increasing teacher salaries should be done to attract more qualified teaching candidates and to retain the excellent teachers we already have.This is how the real world of business operates. In my own company, I pay to keep my best and most experienced employees working so that I don't end up with a team of inexperienced individuals doing the majority of the work, which is what is happening now in education. If we want students to be taught by the best and brightest, we need to compete with better-paying careers.

Especially when you consider that schools are now tasked with teaching a broad range of technologies, including coding, robotics, and advanced science. The field of science has progressed far beyond the average science teacher's level of expertise. Shouldn't we want educators who are up to date with the most recent scientific advancements and technological developments? It would be even better if they had practical experience in the field. There's an old saying, "Those who can, do... and those who can't, teach." If we believe there is even a small measure of truth to this statement, why not pay those who "CAN" so that they will consider teaching? Similarly, teachers who perform well and achieve success in the classroom should be rewarded, just as they would be in a business setting.

But would increasing teacher pay within the current education system actually improve the quality of education in schools? Before we delve deeper into that question, let's take a closer look at what teachers currently earn and how they receive pay raises.

Average Teacher Pay in Order of State Scores 2022

Massachusetts	$77,804	Florida	$49,407
New Jersey	$69,623	Texas	$52,575
Connecticut	$72,561	Maine	$51,077
Wisconsin	$54,998	Rhode Island	$66,477
Virginia	$51,049	Georgia	$54,602
Vermont	$60,187	Michigan	$62,200
Illinois	$61,602	Wyoming	$58,650
Maryland	$66,961	California	$78,711
Minnesota	$57,346	Washington	$54,147
New Hampshire	$57,253	Hawaii	$57,674
Utah	$47,244	South Dakota	$42,668
Kentucky	$52,339	District of Columbia	$76,131
Colorado	$46,506	Alabama	$48,868
New York	$79,637	North Dakota	$51,618
Pennsylvania	$65,863	South Carolina	$48,598
Missouri	$48,293	Idaho	$47,504
Ohio	$57,000	Nevada	$57,376
Tennessee	$48,456	Oregon	$61,631
Iowa	$55,443	Arizona	$47,403
North Carolina	$49,837	West Virginia	$45,701
Indiana	$50,554	Oklahoma	$45,245
Montana	$51,422	Louisiana	$50,000
Nebraska	$52,338	Alaska	$68,138
Arkansas	$48,616	Mississippi	$42,925
Delaware	$60,214	New Mexico	$47,500
Kansas	$47,984		

Important to note that the averages are lower, on average, because 58% of teachers in the system haven't worked more than 3 years.

The average teacher in America earns $58,030 per year, which is comparable to the average salary of $59,124 for individuals with a bachelor's degree, according to the U.S. Census Bureau. Most teachers start with a relatively low salary and receive regular increases based on their years of experience and/or additional education. These increases can come in the form of higher degrees or additional certifications. When teachers retire, their pension is based on a percentage of their highest salary during their active working years. While a teacher can earn between $42,000 and $90,000 a year, based on years of experience and education levels, the average teacher salary stays low because few teachers are staying in education as a career for the long haul.

For example, Georgia teacher's starting salary for the 2023 to 2024 school year is between $48,410 and $58,050 for a beginning teacher with a bachelor's degree and no experience in their first three years and receives raises annually from the fourth year through the tenth year. After that, raises are given every other year until their thirtieth year. However, teachers can increase their income by obtaining a master's degree, a specialist degree (which is above a master's degree but below a doctorate), or a doctorate. In Georgia, a teacher with a master's degree earns an average of $6,000 more per year than a teacher with a bachelor's degree. A teacher with a specialist degree earns an average of $10,000 more, and a teacher with a doctorate earns an average of $22,000 more per year compared to a teacher with only a bachelor's degree. It's important to note that these figures may not be directly applicable to all 50 states, as teacher salaries and benefits vary widely throughout the United States due to different state budgets and cost of living considerations. Additionally, as attrition rates among teachers increase, the average salary decreases since more and more teachers do not stay in the profession long enough to reach higher salary levels. And let's not forget that none of those additional degrees or certifications are free, and so most teachers I know who are increasing their education also have high amounts of student debt. Keep in mind these numbers are averages, because each county can add additional funds to the starting pay or raises to attract teachers to working in their district. For instance, in Georgia, Cobb County's starting pay is the highest starting Salary in the state of Georgia at $58,050. While Henry County has the lowest starting pay at $48,410. The state pays a certain amount of the starting pay and the counties can contribute additional funds to increase the salaries of the teachers working in their counties. Most states operate in this way but the amount that the states contribute is different. For instance, South Dakota has the lowest starting pay for teachers of any state based on 2022 numbers, followed by Mississippi.

I often hear people say, "We don't pay teachers enough, so what do you expect?" This statement reflects low expectations. On the flip side, I've also heard the argument that "teachers do it for the love of the students and teaching, so they don't need to make $100,000 a year for something so altruistic." Both of these statements miss the mark. If we examine a table showing the average teacher pay for K-12 education, we can see that teacher pay and the quality of education do not necessarily go hand in hand. Simply paying teachers more, even when adjusting for the cost of living in their state, does not automatically lead to better educational outcomes. Pay, after all, is not the only reason teachers are leaving the profession.

Given the results of the table comparing average teacher pay to state scores, you might be surprised that I advocate for higher teacher salaries. There are two very simple reasons for this, and I'm drawing on my 20-plus years of experience in business to make this observation.

Firstly, the attrition rate for teachers is alarmingly high. As I write this, there is a teacher shortage in almost every state. According to the Learning Policy Institute, approximately 90percent of open teacher positions are vacant due to teachers leaving the profession, with about two-thirds leaving due to job dissatisfaction[19]. This puts additional strain on an already struggling system, resulting in a shortage of experienced educators. Teachers have the most significant in-school influence on student achievement, and the high turnover rate means that inexperienced and under-qualified teachers are being relied upon to fill the void. From a business perspective, this is akin to losing valuable talent and having to train new employees from scratch. Most large corporations understand the cost of losing experienced employees and the expense of training new, inexperienced ones. If we want our schools to attract and retain the best and most experienced talent, we must be willing to pay what the market demands. As I mentioned earlier, being a teacher is difficult and stressful. Let's pay enough to create a surplus of teachers so that the education system can choose from the best and brightest candidates.

For instance, Mississippi and South Dakota have the lowest average teacher salaries, hovering around the low $40,000s. In these states, it is highly unlikely that a teacher could afford a home and car payment on their salary alone. Can we really expect them to be passionate about working with our children, dealing with parents and administrators, and providing a high-quality education? Would you expect to see the most talented individuals choosing the teaching profession in these states?

Most people carefully weigh the financial remuneration they receive against the stress associated with their job. If the compensation does not adequately compensate for the stress endured, individuals are likely to seek alternative employment opportunities. This phenomenon is particularly evident within the education sector. Teachers and educators, who play a crucial role in shaping the minds of future generations, often face significant levels of stress. The pressure to meet academic standards, manage classrooms, and handle administrative tasks can be overwhelming. In recent times, this stress has led to an increasing number of educators leaving the profession. The discrepancy between the level of compensation and the demands of the job has created a challenging environment for those dedicated to the field of education. As a result, it has become imperative for educational institutions to address this issue and find effective ways to retain talented educators.

The second reason relates to finding teachers with practical experience in the subjects they teach. For example, a science teacher who has worked in the field of science or a coding teacher who has actually produced something using code. In case you are unaware, many public school systems have teachers teaching technology subjects without any real-world experience in those fields. These teachers often only learn the subject matter for the purpose of teaching it to others. While a teacher with a basic understanding of a subject can teach what is written in a curriculum, they may struggle to bring passion to the subject matter or answer deeper questions based on their own experiences. In my own experience, I have been asked by administrators to create content that brings technical subjects to life because the teachers themselves lack sufficient knowledge. Administrators have requested content to show teachers how to teach certain subjects, not for the students' benefit but to compensate for the teachers' lack of expertise. It is not uncommon for many schools to have teachers teaching subjects they are not familiar with, essentially regurgitating content from a textbook. If you were studying engineering in college, you would expect a teacher who truly knows and understands engineering. The solution is to pay more for better-qualified instructors, especially at the high school level. We should also reward teachers who achieve good results with higher pay or bonuses. This last statement may be controversial to teachers' unions, as they often advocate for pay increases based solely on years of experience, even if a teacher has become disengaged and is no longer performing at their best.

Another common argument is that there isn't enough money in school budgets to for pay good teachers. However, as I have emphasized throughout this book, it is not necessary to increase the budget of every school system in America to find the extra funds. Instead, we need to eliminate top-heavy administrative positions, reduce waste, and cut unnecessary expenses. It is frustrating to see more money being spent on micromanaging teachers than on the teachers themselves, who are the ones doing the actual work. This alone suggests that district administration views teachers as the problem and believes they need constant oversight.

Ironically, administrators argue that they require increased oversight due to the influx of new, inexperienced teachers. However, this claim seems to be a mere distraction. If this were indeed the primary concern, the micromanagement would solely focus on supporting and guiding new educators. Furthermore, administrators appear to overlook the fact that excessive micromanagement adds to the stress levels of teachers, leading to a higher turnover rate and exacerbating the issue at hand.

I strongly believe that increasing the pay for exceptional teachers, experienced professionals, and those who consistently deliver outstanding results would significantly enhance the quality of education. While it is true that there are numerous challenges in the education system that extend beyond teachers' salaries, raising their pay would undoubtedly be a crucial step toward achieving better outcomes in the classroom. But let's be realistic: even a $10,000-a-year raise won't help if the teachers do not feel safe or are being told that everything they learned in college about

WHAT IT'S LIKE TRYING TO MAKE LESSON PLANS FOR 40 KIDS WITH...

Different learning abilities/styles/needs, different family/cultural backgrounds, all while making sure they pass the several standardized tests that determine my value as a teacher to the school.

teaching is now thrown out the window to appease the latest teaching program. More money needs to be spent on teachers and in the assistance they receive at the school level. Stress and income are the two best places to start and will make an immediate difference.

Corporations are well aware of the financial advantage that comes with employing experienced individuals. These individuals not only possess a higher level of competence in their roles, but they also require less supervision and guidance to carry out their tasks effectively. Moreover, experienced employees tend to be more self-reliant and proactive in their work, resulting in improved efficiency and productivity. They are often adept at problem-solving and decision-making, allowing them to handle challenges independently and deliver high-quality results. These facts seem to have been missed by most school districts.

Good Teacher, Bad Teacher

Decades of research have consistently demonstrated the profound and enduring impact that a teacher's job performance has on the lives of students. The influence of a highly effective teacher can be transformative, increasing the likelihood of college attendance, reducing the risk of teenage parenthood, boosting lifetime earnings, and promoting retirement savings. Conversely, just one year with a low-performing teacher can set students back academically.

It is important to recognize that there is a distinction between good teachers and bad teachers, and this differentiation has significant implications for the educational system in which your children are enrolled. While the notion of good or bad teaching may seem subjective, it is essential to understand that there are clearly defined criteria by which we assess teacher effectiveness. Unfortunately, many parents who believe they can identify the quality of teachers in their children's schools are often mistaken. Frequently, parental judgments about teachers are based on rumors or isolated negative experiences, which may or may not accurately reflect a teacher's abilities. Additionally, parents sometimes mistakenly assume that if their child had a smooth school year with a particular teacher, they have found an exceptional educator. It is worth noting that teachers and administrators have the authority to select their child's teacher. To identify the most effective teachers in a school, one can examine which teachers have the highest number of other teachers or school administrators entrusting their own children's education to them. Thats not to say that other teachers aren't good teachers or are not effective teachers.

Many teachers I have spoken to refer to a small group of teachers who consistently receive praise from parents and are highly sought after by PTA moms. As mentioned earlier in this chapter, these teachers have a reputation for producing excellent academic results, with students achieving high grades and seemingly never encountering difficulties. However, what many parents may not realize is that these teachers may simply be passing students along without adequately challenging them.

Every teacher in a school is aware of these highly regarded teachers because good teachers often face challenges the following year when parents express concern that their child is falling behind or struggling academically. The good teacher is inevitably compared to the previous year's teacher, who "appeared" to have no trouble teaching their child and consistently awarded them high grades. Consequently, good teacher finds themselves in a situation where parents perceive them as inadequate because their child is not achieving perfect scores, leading parents to desire someone like the previous year's teacher. In reality, parents are reacting to the previous teacher's ability to create an illusion of success and alleviate any concerns they may have had. This cycle perpetuates itself year after year.

Some ineffective teachers adopt this approach to avoid confrontations with parents, as it is easier to apply lenient grading practices. Others relish the attention they receive from being praised for their supposed exceptional work. Some do it to avoid the additional paperwork. A larger portion of ineffective teachers are motivated by the desire to advance quickly within the education system and gain promotions. These teachers, known as "climbers," often cultivate relationships with PTA moms and administrators. Being the teacher who generates no parent complaints and is adored by both parents and the PTA has its advantages. Every good teacher is aware of this dynamic, but they also understand that complaining is futile because the district and school administration values a lack of parental drama. Thus, the system perpetuates itself illogically year after year, reinforcing the notion that this approach works. However, it is important to note that climbers often ascend the ranks for the wrong reasons.

If I were to offer one significant criticism of the teaching profession, it would be the lack of self-regulation in identifying and addressing ineffective teachers. Dismissal of a teacher is exceedingly difficult, even in states without the support of teachers' unions. Consequently, poorly performing teachers continue to teach year after year with minimal or no consequences. Sometimes, I even wonder if a more rigorous evaluation process would be beneficial. However, as I mentioned earlier, teachers are hesitant to criticize their colleagues.

One reason teachers are reluctant to hold each other accountable is the existence of cliques within schools. Most people are familiar with student cliques, but it is worth noting that teachers also form cliques. This occasionally leads to drama as different factions engage in gossip about teachers from other cliques. This observation further supports the notion that adult life often resembles an extended version of grade school. While gossip and drama may not necessarily hinder teachers' ability to fulfill their responsibilities, there are instances where significant drama arises. As in any other profession, when individuals come together, personal relationships and attractions can develop. Unfortunately, teachers engaging in extramarital affairs are more common than the average person realizes. I recall hearing stories about teachers being transferred to different schools to separate them from another teacher with whom they were involved in a romantic relationship. While such behavior occurs in various professional settings, it becomes particularly problematic when it involves children, parents, and other teachers. I witnessed this go on in my own high school experience. In other corporate environments with a larger workforce, it is easier to conceal such relationships. However, in a school setting, it only takes one teacher, parent, or student to voice concerns, and news spreads rapidly.

Now, let's address a more sensitive topic. There are frequent reports of teachers engaging in sexual relationships with students and subsequently being caught. Many women reading this may be quick to condemn male teachers who cannot control their impulses around young girls. However, it is important to acknowledge that there is a growing number of cases involving female teachers engaging in sexual relationships with underage boys. A quick Google search reveals 48 incidents of female teachers having sex with underage boys in just the past three years, with some victims as young as seventh graders.

Nevertheless, it is crucial to recognize that when I discuss bad teachers engaging in inappropriate behavior or making poor choices, they are individuals who, like the general population, sometimes make regrettable decisions. The concern arises when these choices negatively impact the students. While most parents hope for teachers who possess higher moral standards than the average person, it is unrealistic to expect perfection. In the example I shared earlier about the city council relocating teachers to separate them, you may have noticed that I did not mention their eventual termination. This is because teachers rarely get fired, especially in the current climate of teacher shortages. School districts are increasingly hesitant to dismiss teachers.

Allow me to conclude by emphasizing that teachers are human beings who, like everyone else, make mistakes. Instances of adultery, DUIs, and other common problems occur in small businesses, large corporations, and other professional settings. It should only be an issue if it directly affects the students.

Firing Bad Teachers

One well-known aspect of the education system is the difficulty in terminating the employment of teachers. However, it may come as a surprise to many readers just how challenging it truly is. Allow me to elaborate on the intricacies involved. Each state has its own set of rules and regulations when it comes to firing teachers, which are influenced by factors such as state laws and the presence of teachers' unions or collective bargaining agreements. In states like Georgia and Florida, which are right-to-work states with minimal union influence, the process is relatively easier[20]. However, in states where collective bargaining agreements are in place, the task becomes significantly more arduous due to the inclusion of provisions that protect teachers from being fired without a lengthy due process.

The concept of due process may seem fair on the surface, but the time it takes to complete the process in certain states can range from three to five years. Many of you may be familiar with the infamous "rubber rooms" in New York, where up to 700 teachers accused of misconduct were required to report each weekday from 8:30 am to 3:20 pm, mirroring the school day, with a 50-minute lunch break. These teachers were essentially confined to these rooms while awaiting the completion of their due process to determine whether they could be terminated or not. Thanks to the collective bargaining agreements in states like New York, once a teacher achieves tenure, they cannot be fired without engaging in a lengthy legal battle, which some cities and states choose not to pursue[21].

Allow me to provide an example to illustrate the impact of these regulations. In the New York City public school system, there was a case involving Aryeh Eller, who taught orchestral music at Hillcrest High School in Queens. After just two full years of teaching, Eller was suspended in November 1999 for allegedly harassing female students with sexual comments and inappropriate touching. Unfortunately, the school administration delayed involving the authorities, and by the time an investigation was conducted, Eller had already obtained tenure after just three years on the job. As of 2019, Eller had not set foot in a classroom for two decades but had received a total of $1.7 million in salary from New York taxpayers. What's even more astonishing is that he continued to receive mandatory salary increases over the years, and in 2019, he was earning $132,753 annually without doing any work[22].

This is just one of many examples that highlight the issue at hand. Prior to working in education, I was unaware that K-12 teachers could receive tenure. However, in states where teachers' unions hold significant control, it is common for K-12 teachers to obtain tenure, which essentially makes it impossible to terminate their employment. It is important to note that there is a distinction between being vested and having tenure. Most teachers have a vestment period, which requires them to work a certain number of years before becoming eligible for retirement benefits, either partially or in full.

In states where teachers' unions have less influence and are not bound by collective bargaining agreements, terminating a teacher's employment is still challenging but not entirely impossible. I personally know of two teachers who were fired for misconduct that was far less severe than what others have gotten away with. The reality is that once teachers in states like New York achieve tenure, it becomes nearly impossible to replace them, even if they have a documented history of poor performance or engaging in sexual abuse. New York eventually extended the eligibility period for tenure from three to four years and made it more difficult to obtain. From my perspective, I fail to comprehend the necessity of tenure for K-12 teachers or even college professors, for that matter. It is needless to say the teachers' union vehemently opposes any changes to the current system.

Attempting to dismiss a single ineffective teacher can take years and cost taxpayers hundreds of thousands of dollars. Furthermore, even teachers found guilty of severe misconduct, such as missing months of the school year or verbally and physically abusing students, are often reinstated in the classroom based on settled legal precedent, as determined by arbitrators.

However, amidst the political complexities surrounding this issue, a common-sense element seems to be overlooked. In states where tenure makes it impossible to remove underperforming teachers, the quality of education inevitably suffers. It is a matter of common sense that if a district's schools are staffed with underperforming teachers year after year, the overall quality of education will decline. This has even been proven in a court of law.

A high-profile case that challenged similar tenure laws in California, known as Vergara v. California, demonstrated how these laws deprived students of a fair chance at receiving the education they deserve. In a 2014 trial court ruling that overturned the laws, the judge described the evidence presented by the plaintiffs as "shocking to the conscience." Although the decision was later overturned due to questions regarding whether students disadvantaged by California's tenure and dismissal laws constitute a protected class, the findings regarding the detrimental effects of these laws remain unchallenged to this day[23].

Consider how a business would function if it were unable to replace underperforming employees with more qualified individuals. The business would inevitably suffer and lose credibility with its customers. In such a scenario, the business would ultimately fail. However, public schools do not face the same fate. This should be a cause for concern for parents, as their children may be assigned to teachers with a documented history of poor performance. Imagine the outrage if the New York Yankees never replaced underperforming players because of tenure and instead continued to field a team that had little chance of winning. Such a scenario would be unheard of. Yet, the teachers' union would have us believe that once someone becomes a teacher and secures a job, their virtues and overall performance are so exceptional that there is never a need to seek better performance or hold them accountable.

Grading Teachers

For several years, there has been a significant push to implement a system for grading teachers. Many ideas have been proposed and discussed regarding how this could be accomplished. As one might expect, teachers are generally not supportive of this concept. Initially, I was in favor of teacher grading, whether through the average scores of their students on standardized tests that they already take or through another fair means of assessment. However, my perspective has shifted after working closely with classroom teachers and witnessing the challenges that many of them face. Allow me to elaborate on the difficulties associated with evaluating teachers solely based on their students' assessments.

In order to use class assessments as a measure of a teacher's performance or abilities, we would have to assume that all students are starting from the same level of academic readiness, with similar IQ levels and educational backgrounds from the previous grade. Unfortunately, teachers are faced with a diverse range of students each year, each with their own unique personalities and IQ levels. A teacher could be assigned a class with many low-performing students or a class with high-performing students. Which class would you prefer to have if your own pay raise was dependent on their improved performance? Consider the scenario of an "inclusion class" where students with special educational needs are combined with non-disabled students of the same age. In an inclusion class, teachers must accommodate the individualized education plans (IEPs) of each student with special needs, which can vary greatly. This often means providing modified assignments and additional support to ensure all students can succeed. Managing such a diverse classroom environment can be challenging, particularly when teachers no longer have the support of a dedicated special education teacher due to budget cuts.

In order to accurately gauge student growth, it would be

necessary to administer an assessment at the beginning of the school year to establish a baseline for each class. Students already undergo testing at the start of the year, but this assessment would need to include questions aligned with the curriculum they will be taught throughout the year. This would allow us to measure their progress by comparing their performance at the end of the year. However, if we rely on tests designed to assess knowledge from the previous year, we would be evaluating teachers based on the previous teacher's instruction. Creating a baseline and administering additional assessments would require significant time and effort, potentially detracting from valuable instructional time and adding to the already burdensome number of assessments students must complete.

Is there a simpler alternative that could be implemented? Some may argue that teachers should be able to ensure their students meet end-of-year standards. However, this notion assumes that all students begin the year already meeting the standards from the previous grade. If students are not on track with the prior grade's standards, teachers would have to spend valuable time catching them up, making it an unfair comparison. This could also lead to teachers being reluctant to teach students with lower abilities or disabilities due to the potential impact on their employment or pay raise.

One possible solution could involve establishing a baseline for each teacher's class by averaging the performance of the students they received from the previous years. This would require the development of an algorithm or the involvement of an administrator to determine the baseline and appropriate growth expectations for the end of the year. However, even this approach presents complexities and challenges, as there are various factors to consider.

Regardless of how the grading system is implemented, it is bound to have unintended consequences. For example, one disruptive student in a class could negatively impact the progress of the entire class, placing additional stress on the teacher. Additionally, there may be instances where schools are unable to hire enough support for classrooms with struggling students, resulting in an unfair burden on the teacher to provide extra assistance. I have personally witnessed such scenarios where school principals have reached out for additional resources to compensate for cuts in the budget. Let's face it: even a brilliant plan would be opposed by the teacher's unions.

Politics

Back in the '70s, '80s, and even the '90s, teachers had a clear mandate to focus on academic subjects such as reading, science, writing, and arithmetic. Alongside these subjects, there were also gym and shop classes, and for those of us who are a bit older, home economics was a part of the curriculum. Each teacher had their own specialized subject to teach, whether it was math, science, or something else.

Fast forward to today's education landscape, and we see a shift in the decision-making power, with administrators incorporating social and political ideologies into the curriculum. While there is value in teaching basic sex education and promoting inclusivity, many schools are introducing questionable social designs into their teaching materials. In some cases, it seems that schools are intentionally bypassing parental authority or concealing political and social messages from parents.

This situation creates discomfort for teachers who simply want to focus on providing a quality education and leave the social and political education to the parents. Unfortunately, some teachers who disagree with these ideologies find themselves seeking new job opportunities. This not only affects the teachers themselves but also contributes to the ongoing challenge of attracting and retaining talented educators.

Rhode Island high school teacher Ramona Bessinger raised concern over teachers being forced to "adhere to political ideologies in the classroom." Ramona is now receiving threats and harassment due to her views and opposition.

"Teachers are being forced to adhere to these political ideologies in the classroom and contrary to their personal beliefs and what is even right or true. For example, this anti-American content that we are seeing, this anti-girl, anti-boy content that we are seeing.[24]"

In progressive districts, teachers often feel bullied or harassed due to their personal beliefs. This is troubling, as the education profession is already facing difficulties in retaining its best teachers and filling vacant positions. It reflects a broader trend in our society, where disagreements are increasingly met with hostility instead of fostering healthy dialogue.

Unfortunately, some individuals within the education community believe they have a better understanding of what children should be taught about political and social issues than the parents themselves. This ideology is concerning, as it undermines the role of parents in shaping their children's values and beliefs and puts the teachers in the line of fire when the parents come for answers.

The manifestation of this ideology has led to heated encounters at school board meetings across the country, many of which have been documented and shared on platforms like YouTube.

If we truly want to improve education, it is essential to empower teachers to focus on teaching the fundamentals. Parents, on the other hand, should be entrusted with the responsibility of instilling values and guiding their children's moral development, whether through religious institutions, home environments, or a combination of both. While there are a handful of activist teachers, many educators do not want to be tasked with grading a student's political ideology.

ESOL

Allow me to provide an explanation for those who may not be familiar with ESOL. The English for Speakers of Other Languages (ESOL) program is designed to offer English language instruction to English Language Learners (ELLs) in kindergarten through grade 12. This program is mandated by local educational agencies and aims to support students who have been identified as having insufficient language proficiency through language proficiency testing. These students receive language support from certified teachers who possess extensive knowledge of second language acquisition and utilize effective strategies to meet their needs. This comprehensive description is how the Department of Education defines ESOL. In simpler terms, ESOL is a program implemented in most public schools across America to assist students who have limited or no knowledge of the English language. ESOL teachers dedicate a portion of their day to working with grade-level students who qualify for the program, helping them improve their understanding and usage of the English language to enhance their academic performance.

I have included this information in the teacher section of the book due to the current border situation. With the increasing number of immigrants entering the country with children, the impact is being felt in schools nationwide. This influx of immigrant children is placing additional strain on teachers and schools that are already grappling with limited resources. It is important to note that this issue is not confined to the southern border; it is affecting communities across the country. As a resident of a suburb north of Atlanta, I have witnessed a significant rise in the number of children who do not speak fluent English. I should point out that it's not all Latin American students. In many cases, teachers are now faced with the challenge of instructing students who may struggle to comprehend lessons or understand instructions. While ESOL classes provide valuable support, they alone are insufficient, especially considering that most ESOL teachers are only allocated 30 to 45 minutes per day with each student.

Compounding the situation is the fact that in many Latin American households, fathers are the primary breadwinners while mothers stay at home. Often, the mothers do not speak English, relying solely on the father for communication. Consequently, these children are not exposed to English being spoken at home, which can hinder the development of their English language skills. Its no uncommon for a teacher to rely on older children to translate during teacher-parent conferences to effectively communicate with non-English-speaking parents.

This issue is particularly concerning given the existing shortage of teachers. Some schools have resorted to offering free ESOL certification to teachers in order to have a sufficient number of certified educators who can effectively teach classes with students whose English language skills are below average or non-existent. This places an even greater burden on schools as class sizes continue to grow and teachers are tasked with providing special attention to a portion of the class. Unfortunately, there is no indication that this situation will improve in the near future, and it is likely to worsen as the influx of immigrant children shows no signs of slowing down.

---

1. https://www.zippia.com/teacher-jobs/demographics/
2. https://www.zippia.com/answers/what-percentage-of-teachers-quit-in-the-first-five-years/
3. https://soeonline.american.edu/blog/the-current-state-of-teacher-burnout-in-america/
4. https://www.washingtonpost.com/local/education/the-year-of-the-easy-b-how-lowering-grading-standards-may-punish-students/2020/05/01/f97cb206-8898-11ea-9dfd-990f9dcc71fc_story.html
5. https://www.teacherspayteachers.com/
6. https://www.savings.com/insights/teacher-spending-study
7. https://www2.ed.gov/policy/elsec/leg/essa/essa-flex.pdf
8. https://www.kbtx.com/2023/05/01/high-school-students-allegedly-mob-beat-assistant-principal/
9. https://www.edweek.org/technology/at-age-12-they-hacked-their-school-district-the-adults-are-still-trying-to-catch-up/2018/11
    https://www.malwarebytes.com/blog/news/2022/09/when-students-hack-their-schools
    https://www.edsurge.com/news/2019-09-10-a-bored-student-hacked-his-school-s-systems-will-the-edtech-industry-pay-attention
10. https://pittsburgh.momcollective.com/parenting-perspectives/rise-lawnmower-parent/
11. https://ag.nv.gov/Hot_Topics/Issue/Meth_House/

12. https://abcnews.go.com/US/map-shows-us-states-dealing-teaching-shortage-data/story?id=96752632

13. https://www.k12dive.com/news/nces-nearly-half-of-public-schools-impacted-by-staffing-shortage-resignat/619732/

14. https://www.businessinsider.com/costco-worker-loves-new-job-burning-out-teaching-2023-1

15. https://www.k12dive.com/news/survey-48-of-teachers-considering-job-change/610477/

16. https://ce.fresno.edu/news/states-in-every-part-of-the-country-have-teacher-shortages/

17. https://www.insidehighered.com/news/2022/08/29/teacher-shortage-tied-education-programs-enrollment-drop

18. https://newjerseymonitor.com/briefs/governor-murphy-signs-bill-eliminating-test-for-would-be-teachers/

19. https://learningpolicyinstitute.org/press-release/where-have-all-teachers-gone
    https://learningpolicyinstitute.org/product/teacher-turnover-report
    https://learningpolicyinstitute.org/blog/policymakers-should-ring-new-year-action-end-teacher-shortages

20. https://fordhaminstitute.org/national/research/how-strong-are-us-teacher-unions-state-state-comparison

21. https://nypost.com/2020/08/15/nyc-pledged-to-ban-teacher-rubber-rooms-they-went-underground-instead/

22. https://nypost.com/2019/11/02/nyc-pays-rubber-room-teacher-six-figures-20-years-after-sex-abuse-claims/
    https://www.huffpost.com/entry/aryeh-eller-new-york-teac_n_2567546

23. https://www.gse.harvard.edu/ideas/news/14/03/education-courts-vergara-v-california

24. https://www.washingtonexaminer.com/restoring-america/community-family/threatening-messages-reportedly-directed-at-rhode-island-teacher-who-opposes-critical-race-theory

7

STUDENTS

"It is easier to build strong children than to repair broken men."
Frederick Douglass

Black, White, Brown...It must be about Race

Whenever people tell me that the reason for disparagement in education among ethnic groups is systemic racism, I quickly point out that Nigerian parents settle in this country, look like African Americans, and yet outperform white American students academically. Asian students are famous for their academic performance. So much so that Harvard was sued for limiting the number of Asian students accepted into the college. Neither ethnic group is white, yet they perform better on average than white students. Is it because they are genetically more intelligent, have bigger brains, or are born with unique skills? No. The answer lies in what we discussed in the school chapter. Nigerian and Asian parents insist their kids do well in school and continue their education. They consider it a priority and necessary for their child's best possible future. The benefits of being well-educated are drummed into their children from the start of elementary education. Both Nigerian and Asian parents expect their kids to excel in school and focus on their education. In many cases, they do not participate in organized sports; if they do, it is not a more significant part of their lives than school. Nigerian and Asian parents do not point the finger at the teacher when their child doesn't perform well; they expect their kids to buckle down and succeed. One Nigerian parent I spoke with said, "We are old school, so to speak; when it comes to holding our kids accountable for their efforts in school, I don't allow my kids any excuses." BINGO. Expectations are high because they teach their kids that a good education often leads to a better financial life. And excuses are not acceptable[1].

A 2015 study in the Official Journal of the American Academy of Pediatrics found that children whose parents had high expectations and expected them to go to college performed better on tests than those with low expectations[2]. This should be common sense, or at least apparent. The trend occurred among both wealthy and low-income families. Nowhere in this study did it differentiate outcomes based on race. It is intriguing to note the abundance of articles attempting to debunk this notion by asserting that high parental expectations can result in mental health problems and diminished self-esteem. They seem to imply that parents should adopt a more lenient approach towards their children. Yet, are we not already inundated with evidence that suggests our children are already too coddled?

In 2006, Charles Barkley said in an interview with Graham Bensinger, "I do this little science experiment when I speak at schools. Let's say I'm at a white school. I asked how many kids want to play pro sports. Less than 10 percent raise their hand. So I'd ask, what do you want to do? I want to be a doctor, and I want to be a lawyer; I want to be an engineer. But when I speak to predominantly black schools, 90 percent of the kids want to play pro sports, 90 percent! These kids are brainwashed to think they can only play sports or be an entertainer. But they have a better chance of being a doctor or a lawyer than playing in the NBA"[3].

Simply put, the chances of success for individuals in communities where there is a lack of belief in the importance of academic achievement are significantly lower. Perhaps this idea can be rephrased to convey the message more effectively. In communities where people do not believe that their academic accomplishments can lead to a better life, their prospects for long-term success are diminished. This is evident when we observe that certain ethnic groups or communities are not encouraging their children to pursue careers in fields such as medicine, engineering, law, or even skilled trades like welding, which can be financially rewarding.

This situation highlights the need to reassess the messages we are imparting to children from an early age, both in schools and at home. Instead of focusing on the challenges posed by their skin color or income level, we should emphasize the critical importance of education in increasing their chances of success. As someone who has continued to learn and explore new subjects throughout my adult life, I strongly believe that we are doing a disservice to children and jeopardizing the future of our country by failing to instill these fundamental values.

While the initial part of this chapter could have served as an introduction to the section on parents, I chose to establish a premise. This premise is that students who prioritize their education tend to excel, while those who do not often struggle or even drop out. When students do not believe in their ability to pursue higher education or, at the very least, excel in their K-12 education, they may perceive limited options for self-sufficiency beyond what they find on the streets or through government programs.

Behavior

When we compare today's students to those of the 1980s or the 1970s, it becomes evident that there has been a significant change in the level of respect, not just for teachers but for authority figures, adults, and elders in general. As someone who has owned businesses and coached, I have encountered numerous stories that would make people shake their heads in disbelief. While it is important to acknowledge that not all students in schools are disrespectful, it is undeniable that the percentage of disrespectful behavior is much higher than it was in the 1980s. Moreover, the type of disrespectful words and behavior has reached a new level.

One of the primary issues is that teachers have limited power to enforce discipline beyond sending students to the office or reprimanding them. Students are aware of this and know that teachers cannot effectively discipline them. Additionally, administrators often prefer not to see students in the office, so they are instructed to resolve issues within the classroom. While suspensions still occur, they have become less frequent as more parents are inclined to argue against such measures. It is important to note that not all parents fall into this category, but a higher percentage now try to shield their children from disciplinary actions.

Reflecting on my own experience, I recall a time in

middle school when I was spanked by the vice-principal for repeatedly ignoring my teacher and talking out of turn. My parents had given permission for this form of punishment, which meant that I faced consequences both at school and at home. This incident served as a wake-up call for me, and I made a conscious effort to be less disruptive in the classroom.

It is crucial to clarify that I am not advocating for spanking as a disciplinary measure. Rather, I believe that disciplinary actions should have leverage with the students and work to the advantage of the teachers. In some cases, corporal punishment may be effective for boys, who can be particularly challenging. However, both teachers and administrators need disciplinary measures that carry weight. Unfortunately, many parents today do not enforce strict discipline at home, and this has been exacerbated by the notion that punishment is detrimental to children. As a result, some parents have shifted the responsibility of correcting bad behavior to schools.

Teenagers, especially boys, often exhibit unruly behavior due to their hormones and natural rambunctiousness. While this may be considered normal, part of raising a child involves guiding them on how to behave and treat others. I can assure you that I grew up with loud and selfish kids, but in most cases, they did not want their parents involved in addressing their behavior because they knew their parents would not support their foolish actions or disrespect towards teachers. They understood that they would face even harsher consequences at home.

Many students today do not fear going home to parents who are aware of their misbehavior and the school's intervention because they know their parents will take their side. It is no wonder that we are witnessing an increase in disrup-

tive behavior in schools. For these students, the only consequence they may face is dealing with angry parents who are
inconvenienced by having to visit the school.

Furthermore, students today are heavily influenced by
social media, music, and shows/movies that cater to their
age group. From the rebellious characters portrayed by
James Dean in the 1950s to the present, there has been a
recurring theme of defiance and a lack of respect for
authority figures. While I grew up with the "brat pack" and
admired rock stars who smashed hotel rooms and defied
authority, I also had a more balanced message at home that
helped me understand societal boundaries as a student and
later as an adult.

If you have read the chapter on educators, you are aware
of the threats that teachers face. Incidents of physical harm
by students have dramatically increased over the past two
decades. I have personally witnessed high school students
sharing videos of teacher-student altercations on platforms
like YouTube. While it is unlikely that these videos directly
lead to copycat behavior, they can serve as reinforcement for
students who are already angry and contemplating ways to
lash out at their teachers or administrators. It is important
to note that physical attacks on teachers by students as
young as seven are not isolated incidents, although they are
not commonplace either. Some may argue that the appropriate response would be to physically remove the student.
Teachers and administrators are no longer able to take such
actions due to protocols that prioritize minimizing the
school's risk of lawsuits or negative media coverage.

Comparing how students of the past treated teachers
and authority figures is challenging since little data is
collected and released for public consumption.

Therefore, I have relied on

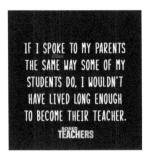

IF I SPOKE TO MY PARENTS THE SAME WAY SOME OF MY STUDENTS DO, I WOULDN'T HAVE LIVED LONG ENOUGH TO BECOME THEIR TEACHER.

BORED TEACHERS

interviews with retired teachers and administrators to gain insight into their experiences.

Throughout my interviews, it has become evident that behavior issues among students have worsened across the board. While there may not be specific statistical data or surveys to support this claim, there is a consensus among educators that behavior problems have increased significantly, perhaps even tenfold, depending on the community or area of the country. Quantifying this increase is challenging due to the tendency of schools and districts to turn a blind eye to bad behavior, hoping it will resolve itself. Pinpointing a single reason for this trend is difficult, so let's explore some of the causes that were frequently mentioned in my interviews. These causes are listed in the order of how many interviewees brought them up:

1. Parents - Many parents are less disciplined at home and often fail to impose meaningful consequences when their children get into trouble. Without facing any repercussions, children feel no concern about losing privileges or facing restrictions for misbehavior, whether in public or at school.

2. Lack of respect for authority - A significant number of students believe that they are not obligated to listen, obey, or follow basic rules because they perceive teachers and administrators as insignificant figures who exist solely to oppress them. This lack of respect

makes it challenging for educators to establish control in the classroom, as compliance from students is crucial for following instructions, completing assignments, or even maintaining a quiet environment for other students to focus on their work.

3. Decline in disciplinary measures - If students can engage in behaviors or utter words that would have resulted in expulsion in the past, they have no incentive to correct their behavior. Unfortunately, it is often the most disruptive students who take full advantage of this leniency.

4. Fear of lawsuits - Like the rest of society, schools and school districts are increasingly concerned about legal challenges. From allegations of racial discrimination to claims of inappropriate behavior by teachers or staff, the fear of litigation has led to a more lenient approach to addressing problems. This aligns with the previous point.

5. Influence of social media - Social media platforms such as Instagram, TikTok, and YouTube have become breeding grounds for showcasing and normalizing bad behavior among students. Every day, new videos emerge depicting students misbehaving, conflicts between educators and students, or even student-on-student fights. While studies may argue that video game violence does not directly lead to real-life violence, it is essential to approach this issue with common sense. Students can draw ideas from such content, especially if they are already angry or seeking ways to retaliate against others or their teachers. Social media provides a

plethora of options for them to emulate. This phenomenon is also observed in copycat incidents of mass shootings. Even if it is just vulgar language, it can be repeated and acted out by impressionable children who want to replicate the perceived coolness portrayed in the videos.

6. Erosion of caring - Over the past two or three decades, many educators have witnessed a decline in students' sense of caring about their achievements and doing their best. While there have always been students who seemed indifferent, it has now become socially acceptable and even "cool" to adopt an apathetic attitude. This is particularly prevalent in inner-city schools, where caring about grades and achievements is often ridiculed. In fact, I personally know students who have been mocked for striving to improve their grades.

When people argue that student behavior has not deteriorated significantly compared to when they were children, they overlook a crucial fact: bad behavior is a major contributing factor to teachers leaving the profession. Unfortunately, addressing this situation requires two key factors. Firstly, the punishment for student misconduct must be proportionate to the offense and carry significant consequences. Secondly, parents must demonstrate enough concern to hold their children accountable and respect the punishments imposed without attempting to circumvent them. Without alignment between parents, teachers, and school administrators in creating a better learning environment, the goal of nurturing better-educated students will never fully materialize.

Send them to Alternative School

When engaging in discussions with educators and administrators regarding the performance of private schools, it is often highlighted that private schools have the ability to remove students who exhibit disruptive behavior or fail to adhere to the rules. This aspect resonates positively with me, as well as with many other adults who prioritize the quality of their child's classroom environment throughout the school year. In the past, most states had alternative schools as an option for students who were expelled or proved to be excessively disruptive for their original schools to handle. If removing problematic students from the school setting is indeed the most effective way to maintain a conducive learning environment, then I wholeheartedly support it, and I would be surprised if most parents did not share the same sentiment.

To be fair, alternative schools still exist, albeit in a much more limited capacity. Moreover, they primarily cater to high school-aged students. However, with the emergence of online schooling, students who struggle to cooperate with their peers and teachers in a traditional school setting should be relocated and provided with an online or alternative educational option. Critics of alternative schools argue that students who enroll in such programs face greater challenges when it comes to college acceptance, experience diminished self-esteem due to attending a school labeled for students who are not academically advanced, and contend that grouping poorly behaved students together, much like in a prison setting, only leads to further misconduct. However, let us be realistic. A student who has been expelled from a school due to behavioral issues is unlikely to be a valedictorian or possess the necessary focus to prioritize college education. Even if that were the case, there are numerous junior colleges that would readily accept students at the junior level. The problem seems to lie in the concept of a school specifically designed for misfit students, which can negatively impact their self-worth and expose them to peers who may not serve as positive role models. Let's also acknowledge that by the time a student reaches an alternative school, the regular school system has provided ample opportunities and time for the student to rectify their behavior and avoid expulsion.

Several teachers I spoke with regarding the permanent removal of a student from school informed me that the process could take anywhere from 1 to 3 years, and would involve an overwhelming amount of documentation, leading many teachers to pass the problem onto the next grade level.

I find it difficult to comprehend how any parent can rationalize such a notion other than the fact that some parents today tend to prioritize their child's perspective over that of the school administration or teachers and may be convinced that all the adults involved are somehow biased against their precious child. It is important to acknowledge that some teachers may be more challenging to get along with than others, just as it is in the real world. Different teachers have varying levels of strictness. However, to believe that one's child has been consistently targeted for multiple years by multiple teachers is to disregard the previous incidents in which the child has been involved.

Social Media & Smart Devices

In today's society, the pervasive influence of social media cannot be ignored. It has become an integral part of our daily lives, with people easily accessing a wealth of information through their mobile phones and computers. Platforms like TikTok, Facebook, and Instagram are particularly popular among students. Extensive research has been conducted to investigate the impact of social media usage, revealing both positive and negative effects on its users. Parents who are vigilant about their children's activities can attest to the benefits and drawbacks of social media use among students.

Since their inception, social networking sites have captivated the attention of many adolescents. Concerns have been raised about the potential effects of excessive internet browsing, which often extends into the late hours of the night, on students' psychosocial behaviors[4]. Additionally, many students rely heavily on social networking sites as a quick source of information, leading to a decreased focus on learning and reduced knowledge retention[5]. Furthermore, their writing and communication skills, both personal and academic, have been negatively impacted as students attempt to multitask with social media while studying.

Adolescents frequently encounter negative experiences on social media, with online bullying being a particularly alarming issue. The anonymity provided by digital platforms allows bullies to escape the consequences of their actions, treating the act of bullying as a game where they strive to outdo one another in cruelty[6].

Some adolescents may be more susceptible to developing indicators of internet addiction, while others may experience psychological symptoms such as depression,

ADHD, or aggression. Moreover, excessive internet use among adolescents has been linked to psychological and intellectual problems, including anxiety, despair, and loneliness. Researchers have even suggested a correlation between the rise in attention deficit disorders and the prevalence of screens in children's lives from an early age[7]. Growing up surrounded by televisions, video games, smartphones, and computers, today's generation is constantly exposed to stimuli, potentially leading to a diminished ability to focus on less stimulating tasks[8]. Even Steve Jobs, the late co-founder of Apple, recognized the importance of disconnecting from devices, as he required his own children to turn them off after dinner to encourage engagement with the world around them.

Anyone who has seen "The Social Dilemma" on Netflix should understand the addictive nature of social media apps and how they are intentionally designed to be addictive. This thought-provoking 2020 docudrama sheds light on the dark side of social media, especially its impact on adolescents. The film delves into the detrimental effects on mental health that arise from excessive social media usage[9].

It is disheartening to observe how social media has replaced genuine human interaction. Although some argue that digital interaction still involves communication with other individuals, it lacks the warmth and empathy that comes with face-to-face interaction. This cold and impersonal nature of online communication makes it easier for individuals to express hateful sentiments without having to confront the consequences of their words.

While there are proponents of social media who highlight its positive aspects, the majority of research suggests that the negative impact outweighs the benefits. Excessive use of social media has been found to have detrimental effects on students' physical, psychological, and familial well-being[10].

In today's modern society, social media has become an integral part of students' lives, leading to widespread misuse among this demographic. Unfortunately, many parents remain unaware or neglect to monitor their children's activities on these platforms, allowing them to engage in whatever they please, upload inappropriate content, and communicate with unknown individuals. I have personally witnessed young girls posting questionable pictures that reveal too much skin or engage in inappropriate behavior. It is alarming to see how many parents fail to monitor their children's social media usage and the individuals they interact with. I recall an incident where a 33-year-old man showed up at a mother's doorstep to meet her 13-year-old daughter, whom he had been interacting with on Snapchat. The lack of parental supervision and awareness is truly concerning.

While there is limited research on the direct impact of social media on students' grades and behavior, numerous studies have explored its effects on overall behavior and self-esteem. Similar to the studies conducted on the harmful effects of smoking in the 1970s and '80s, the few studies that highlight the positive aspects of devices and social media are often funded by the very entities that benefit from continued social media usage.

However, if we apply the research on general changes in attention span, behavior, and personality to students, there are significant red flags. The rise in personality disorders has been associated with the use of social media. Never before have children been so consumed with seeking attention and validation, which, anecdotally, seems to contribute to a more narcissistic outlook. Today's youth believe that the number of connections and likes on their posts determines their worth, constantly seeking validation while navigating through negative comments[11].

When it comes to online bullying, it appears that girls are often the instigators. Many women have shared their experiences with me, highlighting the viciousness that can occur among girls. These attacks often occur in groups, with friends and acquaintances of the instigator joining in on the bullying. While this is not to say that boys are exempt from engaging in online fights, I have never had to confiscate or restrict phones to intervene in online conflicts between our sons. However, we have had to do so on multiple occasions with our daughters.

Social media exposes children to various trends and ideas that they may perceive as cool and seek to replicate. Numerous stories over the past 5 years of kids dying while trying the latest TikTok challenge[12]. Unfortunately, not all of these ideas are beneficial. Moreover, social media has become a breeding ground for shaming, enabling acts of humiliation that were previously unimaginable. I personally know someone whose child fell victim to such an incident. She accepted something from another student at school, which turned out to be a bad idea. She ended up having a seizure, which was recorded on video by multiple students and shared on social media platforms. The subsequent teasing and embarrassment were so severe that she had to change schools to complete her high school education. This is just one example, but similar scenarios occur regularly in schools across the country. It is no wonder that social media can lead to anxiety, depression, and even self-harm among some children.

Perhaps as parents, we should not be completely oblivious to our children's activities on social media or the individuals they interact with. Let's not forget the impact of gaming devices. Many young children are now being babysat by video games. While video games can be entertaining, they should have limits, just like any other aspect of life. They should not be used as a substitute for parenting. Boys, in particular, can spend the entire day playing if given the opportunity. To address this, I implemented a system where my son had to earn his video game time during the summer and on weekends. For example, an hour of chores would earn him an hour of video game time, or completing five laps in our neighborhood junior Olympic pool would also earn him an hour of video game time. I believed that the exercise he received would offset the sedentary nature of playing video games for extended periods.

My son started swimming 25 laps for 5 hours of video game time, which was alarming, but I set the rules, and I stuck by what he earned. However, I was also thinking, "I couldn't swim 25 laps, so clearly the additional exercise is working towards a positive outcome".

Sleep & Screen Time

As someone who is a night owl myself, I can relate to the importance of having a set bedtime. My parents understood that a good night's sleep was crucial for my brain power and overall performance in school. However, it's disheartening to hear that many elementary and middle school teachers have encountered parents who either have no bedtime routine or are unsure about what a reasonable bedtime should be for their child. In this day and age, with all the information available at our fingertips, it's surprising that parents don't utilize the screens in their hands to look up recommended sleep times for children[13].

Speaking of which, here are the recommended sleep times for kids:

- • 1 to 2-year-olds need 11-12.5 hours of sleep per night.
- • 3 to 5-year-olds need 10.5-11.5 hours.
- • 6 to 7-year-olds need about 10.5 hours.
- • 7 to 13-year-olds need about 10 hours.
- • Even 18-year-olds need about 9 hours of sleep each night.

However, nowadays, the problem goes beyond parents setting a reasonable bedtime. It extends to parents regulating the screens and devices in the bedroom, and for good reason.

Sleep is an essential part of our development and well-being. It is vital for learning, memory, emotions, behaviors, and overall health. Unfortunately, the total amount of sleep that children and adolescents get continues to decrease.

When it comes to my own children, we used to take their phones at night until they reached high school. We also did not allow TVs in their bedrooms until their junior year in high school. I understand that some people might find this strict, but we firmly believed that it was in their best interest. In a society where parents are often unaware of their children's late-night phone or device usage, the problem only worsens.

It is evident that screen time, whether from watching television or using computers, mobile phones, and other electronic devices, can significantly and negatively impact children's sleep. Almost 72 percent of young people between the ages of 6 and 17 have at least one electronic device in their bedroom, as reported by a 2014 National Sleep Foundation survey[14]. The survey also revealed that children who keep these devices on during the night tend to sleep an average of one hour less per night. The number of devices and screen time that children and adolescents are exposed to continues to increase. With the rise in exposure to electronic screens, particularly in the hours before bedtime, it is not surprising that screen time is now associated with insufficient and poor-quality sleep[15].

A review of 8 sleep studies found consistent evidence that screen time hampers sleep, primarily by shortening sleep duration and delaying the timing of sleep. The latter finding was reported in nearly all of the studies reviewed.

However, the relationship between screen time and sleep is more complex than it seems. Screen time could be negatively influencing sleep in many ways. These negative impacts on sleep can be attributed to screen time in the evening cutting into the time that children would typically spend preparing for bed and sleeping, thus delaying sleep onset and reducing the overall duration of sleep.

Screen time in the hours directly before sleep is problematic in several ways other than just displacing children and adolescents' bed and sleep times. The content that we engage with on screens can also harm sleep. For example, exciting video games, dramatic or scary television shows, or even stimulating phone conversations can engage the brain and release hormones such as adrenaline. This, in turn, can make it more difficult to fall asleep or maintain sleep[16].

Anyone sleeping with their phone in their hand or having it lying on their nightstand or not on Do Not Disturb will constantly have their sleep patterns interrupted by the ding or vibration of incoming text, push notices, or phone calls. A steady stream of notices that keep the mind from falling into REM sleep. REM is important because it stimulates the areas of the brain that help with learning and is associated with increased production of proteins

Babies have a significantly higher amount of REM sleep compared to adults. In fact, it is not uncommon for babies to spend up to 50percent of their sleep time in the REM stage, while adults typically experience only about 20percent of their sleep in REM.

Another factor that is often overlooked but just as important is the impact of light on sleep and our sleep-wake patterns in general. Bright light at night can disrupt the body's naturally occurring circadian rhythms by suppressing the release of the hormone melatonin, which is essential for maintaining and regulating our sleep-wake cycle[17].

It is becoming increasingly clear that limiting screen time in the period leading up to bedtime is beneficial for sleep. In relation to this, removing electronic devices from the bedroom provides a good sleep environment and promotes sound sleep practices. Dr. Michael Breus, Ph.D., DABSM, FAASM, a Clinical Psychologist and Sleep Medicine Expert, recommends that children not have a screen in front of them for at least 1 hour before bedtime[18].

Boredom is Good for your Child

When I was growing up, it seemed like kids were always complaining about being bored. However, in today's age, the concept of boredom is becoming increasingly rare. With the abundance of activities available to combat boredom, such as apps, podcasts, webisodes, video games, viral videos, and texting friends with the classic "I'm bored" message, it's no wonder that the idea of being bored is becoming endangered.

If you search the internet for "boredom is good for kids," you will come across a wealth of research that supports this statement. Prominent sources such as PBS Kids, Psychology Today, and Parent Magazine have all conducted studies that clearly demonstrate the benefits of allowing children to find things to do, make up games, and explore their surroundings without constant stimulation from screens or other forms of technology. While constant video stimulation may be captivating, it keeps our minds fixated on the screen rather than the world around us. We've all heard stories of people walking into things while staring at their smartphones, highlighting the importance of having moments where our minds are free from external distractions and focused solely on our own thoughts. Numerous studies have shown that this practice is not only beneficial for children but also for adults, as it allows us to clear our heads of the constant noise and find mental clarity.

While boredom has been associated with negative behaviors such as mindless snacking, poor driving, and engaging in risky activities, it also has intriguing positive effects. Boredom can actually spur creativity and help cultivate essential traits such as curiosity, perseverance, playfulness, interest, and confidence. These are the very qualities that contribute to the development of intelligent and engaging individuals. So, embracing moments of boredom can actually be a catalyst for personal growth and self-discovery[19].

In short, if your kids come to you and say I'm bored, you do not need to find a movie, game, or YouTube video for them to watch. Tell them to figure it out by being creative. They will be much better for it in the future. Better yet, tell them to go outside.

Bored in the Classroom

There seem to be two conflicting opinions on the topic of boredom in the classroom. On the one hand, some people believe that teachers should make their lessons more interesting and exciting to hold the attention of today's kids, who are used to constant stimulation. However, the other side believes that learning is about listening, reading, watching, and absorbing information in order to be considered educated on the subject matter being taught. Both sides present valid points, but let's be realistic: a teacher can't perform a song and dance for every educational topic.

Let's not overlook the fact that kids today need constant stimulation because they've grown up in a world where screens have their constant attention, and the content changes rapidly. From YouTube to Facebook to Twitter and Instagram, where they read headlines, watch short videos, look at pictures, and now even watch shorter videos on TikTok. And let us not forget all the sugar they are getting dosed with their food and drinks.

I believe it is true that we must teach our kids that it's necessary to sit, listen, read, and learn. When I ask people how to make education more exciting and fun, they often don't have the answers; they just know it should be more interesting. Many school districts have indeed restricted how often a teacher can do science experiments, opting for a video showing the experiment. However, watching a video is not the same as experiencing a science experiment first-hand. Some argue that kids are used to watching videos, so seeing a science experiment on video is comfortable. While that may be true for today's kids, the videos they watch are typically short, and they quickly move on if the video isn't interesting enough. A video cannot replicate watching an experiment in person as your teacher explains and challenges the class to make a guess as to the outcome of the experiment. In-person experiments allow the students to experience the activity, not just visually but physically.

Teachers will tell you that when they do science experiments or demonstrations with their class, they fascinated and totally engaged. Asking the kids to describe what they think the outcome of the experiment will be brings a lot of excitement that a video just can not engender.

As a "hands-on" learner myself, I find that I learn best when I can actively engage with the material. I'm also a visual learner, which is why I helped create our video education company. However, over the years, I've had to teach myself to read something, turn off the voices in my head, absorb the knowledge, and retain it. I've become proficient at this out of necessity. As mentioned earlier, people learn in different ways. If we want to make education more enjoyable, we should incorporate more hands-on activities whenever possible, especially in subjects like science that shouldn't be primarily experienced through videos. Let the kids witness the lab experiments, participate in them, and engage in discussions about the lessons. It may not be as exciting as a video game, but it's certainly more engaging than listening to a lecture. This approach can be applied to many subjects where real-life demonstrations would be more interesting than simply reading from a book or listening to someone talk at the front of the room.

While it is necessary for a teacher to deliver information through lectures, it should also be possible to mix things up. Invite engaging presenters to speak to the children more frequently. Unfortunately, many schools make it difficult to have guest presenters come in. Part of that decision is budget-related. I can remember when I was in middle school, and someone from NASA came and did a demonstration of how the shuttle would weather the extremes of space and reentry. I'm 55 now, and that is still ingrained in my mind. We also had many other great assembly presenters of science when I was in school, and I remember most of their demonstrations.

Of course, implementing these changes would require more time, and extra time is not something that teachers have an abundance of. However, that's a topic for another chapter. Nowadays, with the increasing emphasis on social and emotional learning, most teachers will tell you that they barely have 30 minutes to spend on each subject, especially at the elementary level. How can we expect students to be more interested when they move on to a new subject before they have had time to fully grasp the previous one?

Alternatively, we could consider teaching basic subjects like math, English, language arts, literature, science, and history by middle school and then allow students from 8th grade through graduation to choose their own subjects based on their interest. This would enable them to select subjects that genuinely interest them and allow for a deeper dive into those areas. Podcasts, which can range from 1 to 3 hours, are very popular among high school-age kids. In fact, students between the ages of 12 and 24 are the fastest-growing audience for podcasts in 2022, with roughly 40percent in that age range regularly listening to podcasts each month. This indicates that students are not necessarily opposed to long-form discussions or listening to someone talk about a subject they care about for extended periods of time. So why not let high school kids choose their topics and select the lectures they want to hear and learn more about? In this way, a high school could curate topics with qualified lecturers to teach the subjects. Instead of force-feeding them things they are not interested in or are unlikely to use in the future, like translating the graph of trigonometric functions in a math class. Some students will choose to pursue higher-level math. I know many individuals who loved math and found it exhilarating. I may consider them weirdos, but they do exist, and my personal dislike for math should not influence anyone's future decisions. Let the students make the decision for themselves, and maybe they won't be so bored in the classroom.

Autism

This section will be kept brief as I am not a medical researcher and cannot make any definitive statements about the increase in autism among school-age children. However, it is indeed a concern and is impacting education in ways that may not be fully understood. Due to the growing number of autistic children, schools are having to make adjustments to their special education classes. This creates an increased demand for qualified special education teachers, a field that already faces shortages.

While some argue that the rise in autism cases is simply due to different standards for recognition and improved testing methods, this is not the prevailing opinion among teachers with more than a decade of experience, particularly those who have been teaching for 20 years or more. Many autistic children display notable behavioral patterns, and the most severe cases are easily recognized. Additionally, many autistic individuals possess exceptional intelligence in a specific subject or area but very often lack the social skills to go along with their intelligence.

According to the National Institute of Mental Health, autism spectrum disorder (ASD) is a neurological and developmental condition that affects how individuals interact with others, communicate, learn, and behave. Although autism can be diagnosed at any age, it is considered a "developmental disorder" because symptoms typically appear within the first two years of life[20].

The term "spectrum" refers to the range of severity within autism. Individuals who are high-functioning demonstrate fewer obvious symptoms compared to those on the more severe end of the spectrum. Common symptoms, as outlined by the Mayo Clinic, include limited or inconsistent eye contact, seeming disinterested in or unaware of people speaking, infrequent sharing of interests or emotions, difficulty responding to their name or verbal cues, challenges in maintaining back-and-forth conversations, extensive monologues on personal interests without regard for others' interest or input, facial expressions and gestures that do not correspond to spoken words, a distinctive or robotic tone of voice, difficulty understanding others' perspectives or predicting their actions, struggles in adapting behavior to various social situations, and difficulties in engaging in imaginative play or forming friendships[21].

As for the cause of the increase in autism cases, it remains uncertain. Various theories exist, and there is currently no scientific consensus. In 2023, Robert F.

Kennedy sparked controversy by suggesting a possible link between autism and the mercury or aluminum content in vaccines administered during the first two years of a child's life[22]. The number of vaccines has significantly risen over time. In the 1940s, children received only four vaccines before the age of two, which doubled by the 1960s. As of 2023, according to the Children's Hospital of Philadelphia, children could receive up to 27 shots by the age of two, with six shots administered in a single visit[23].

An article published in USA Today in February 2023 noted that autism diagnosis rates had tripled in less than two decades[24]. While the article acknowledges theories attributing this increase to improved diagnostic tools, it emphasizes that vaccines are not the cause. It is important to clarify that I am not asserting that vaccines are responsible for the rise in autism cases. However, it is worth examining the correlation between the increased prevalence of autism and the increased number of vaccinations. While this does not constitute scientific evidence, it prompts us to consider the impact of our environment and the substances we introduce into our bodies.

Today, many individuals consume a variety of chemicals through processed foods containing ingredients they struggle to pronounce or recognize. They also take medications designed to alter or control moods through chemical manipulation of hormones and other bodily processes. Alarming as well is the fact that most of these medications and chemical additives are considered safe for pregnant women. Pharmaceutical and food companies often cite studies, often funded by themselves, to support the safety of mood-altering drugs and other chemicals. However, we must recognize that what is deemed safe by manufacturers and regulatory bodies may not always be as safe as we are led to believe. Over time, numerous food additives and medications have been pulled from the market due to unforeseen health issues. These chemicals were approved based on studies that failed to identify the long-term problems that eventually led to their removal from the market.

History provides us with numerous examples of chemicals, preservatives, and additives that were initially deemed safe but later proven to be harmful. Vioxx, red dye No. 3, and glyphosate are just a few examples. In each case, companies provided data to the FDA to approve these substances, claiming their safety. On April 2021, the world received an enlightening lesson on the concept of a "taint" courtesy of Joe Rogan. He brought attention to the work of Shannah H. Swan, Ph.D., and her book titled "Count Down: How Our Modern World Is Threatening Sperm Counts, Altering Male and Female Reproductive Development, and Imperiling the Future of the Human Race." This insightful book explores the profound impact of chemicals found in the contemporary environment, shedding light on how these substances are fundamentally altering and jeopardizing human sexuality and fertility on a global level[25].

As Robert F. Kennedy highlights, individuals over the age of 40 likely did not encounter autistic peers during their schooling years. Reading the research on the causes of autism is a time-consuming undertaking, as there is no scientific consensus. Various researchers "think" they understand what is driving the increase in autism cases. But no one is certain of the cause or causes. It seems that a lot more funding for this research is needed to get as many bright minds on the problem as possible.

I bring up this issue in the book to encourage continued discussion and to help readers grasp the additional challenges that the rising prevalence of autism poses to teachers and schools. Autistic students often require individualized education plans tailored to their specific needs. Low-functioning students require extra support to navigate their daily activities at school. Most autistic students benefit from personalized guidance, yet schools are facing dwindling resources and a shortage of educators trained to effectively address the issues accompanying the teaching of autistic students. I also hope that people will pay more attention to what they are putting into their bodies.

Mental Health and Prescribed Drugs

In the previous chapter, I discussed the concerning issue of teachers using prescription medication for depression and anxiety. While there is a lack of concrete data on the number of educators relying on these medications, there is alarming evidence regarding the high prescription rates for young children. Through personal anecdotes from friends and teachers, I have witnessed how easily children can be put on medication. In my opinion, psychiatrists and physicians sometimes fail to consider the best interests of our children when prescribing psychotropic medications. And from the stories that have been relayed to me, there doesn't seem to be very much clinical evaluation taking place to justify these medications.

Allow me to share two specific cases that highlight this issue. I personally know two parents who were going through a divorce, and their children were acting out and displaying anger. In both instances, a psychiatrist quickly diagnosed the children with bipolar disorder and prescribed medication within just 30 minutes. However, a brief internet search reveals that such a diagnosis cannot be accurately made in such a short timeframe. Fortunately, both children did not respond well to the medication and discontinued its use after a short period.

Now, some may argue that I am not a doctor and therefore cannot definitively claim that a diagnosis of bipolar disorder cannot be made within an hour for 12 and 14-year-olds. However, Dr. Kay Redfield Jamison, a renowned professor of psychiatry at Johns Hopkins School of Medicine, provides valuable insight into the challenges of diagnosing bipolar disorder. She explains that the symptoms can vary widely and are often influenced by other factors such as concurrent drug use or symptom remission. Additionally, the average time between a person's first episode and receiving the correct diagnosis is eight years. Some studies even suggest that it can take up to ten years to diagnose bipolar disorder when the patient primarily presents with depression. The use of assessment scales and gathering information from relatives can aid in the diagnostic process. It is important to note that most individuals with bipolar disorder are diagnosed in early adulthood after experiencing persistent symptoms for several years[26].

One story shared with me by a teacher involved a parent who repeatedly took their child to their pediatrician in search of a medication that would address their behavioral issues. He had already been on several different medications. Shockingly, one doctor simply opened a book with various medications and asked the parent to choose which one they wanted to try next. It is evident that a significant number of doctors place unwavering trust in these pills and prescribe them without thorough consideration, almost as if they were handing out candy. This approach to prescribing behavior medications can be likened to the strategy of throwing noodles on the wall to see what sticks. However, what is concerning is the apparent lack of counseling with children to understand the underlying issues they may be facing. Are pharmaceutical companies and doctors under the illusion that giving a child a pill will somehow make them feel better about the real problems they are experiencing at home, such as divorce or abuse? It seems to suggest that if we simply feel good about our problems, they will magically disappear. Unfortunately, in cases like this, the problems are not being addressed but rather masked through a "numbing" approach.

Now, let me clarify that I am not a doctor or medical researcher. However, I do possess common sense and a logical perspective. These medications directly impact the brain's chemistry, which should raise concerns. Yet, as demonstrated by the Milgram experiment in 1961, many individuals unquestioningly believe everything someone in a white coat or a position of authority says[27].

As a former restaurant owner, I was astonished to discover that many of the young girls working for me, some as young as 16, were already on medication for anxiety and depression. They had been relying on these medications for multiple years. When I discussed this topic with a psychiatrist and a parent whose daughter took two different medications daily, I was taken aback by their lack of consideration. They had not given much thought to the potential consequences of long-term medication use. Unfortunately, I could not find reliable data on the number of children who eventually discontinue medication, but it appears to be a small percentage. There is significant debate surrounding the positive and negative effects of these medications on young children. Interestingly, studies sponsored by pharmaceutical companies always claim no long-term problems.

However, anyone who has witnessed someone abruptly stop taking these drugs knows that it can have severe consequences. The individual's brain chemistry attempts to readjust, resulting in intense mood swings from happiness to anguish. The human body constantly strives for balance, so abruptly discontinuing a psychotropic medication can disrupt the system and lead to uncomfortable and potentially dangerous withdrawal symptoms.

I raise this issue because many parents entrust their children to take their medication independently once they reach the ages of 9 or 10.

However, most children are not consistently responsible in various aspects of their lives and may forget to take their medications regularly. I have encountered numerous high school students working for me who experienced significant mood swings because they had forgotten to take their medication for several days. One particular incident involved a sophomore in high school who had been working at my establishment for about six months. She was usually sweet and had a great sense of humor, and we had a positive working relationship. I genuinely loved joking around with her. One day, she failed to show up for her shift, so I reached out to her via text to inquire about her absence. The response I received was an emotional rant, barely coherent, expressing how she had been treated poorly at work and was contemplating quitting. This sudden outburst caught me off guard, as it seemed to come out of nowhere. A few days later, her mother visited the business and apologized on her daughter's behalf. She explained that her daughter loved working there and was embarrassed about the text she had sent. The mother revealed that her daughter had forgotten to take her depression and anxiety medication for several days, which had contributed to her emotional state. I later learned that she had even contemplated self-harm.

I bring up these examples because it appears to me, and many others who are not affiliated with pharmaceutical companies, that we are tampering with our children's minds. This may potentially lead to more significant short-term and long-term problems. Could this be contributing to an increase in self-harm and violent behavior? Some psychotropic drugs dull the senses, and it is worth considering whether there is a connection between these medications and school shootings committed by students or former students.

Developing the ability to handle stress and the challenges of everyday life is crucial for mental resilience. It seems that by relying on medication to mute their emotions and stress, we are attaching our children to a lifelong dependency, depriving them of the necessary coping skills to navigate adulthood. They may struggle to manage overwhelming situations when they lack the necessary tools. While this is solely my opinion, it does prompt us to question how humans have evolved to survive daily challenges without resorting to constant medication. Humans, throughout time, were not as comfy and secure as humans today. Figuring out how not to starve or feed your family and not become food for another predator was the order of the day. How did they cope without medication? Or perhaps, as some people joke, are our children and their parents have become too soft?

The table shows the total number of children on all psychiatric drugs. The information is extracted from the most accurate data available on the number of children and adolescents prescribed psychiatric drugs in the United States, including 0-5-year-olds. The information is from IQVia (formerly IMS Health), the largest vendor of U.S. physician prescribing data. The following data was taken from the IQVia Total Patient Tracker Database for the Year 2020, extracted in January 2021.

Note: The total number of individual children on psychiatric drugs was cited by IQVia as 6.155,852. The totals for each class of drug (i.e. ADHD or Antidepressant drugs) may include children on more than one class of drug or children who were also counted in the next year's age bracket during a one-year period. The total number of children on all psychiatric drugs, including age break-down, have been deduplicated, so these are the total number of children prescribed drugs for the year.

It is important to note that most of the young employees I have encountered who believe they need antidepressants and anxiety medication to function daily are predominantly female. When I inquire about their reasons, they often claim that I cannot comprehend the level of stress they experience due to school, dating, work, and dealing with their parents. They seem to believe that their generation is the first and only one to face such problems. Alarming conversations with parents who have visited doctors to obtain these medications further highlight the issue. Doctors often guilt parents into believing that without these medications, their children may harm themselves or struggle to cope with school and life. Personally, I find it difficult to fully embrace this line of thinking.

If you search for the adverse effects or drawbacks of anxiety medication, you will find yourself scrolling through approximately 20 pages before encountering any significant cons.

Drug Class		Age Group	Number of Children
All Psychiatric Drugs		0-17 Years	6,155,852
		0-5 Years	418,425
	Age Breakdown		
		0-1 Years	85,003
		2-3 Years	138,822
		4-5 Years	215,120
		6-12 Years	2,652,554
		13-17 Years	3,188,966
ADHD Drugs		0-17 Years	3,155,441
		0-5 Years	58,091
	Age Breakdown		
		0-1 Years	310
		2-3 Years	1,300
		4-5 Years	57,010
		6-12 Years	1,750,481
		13-17 Years	1,409,438
Antidepressants		0-17 Years	2,154,118
		0-5 Years	35,216
	Age Breakdown		
		0-1 Years	7,811
		2-3 Years	12,137
		4-5 Years	18,911
		6-12 Years	543,120
		13-17 Years	1,605,375

Most websites simply echo the pharmaceutical industry's claims that there are no noteworthy negative aspects to
these medications, aside from the usual side effects such as
headaches or loss of appetite.

Drug Class		Age Group	Number of Children
Antipsychotics		0-17 Years	829,372
		0-5 Years	30,632
	Age Breakdown		
		0-1 Years	1,318
		2-3 Years	7,873
		4-5 Years	22,180
		6-12 Years	304,754
		13-17 Years	502,372
Anti-anxiety Drugs		0-17 Years	1,153,351
		0-5 Years	233,125
	Age Breakdown		
		0-1 Years	60,068
		2-3 Years	89,453
		4-5 Years	90,716
		6-12 Years	357,976
		13-17 Years	571,210
Mood Stabilizers		0-17 Years	794,715
		0-5 Years	100,233
	Age Breakdown		
		0-1 Years	21,593
		2-3 Years	36,986
		4-5 Years	50,206
		6-12 Years	289,262
		13-17 Years	419,221

Let me be clear: I am not suggesting that these medications are universally wrong or bad. However, when we examine the numbers, it should give the average person pause to consider the overall impact on the population of children under 17 years old. The United States already has the highest rate of pharmaceutical prescriptions in the world, and we are raising children to trust individuals who have a financial interest in them staying medicated. They believe that there is a pill to solve all their problems rather than examining themselves, their habits, or their behavior.

In August 2017, Consumer Reports published an article titled "Too Many Meds? America's Love Affair With Prescription Medication...We now take more pills than ever. Is that doing more harm than good?" The title itself encapsulates the issue, but one particular story within the article highlights a common problem, even among young individuals. Nicole Lamber's troubles began with a single prescription medication when, overwhelmed by stress in her first job as a physician's assistant, a colleague prescribed alprazolam (Xanax). She recalls receiving no warning about the potential risks associated with the drug. Within a few months, Lamber, now 38, found herself depressed and even contemplating suicide. Over the next five years, she encountered a series of doctors who prescribed an increasing number of drugs: Adderall for ADHD to improve her mood and focus, another medication to counter the side effects of Adderall, additional drugs to enhance her appetite and aid sleep, and yet another sedative when her anxiety worsened[28].

Proponents of psychotropic medication may argue that society has become more complex, placing greater demands on children who are required to do more than ever before. These are valid points. However, one area where I do agree that the risk of depression and anxiety has increased is social media. As discussed earlier in this chapter, bullying, comparing oneself to others, and the overall perception on social media that one's life is inferior to others can contribute to depression and anxiety, particularly among young girls. As parents, it is our responsibility to educate our children about the reality behind these feelings and the false representation of life on social media. I have made a conscious effort to emphasize these points to my children, ensuring they understand that social media bullying and the pursuit of likes do not reflect real life but rather a distorted version of reality.

Teach Your Kids to Care and Why its Important

When teachers observe the student body, they encounter a diverse range of students. Some students demonstrate a strong commitment and put in the effort to succeed, while others seem content with just getting by or show a lack of interest in passing. It is crucial for everyone involved to care about education.

When you survey teachers about the most successful groups of students or the students that do well and are respectful, it's often Indian, Asian, and Nigerian students. The answer to this is easy. Failure due to a lack of effort is not tolerated. Teachers have told me that Indian and Asian parents will often ask for a curriculum map for their child's grade level so they can begin working with them at home or making sure they are keeping up with their assignments. Teachers will tell you that most Indian parents thank her for educating their children. They are grateful for the work and effort the teacher is putting in for their children. You will not find helicopter or lawnmower parenting in these ethnic groups because they want their kids to grow up to take care of themselves and be productive members of society. They are not raising kids to live at home and live off of mommy and daddy. The parents in these ethnic groups care about the outcome of their children as adults and want them to be doing well. Of course, most American families care about their children's future development, but the priorities and attitudes towards school, grades, and the teacher are often very different. Some parents might think that these ethnic groups work too hard and do not leave room for fun and enjoyment. I'm not sure that's true, but if so, a balance can be achieved with a little effort.

As parents, we have always prioritized instilling in our children a strong work ethic and the importance of giving their best effort. We consistently reinforce this message and emphasize its significance in every way possible. However, once our children entered the school environment, we understood that the responsibility for excelling and achieving their goals rested with them. Consequently, many evenings were spent engaged in arguments and disagreements about grades, homework, and even instances where they received a zero in the grade book. Nonetheless, we firmly believed that it was ultimately up to our kids to complete their assignments and strive for excellence. We viewed this as a crucial investment in their future. Our children had the opportunity to witness firsthand the significance of putting in the effort, as we never wavered in our commitment to combat laziness. We firmly believe that by encouraging our children to make that extra push, even a small one, parents can empower them to thrive academically and succeed in life beyond school. While we may not have turned them into straight-A students, we were able to instill in them a sense of caring and understanding as to why it matters.

However, it is important not to overlook the underlying reasons for our approach. When all four of our children were living at home, I gathered them together with yellow notepads and pens. I instructed them to write down the numbers that I was about to call out. I started by saying numbers like $1850, $434, $744, and so on. Once I finished, I had them write a second column of numbers as I called them out once again. After they had finished, I asked if they knew what these numbers represented. They had their guesses, but none of them were correct. I proceeded to explain that the first column represented all the monthly bills we have to pay, while the second column represented the bills we pay once a year. I then pointed out that neither column accounted for entertainment or vacations. I told them to circle the numbers on their notepads, and when they were done, I said, "This is the amount of money you need to make each year in order to have at least the same level of comfort that we have today." I explained that this was their goal if they wanted to have a middle-class life like ours. Keep in mind that all of our kids were under 20 years old at the time. They were taken aback by the amount of money we had to spend each month to ensure their comfort and well-being. This eye-opening exercise provided them with a goal and a clear understanding of why it is important to work hard, give their best effort, and care about their grades. It highlighted why all their efforts and dedication were essential. Even if they chose a trade over a four-year college degree, setting the bar is what matters the most.

---

1. https://medium.com/@joecarleton/why-nigerian-immigrants-are-the-most-successful-ethnic-group-in-the-u-s-23a7ea5a0832

   https://www.theroot.com/the-tiger-mom-on-why-nigerian-americans-are-more-succes-1790874731

   https://www.yahoo.com/now/u-could-actually-more-nigerian-133011858.html?guccounter=1&guce_referrer=aHR0cHM6Ly9zZWFyY2guYnJhdmUuY29tLw&guce_referrer_sig=AQAAAE4aW7jsEmHq G7ItxAFcrvaoJCQlJmAA2GLi7u9wPhYF3X8mq2Xuyr7IJe77wJeEILOMF-6Df3lpBsZLObD7Qi2uXAS9NH2BI7jwM0D9y-2RhZeU3_S5gtWdhi PF8_PixnQOBg5tjDFQUcS7V3f-FaspnR92trXsYR59EUbYLsbb

BRYAN THOMAS WETZEL

2. https://publications.aap.org/pediatrics/article-abstract/135/2/e440/
    33377/Cognitive-Ability-at-Kindergarten-Entry-and?redirectedFrom=
    fulltext
    https://www.businessinsider.com/how-your-parents-behaviors-
    shape-who-you-are-today-2019-7#if-your-parents-set-high-expecta
    tions-for-you-you-probably-did-better-in-school-5
3. https://youtu.be/zGFWBddzaAw?si=1OIXjuwL2zTWCmUJ
4. https://www.theguardian.com/society/2015/sep/11/teens-social-media-
    night-risk-harm-mental-health-research
    https://www.ncbi.nlm.nih.gov/pmc/articles/PMC8233562/
5. https://digitalcommons.unl.edu/cgi/viewcontent.cgi?article=4687&
    context=libphilprac
6. https://kidshealth.org/en/parents/cyberbullying.html
    https://www.mcleanhospital.org/essential/bullying-kids-teens
7. https://www.addictioncenter.com/drugs/internet-addiction/
    https://www.ncbi.nlm.nih.gov/pmc/articles/PMC3480687/
8. https://www.webmd.com/add-adhd/adult-adhd-internet-addiction
    https://www.ncbi.nlm.nih.gov/pmc/articles/PMC5517818/
9. https://www.thesocialdilemma.com/the-film/
10. https://www.reuters.com/article/us-health-internet-depression/good-
    social-media-experiences-dont-outweigh-bad-ones-for-young-adults-
    idUSKBN1JF37S/
11. https://countercurrents.org/2021/04/impact-of-social-media-on-our-
    attention-span-and-its-drastic-aftermath/
    https://www.cbsnews.com/pittsburgh/news/how-social-media-
    could-be-harming-your-childs-attention-span/
12. https://nypost.com/2023/09/20/tiktok-challenges-killed-my-kid-and-
    now-im-fighting-back/
13. https://www.nationwidechildrens.org/specialties/sleep-disorder-
    center/sleep-in-adolescents
    https://www.cdc.gov/healthyschools/features/students-sleep.htm
    https://www.sleepfoundation.org/teens-and-sleep
14. https://www.healthday.com/health-news/child-health/ban-electronics-
    in-kids-bedrooms-expert-says-691503.html#:~:text=Almostper-
    cent2072percent20percentpercent20ofpercent20young,eachper-
    cent20nightpercent2Cpercent20thepercent20grouppercent20found.
15. https://www.ncbi.nlm.nih.gov/pmc/articles/PMC5839336/
    https://www.sciencedirect.com/science/article/abs/pii/
    S1389945719302886
16. https://www.iflscience.com/why-screen-time-bed-bad-children-30639
17. https://health.clevelandclinic.org/put-the-phone-away-3-reasons-why-
    looking-at-it-before-bed-is-a-bad-habit/
18. https://sleepdoctor.com/technology/
19. https://www.parent.com/blogs/conversations/2023-5-surprising-bene
    fits-of-letting-your-children-get-bored

https://www.psychologytoday.com/us/blog/shouldstorm/201812/boredomtunity-why-boredom-is-the-best-thing-our-kids

https://www.pbs.org/parents/thrive/boredom-isnt-a-bad-thing-for-kids

20. https://www.nimh.nih.gov/health/topics/autism-spectrum-disorders-asd

21. https://www.mayoclinic.org/diseases-conditions/autism-spectrum-disorder/symptoms-causes/syc-20352928

22. https://childrenshealthdefense.org/news/salons-retraction-deadly-immunity-article-real-reason-behind/

23. https://www.chop.edu/centers-programs/vaccine-education-center/vaccine-history/developments-by-year

24. https://www.usatoday.com/story/news/education/2023/02/02/new-study-indicates-percentage-children-autism-climbing/11156966002/

25. https://theprepared.com/blog/review-count-down-presents-a-grim-plastic-coated-view-of-humanitys-infertile-future/

26. https://www.nbcnews.com/health/mental-health/why-does-it-take-so-long-diagnose-bipolar-disorder-n865171

27. https://www.britannica.com/science/Milgram-experiment

28. https://www.consumerreports.org/prescription-drugs/too-many-meds-americas-love-affair-with-prescription-medication/

8

PARENTS

Dear Parents,

If you promise not believe everything your child says happens at school, I'll promise not to believe everything they say happens at home.

Anonymous

Anyone over 25 should recognize that children often exhibit laziness and tend to do the bare minimum to get by. Without strong leadership in the home, many children will become average or below-average students. It is crucial for parents to guide their children throughout their formative years, emphasizing the importance of giving their best effort and achieving the highest grades possible. Settling for mediocrity should never be acceptable. You may not be able to turn them into valedictorians, but the constant reminder that your success in life is based on your effort, not your parents, will bear results over the long term.

In other words, children need to be taught to value education and strive for excellence. They require a parent who sets high expectations and serves as a role model. It is the responsibility of parents to raise and prepare their children for success in the world, whether that means pursuing higher education or entering the workforce after trade school. Of course, there are numerous life lessons that must be imparted before they leave the nest. Ultimately, the goal is to raise functional, self-sufficient young adults who can effectively navigate the challenges life presents.

While every parent would wholeheartedly agree with this final statement when confronted, fewer and fewer are effectively fulfilling this role. It is important to note that the parents being criticized here are not abusive or uncaring. Rather, their parenting methods are counterproductive to the aforementioned goals. They may not realize it, but many parents strive to shield their children from failure. However, it is through failure that we learn and grow. For example, a child who touches a hot stove quickly learns not to do so again. This is a simple example, but it holds true.

Frankly, too many parents today allow their children to run the household. Why are moms and dads so hesitant to establish rules and boundaries for their children? Why do they succumb to their children's demands and fear their temper tantrums? These are questions that traditional parents often ponder. However, it may be perceived as a weakness or influenced by the parenting books they have read, which advise against breaking a child's spirit. It is important to remember that a child's spirit can be both positive and negative, and it is the parent's responsibility to guide them when they veer off track and acknowledge their efforts when they are doing their best.

We are fortunate to live in a country where many luxuries are readily available. However, as parents, we must resist the temptation to spoil our children. This is why numerous teachers have reported an increase in both misbehavior and entitlement among students. Perhaps it is time for parents to mature alongside their children. Teachers have told me stories about parents telling them their child won't go get off the video games at night or refuses to do their homework. I would be embarrassed to tell another adult such a thing, but many parents are not fully in charge of their household. They probably didn't have strong parents as role models themselves. By the way, every good parent is still rolling their eyes at the video game excuse. If your child won't get off of the iPad or video games at night, you take them away and let them know they won't be getting them back until they shape up. It"s that simple.

First Days of School

Some of the best research about raising kids who are self-sufficient and confident reveals that it's best if parents let their children slowly begin to navigate routine life skills on their own. And this starts in elementary school. If you were to stand in the halls of most elementary schools in the morning, you would observe parents accompanying their children to class. However, it is important to consider the impact of this behavior on the child's confidence and independence. Elementary teachers, if given the opportunity, would advise parents to refrain from walking their children to class. While it may seem like a small matter, allowing children to navigate their own way, solve problems, and develop independence is crucial for their personal growth and future success. By encouraging children to take responsibility for finding their classrooms, parents empower them to build confidence and self-reliance. Anyone who has had young kids knows the smile and pride your kids had when they tell you, "I did this all by myself." This is especially important because a child's confidence level often plays a significant role in their overall school experience. Additionally, it is worth noting that children with low self-esteem are more likely to become targets of bullying. Therefore, fostering independence and self-assurance from an early age can help protect children from such negative experiences. Consider that you are releasing them into a school with lots of adult supervision, not the local mall.

Teachers are loaded with stories of elementary students crying when their parents walk them to class because they don't want their parents to leave. But as soon as the parent is out of sight, the child is fine. Parents should understand that kids learn how to pull on their heartstrings before they are a year old. That's all the more reason to let your kids know that you trust them to make it to class on their own.

Bullying or Teasing

For quite some time, addressing the issue of bullying has been a prominent focus for schools in our country. As an individual who has personally experienced the effects of bullying and even had to stand up against it, I strongly believe in the significance of tackling this problem. Creating a safe and supportive environment for all students is a cause that holds great value. Thankfully, it appears that the majority of people are not opposed to promoting anti-bullying messages.

Over the past 15 years, bullying has become more prevalent in our country. This raises the question of whether this increase is due to social media shedding light on the issue or if social media itself is exacerbating the problem. In my opinion, it's a combination of both factors. Social media platforms have provided a stage for bullies to showcase their behavior, as their friends capture videos to share. This exposure has brought attention to what was already a growing problem.

When I was growing up, fights rarely involved one person against a larger group. The gang or pack mentality that often accompanies bullying is especially disturbing, especially when it escalates to the use of weapons such as knives or guns. Even without weapons, a group of kids ganging up on one individual, particularly after they have been knocked unconscious, is a recipe for life-threatening injuries or long-term disabilities. Tragically, there have been cases where children have lost their lives as a result of severe beatings by groups of thirteen to seventeen-year-olds, such as the devastating incident that occurred in Las Vegas in 2023[1].

Unfortunately, many teenagers, who probably do not have children of their own, watch these videos of bullying without displaying any emotion. They then share these videos with their friends, perpetuating the cycle. While this may seem like a personal observation, the reality of cyberbullying is undeniable. With the rise of cell phones and social media, cyberbullying has become an incredibly serious issue that demands immediate attention.

In simple terms, cyberbullying refers to a form of harassment that takes place through electronic means. It encompasses various types of aggressive behavior, including hate speech, sexual remarks, stalking, trolling, and ridicule. Ignoring this toxic behavior can lead to further escalation, including physical harm.

The statistics are startling: 46 percent of U.S. teens aged 13 to 17 have experienced online bullying. The impact of online bullying can be devastating, with some victims being pushed to contemplate suicide. Studies have shown that cyberbullying victims are 1.9 times more likely to take their own lives, while the bullies themselves are also 1.7 times more likely to do so. Clearly, bullies often come from unhappy places, and hurting others becomes an outlet for their own issues. These statistics underscore the urgent need for anti-bullying programs in schools in order to effectively address this problem[2].

Cyberbullying takes on various forms:

Offensive name-calling
Spreading false rumors about the victim
Receiving explicit images they didn't ask for
Physical threats
Having explicit images of them shared without consent

According to the CDC, nearly 14 percent of public schools report that bullying is a disciplinary problem that occurs on a daily or weekly basis. Middle schools have the highest rate of bullying at 28 percent, followed by high schools at 16 percent, and combined and primary schools at 12 percent and 9 percent, respectively[3].

Interestingly, cyberbullying is most prevalent among middle schoolers, affecting 33 percent of students in that age group. High schoolers closely follow at 30 percent, while combined schoolers and primary school children experience cyberbullying at rates of 20 percent and 5 percent, respectively[4].

Surprisingly, Instagram has the highest percentage of cyberbullying incidents among various social media platforms. Statistics show that 42 percent of youths have been bullied on Instagram, surpassing other platforms like Facebook (37 percent), Snapchat (31 percent), WhatsApp (12 percent), and YouTube (10 percent)[5].

Unsurprisingly, women are often the preferred targets of online harassment. A survey among over 5,700 respondents revealed that 1 in 3 girls falls victim to cyberbullying. On the other hand, 1 in 10 admits to having been a cyber bully themselves[6].

According to a national survey, cyberbullying attacks can be categorized as follows:

Appearance - 61%	Financial Status - 15%
Academic Achievement - 25%	Religion - 11%
Race - 17%	Other - 20%
Sexuality - 15%	

Bullying can have a profound impact on young children, leading to issues with self-esteem. In the past, when cell phones and social media weren't as prevalent, victims of bullying at school could at least find solace by going home. Nowadays, bullies don't need to confront their targets physically in person. Social media has provided new avenues for targeting and piling on their victims.

As a parent, I have found myself needing to take cell phones away from our daughters on multiple occasions. They felt compelled to involve themselves in social media fights or attacks, always wanting to defend their friends. However, we taught them the phrase "not your circus" and confiscated their phones to prevent them from getting further entangled in these situations.

I must admit that, as a father, I was not prepared for the

level of viciousness that girls can exhibit towards each other and how early it begins. On social media, groups form, and they act like packs of wild dogs, ganging up on others.

When it comes to handling in-person bullying, we take a somewhat old-fashioned approach. We've encouraged our children never to start a fight but also not to allow someone to abuse them without defending themselves. There have been incidents that needed to be addressed on more than one occasion. Although it may sound old-fashioned and politically incorrect, we've noticed that when our kids stand up to bullying, the bullies tend to move on to easier targets.

However, it's important to distinguish between bullying and teasing. Many teachers have stories about overprotective parents who complain that their child is being bullied when it is actually just immature teasing. In some cases, these parents want the school to escalate the situation. Teachers have shared instances where a parent called or emailed because another elementary school student made fun of their child's lunch. Making fun of someone's lunch is not bullying. Bullying would involve taking your child's lunch and destroying it or threatening to beat up your child if they tell on the bully.

We seem to have lost sight of what real bullying looks like, and now everything falls under the umbrella label of bullying for some parents. Perhaps this is why many young adults today have such thin skin when it comes to dealing with drama or problems. When parents constantly swoop in to take care of every incident, children learn nothing about how to handle similar situations that will inevitably arise in the future. Conflict resolution is a critical life skill that goes a long way in helping individuals navigate challenges throughout their lives.

Let me be clear: I'm not referring to violent situations.

When someone threatens the safety of your child, it is best to bring it to the attention of the school authorities and, in cases of terroristic threats, possibly involve the police. However, before escalating the issue, it is crucial to determine whether it was teasing or making fun of something. Teasing, especially in elementary school, is not bullying, and parents should not intervene in these situations. Instead, we should teach our children to develop the self-esteem to ignore immature teasing and equip them with the skills to resolve minor confrontations themselves without violence.

It is an unfortunate reality of life that people will talk about you, make fun of you, tease you, and be rude. We cannot run to authorities or school administrations for every incident, or we would be constantly having conferences with our children's schools. Many bullies who are told by adults to stop eventually return to taunt their victims. Bullies often seek out easy or weaker targets. Therefore, it is crucial to teach our children how to deal with these situations. Engaging in sports can greatly boost a child's self-esteem, and for those who aren't particularly athletic, martial arts classes can be a beneficial option. In fact, I know several parents who enrolled their children in martial arts to help them overcome the fear of confrontation, as it teaches discipline and good values and skills for de-escalating confrontations and self-defense.

If you speak to counselors or childcare advocates, they will tell you that teasing that becomes repetitive can evolve into bullying. However, it could also just be annoying. As a father, I didn't want my children to be scared by every little thing that didn't make them feel special. It is important to consider the maturity level of those involved when distinguishing between teasing in elementary school and older grades. This is a critical time to teach our children how to handle themselves and to identify kids who may be on the path to becoming bullies, as early intervention may be the key to helping kids who have a propensity for bullying others.

I often drummed into my kids' heads that just because someone said something about them, it doesn't make it true and that they should take it as though the offender's comments have no basis in reality except for their own head. If your child is confident, then they will brush off what some might consider harmful comments and verbal attacks.

Parents often find themselves hesitant to confiscate their children's phones and restrict their access to social media despite the fact that these platforms can often be the source of cyberbullying that harms their own children. This hesitation may stem from the fact that many parents themselves heavily rely on their own cell phones and cannot imagine going without them, which may lead them to overlook the option of taking away their kids' phones. However, it is crucial for parents to take action if their child is being bullied through texts or on social media. By temporarily removing the device, parents can help their child refocus on life and break free from the negativity that cyberbullying brings. It's important to remember that your child will not suffer drastically without their phone, and this experience can serve as a valuable lesson. Taking a break from technology when things aren't going in a positive direction can provide an opportunity to regain perspective and prioritize their emotional well-being.

The Rise of Narcissistic Parenting

A significant study conducted by Dr. Jean Twenge from San Diego State University sheds light on the escalating narcissistic traits among American college students. The study, spanning over 27 years from 1982 to 2009, unearthed a disconcerting trend - a noticeable rise in narcissistic tendencies. These findings were further corroborated by the National Institute of Health's extensive survey of 35,000 Americans. Notably, both studies highlighted that the surge in narcissism was particularly pronounced among women, and worryingly, this upward trajectory shows no signs of abating[7].

One significant factor that has greatly contributed to this trend is the pervasive influence of social media. Platforms such as Facebook, Instagram, and Twitter have provided a platform for every young adult to seek constant attention and validation, creating a culture of "15 minutes of fame." Through these platforms, individuals have the opportunity to showcase their lives, achievements, and even their most mundane activities to an audience of followers, all in the pursuit of garnering likes, comments, and shares.

Furthermore, the rise of reality TV shows featuring individuals who lack any real value or talent has set a precedent for the younger generation. These shows highlight how one can attain fame and fortune without making any substantial contributions to society or even having good moral character. As a result, many young people have become enamored with the idea of becoming famous simply for the sake of being famous, without considering the impact or meaning behind their actions.

This self-obsession is further exemplified by the prevalence of teenagers and their peers engaging in excessive selfie-taking. Taking endless selfies and sharing them on social media has become a common practice, serving as a starting point for cultivating a "look at me" personality trait. This constant need for attention and validation can be seen as an initial step towards developing narcissistic tendencies, as individuals become increasingly focused on their own image and how others perceive them. You can see this demonstrated in videos of people doing stupid and dangerous stunts to get clicks, likes, and views. Always upping the game to keep the 15 minutes of fame rolling has, at times, cost some people their lives.

While numerous articles and studies, such as those featuring Dr. Twenge's research, have identified various signs and social indicators associated with the rise of narcissistic personalities, there is one specific factor that has received relatively less attention.

This factor centers around the influence of narcissistic parenting or the inadvertent promotion of narcissistic behaviors in children. Specifically, I am referring to the attitudes and actions of parents who firmly believe that their children are never at fault when it comes to their academic performance or their behavior[8]. It is quite common for teachers, especially those with more than a year of experience, to come across parents who vehemently defend their child's innocence in every situation. In their interactions with parents, teachers often hear statements such as:

- "My child said they didn't do it." - "It wasn't my child's fault." - "My child said it was someone else."

or

- "I demand to know why my kid received a B. My child has an A in all the other classes except yours."

and my personal favorite:

- "My kid cannot have a learning issue; both mom and I have college degrees."

Are we currently living in a society that is so narcissistic that we expect others to believe that our children are flawless, even if it inhibits their personal growth and development? Or do some parents genuinely think their child's teacher enjoys singling out their child for criticism? When I was in school, I would face consequences at home if I received a note about something I had done wrong. I might have even attempted to shift the blame onto my teacher or a classmate. I often told my kids that any excuse that begins or ends with someone else's name will not be taken seriously.

However, many of today's parents not only vehemently advocate for their child's innocence but also escalate the situation by seeking intervention from higher authorities, bypassing the teacher altogether. Teachers often recount stories of students who consistently exhibit disruptive and problematic behavior. Yet, their parents go to great lengths to absolve them of any punishment. Essentially, these parents teach their children that they are not obligated to follow the rules that everyone else follows. Unfortunately, this lack of respect for authority figures is already well-documented. Numerous YouTube videos and articles have shed light on the fact that many students today display minimal respect toward their teachers and those in positions of authority. Additionally, the Nickelodeon and Disney Channel shows that parents often use as a means of entertainment for their children may inadvertently reinforce this lack of respect for authority figures, as many of these programs depict children as the ones in control while portraying adults as fools.

It is crucial to address the fact that some parents may have initially engaged in this protective behavior with good intentions, simply wanting to believe in their child's innocence. However, after conversing with teachers, especially those who instruct elementary school students, it becomes evident that they experience significant frustration towards parents who consistently undermine their authority. If only these parents could realize that by consistently rushing to their child's defense, they inadvertently enable their children to engage in further inappropriate behavior, secure in the knowledge that their parents will take care of any issues that arise. Consider how that attitude will play out in the future.

This raises an important question: Do parents possess such high levels of self-absorption that they are incapable of acknowledging their child's wrongdoings? Furthermore, are we unintentionally shaping a new generation of narcissistic individuals by teaching our children that authority figures, both within and outside of school, are undeserving of their respect?

This prevailing phenomenon can pose challenges for schools, as they often find themselves grappling with parents who swiftly leap to outrageous conclusions based solely on their child's account. For instance, a child might claim that they were forcefully pushed by another student or even by a teacher. Without giving it a second thought or employing rational judgment to determine the veracity of such stories, some parents immediately storm into the school, commencing a tumultuous uproar.

I have personally come across numerous tales of parents levying allegations of abuse against teachers or fellow students, prompting schools to review video footage in order to ascertain the accuracy of these claims. In every case that I am familiar with, these recordings have shown that no incident occurred. Nevertheless, this necessitates valuable time and resources being squandered on investigations, the creation of reports by teachers, and the subsequent dissemination of emails to all parents in the class, elucidating the evolving situation and its ultimate outcome.

Of course, there have been instances where teachers or even students have indeed acted inappropriately, engaging in physical altercations with young students. Such incidents have been captured on video, providing tangible evidence to support the child's claim. However, it is essential to acknowledge that the majority of these cases involve baseless assertions made by students. What is truly bewildering is that, despite the testimonies of teachers and administrators that I have had the opportunity to interview, certain parents steadfastly retain their belief in their child's account, even after interviews and video have concluded that nothing happened.

Let's delve deeper into another noteworthy characteristic that can be associated with narcissism or, at the very least, entitlement. Within the realm of education, a concerning trend has emerged: the growing demand from parents to have their child placed in a specific class solely based on the presence of their friends. These parents assert that their children would experience unhappiness or disappointment if they were not assigned to the same class. While it has long been the norm for schools to have the final say in assigning classes and teachers, an increasing number of parents are making requests and pleas to have their children moved to their preferred class.

Schools have established a longstanding policy that parents cannot have a say in determining their child's class for the school year. This policy is in place to prevent the situation from spiraling out of control. If one parent is allowed to move their child to a different class before the start of the school year, it would set a precedent and lead to every parent demanding the same consideration. This issue presents a significant challenge for school administrators, who are constantly faced with pressure from dissatisfied parents. Despite the explicit policy of not accommodating such requests, schools frequently find themselves succumbing to the demands of these parents. Unfortunately, this only exacerbates the problem, as it encourages other parents to follow suit and seek preferential treatment for their children.

Teachers, on the other hand, are given the freedom to choose their child's class or teacher as long as it is within the county they work in. However, this is a perk or benefit of being employed by the county school system. Unfortunately, the pressure on school administrators to move a child to a class where their friends are assigned has become more frequent over the past decade, and these requests have transformed into demands. Some administrators, in an effort to avoid confrontation at the start of the year, choose to honor these demands and move the child. This is quite absurd, as it essentially allows parents to create a problem that will only escalate when other parents realize they can bully the school administration into getting what they want.

This particular situation serves as a compelling illustration of the prevailing mindset among many parents today, who feel entitled to dictate the terms and conditions of their child's education. It is important to note that my previous statement may have inadvertently conveyed a lack of support for parental rights. On the contrary, I firmly believe that parents should have a voice in crucial aspects such as curriculum and the content being taught. Nonetheless, it is imperative that administrators do not succumb to the pressure of aligning a child with their specific friend group. The consequences of

this behavior, regardless of how it is perceived, can be categorized as a sense of entitlement that is passed down to the
students. It also exemplifies how parents frequently intervene
to shape their child's life according to their own preferences.

Helicopter to Lawnmower Parents

When discussing parenting styles, one term that often
comes up is "helicopter parents." These are parents who are
known for being overly protective and excessively involved
in their children's lives, sometimes to the point of causing
harm. Helicopter parents closely monitor their children's
activities, academic performance, and social interactions
with the intention of shielding them from any potential pain
or disappointment while ensuring their success. They have
a tendency to micromanage their children's lives and
become deeply intertwined with every aspect. The term
"helicopter parent" was first coined in 1969 by Dr. Haim
Ginott in his best-selling book "Between Parent & Teenager,"
where teenagers complains about their mother constantly
hovering over them like a helicopter[9].

Helicopter parents are often driven by a deep love and
concern for their children. They want the best for them and
believe that by being involved in every aspect of their lives,
they can protect them from harm and pave the way for their
future success. However, this parenting style can have negative consequences. The amusing aspect of helicopter
parents is that they are often unaware of their behavior.

One of the downsides of helicopter parenting is that it
can hinder children's development of independence and

problem-solving skills. When parents constantly intervene and make decisions for their children, it deprives them of the opportunity to learn from their own mistakes and develop important life skills. This can result in children who struggle with decision-making, lack resilience, and have difficulty adapting to new situations[10].

Being cautious and careful appears to be the guiding principle for overprotective parents. Their kids have been raised in an atmosphere clouded by apprehension, constantly fearing to take any chances, too wary of exerting their own judgment, and lacking the self-assurance to assert themselves. Throughout their formative years, their parents made all the choices on their behalf, leaving them ill-equipped to navigate the obstacles that arise during early adulthood.

A Huffington Post article titled "Helicopter Parenting Leads To Serious Workplace Setbacks" highlights that helicopter parents have raised children who struggle to thrive in the workforce[11].

A recent study conducted by the University of Houston has shed light on the profound influence of helicopter parenting on millennials. Being the generation that has experienced the most protection and programming in history, millennials are undoubtedly affected by this phenomenon. Interestingly, this impact goes beyond their personal lives and has a significant influence on the recruitment process as well. The study highlights the long-lasting effects of helicopter parenting on millennials' ability to navigate the workplace. These individuals, who have been closely monitored and guided throughout their upbringing, often struggle with the challenges of independence and decision-making in a professional setting. Their constant need for reassurance and validation can hinder their ability to adapt to the demands of the job market[12].

A survey conducted by Michigan State University revealed some alarming trends among employers seeking to hire recent college graduates. According to the survey, nearly one-third of employers reported that parents had submitted resumes on behalf of their children. This indicates a growing trend of parental involvement in the job application process. Furthermore, one-quarter of employers had received calls from parents urging them to hire their son or daughter. This kind of parental intervention can create an uncomfortable situation for employers, as they are expecting to interact directly with the candidates themselves. Shockingly, the survey also found that 4 percent of respondents had even encountered instances where a parent showed up for the candidate's job interview. This level of parental involvement raises concerns about the independence and professionalism of the candidates[13].

As an employer, I have personally experienced parents calling me to convince me to rehire their young adult child after they were fired for reasons such as chronic tardiness. This kind of interference from parents can undermine the employer-employee relationship and hinder the development of essential skills such as responsibility and accountability. It is important for young adults to learn how to handle workplace challenges on their own and take ownership of their actions. Even if I had asked my own mother to make such a call on my behalf, she would have advised me to address the situation myself, understanding the importance of personal responsibility in professional settings.

This hyper-parenting style has undoubtedly had a detrimental impact on this young generation[14].

Here are some of the ways in which helicopter parents have sabotaged their children's future:

- Lack of decision-making power
- Low self-esteem
- Poor leadership skills
- Inability to handle problems independently
- Diminished earning potential

As I mentioned earlier, most helicopter parents aren't even aware of their overbearing activities. And they do not see their child as having low self-esteem or poor leadership skills.

Forbes published an insightful article back in 2016 titled "Want A Well-Adjusted College Student? Stop Helicopter Parenting." In this article, they shed light on a study conducted at Florida State University. The study defined helicopter parents as those who excessively involve themselves in their emerging adult children's lives, providing extensive support (such as financial assistance, emotional guidance, and health advice), frequently interfering in their affairs, and even making decisions on their behalf[15].

Dr. Kayla Reed and her co-author, Mallory Lucier-Greer, who are notable figures in the field, shared a thought-provoking quote in the article. She stated, "Individuals with parents who engage in highly controlling, overprotective behaviors have been characterized as being overly needy in terms of seeking attention, approval, and direction from others." The authors also mentioned, "In addition, they have been found to utilize more ineffective coping skills, express higher levels of narcissism, and demonstrate lower self-efficacy," summarizing past research[16].

The researchers utilized a novel assessment scale known as the "Helicopter Parenting Behaviors measure." This scale aims to distinguish between intrusive parenting behaviors and those that are supportive, fostering a child's autonomy. In order to gauge autonomy, students were presented with various statements and asked to indicate their level of agreement or disagreement. For instance, participants were asked to express their views on whether their mother encourages them to make their own decisions and take responsibility for the choices they make. Another statement focused on whether their mother supports them in resolving interpersonal conflicts with roommates or friends independently. On the other hand, items pertaining to helicoptering behaviors examined the extent to which mothers engage in excessive monitoring. Examples of such items include whether their mother regularly expects them to call or text her to inform her of their whereabouts and whether their mother monitors their diet[17].

Furthermore, a study conducted among college professors revealed a concerning trend: an increasing number of complaints from professors and college administrators about the growing dependence of college students on their parents. Professors find themselves receiving more calls from parents regarding absences or grade disputes compared to a generation ago. Countless articles have expressed their concerns, emphasizing how helicopter parenting is negatively impacting college students, rendering them more fragile and ill-equipped to handle the challenges that come with young adulthood[18].

If that weren't alarming enough, a new phenomenon is emerging—a cottage industry where parents can hire individuals in the same state as their college-bound children to check on them regularly. These "proxy helicopter parents" serve as substitutes, ensuring that their children's daily needs are met, from doing laundry to stocking up their fridges, making their beds, and even waking them up in the mornings. Providing regular reports to the parent about how their child is doing[19].

In addition to the concern of being a helicopter parent, a new parenting style has emerged in recent years, known as "lawnmower parenting" or "Snowplow parenting" in the North. This parenting style involves parents taking proactive measures to eliminate any obstacles or challenges that their child may face. They do not wait for problems to arise; instead, they actively remove any opposition or difficulties that come their child's way. The term "lawnmower" is used metaphorically to convey the act of mowing down any problems or opposition that could hinder their child's progress or success. Here are some examples of what lawnmower parents may do:

- - Complete homework or projects for their child
- - Email teachers to argue about grades
- - Remove their child from difficult activities
- - Blame others for their child's mistakes
- - Intervene in conflicts with friends, teachers, coaches, and others
- - Request unreasonable accommodations for their child
- - Contact teachers about grades or extensions
- - Reach out to potential employers about interviews

Lawnmower parents often take it upon themselves to micromanage their children's lives in an attempt to shield them from any form of suffering or adversity. Unfortunately, this well-intentioned approach can inadvertently impede the development of crucial life skills. Children who have lawnmower parents may struggle with feelings of insecurity and find it challenging to handle failure. They might become overwhelmed or shut down when confronted with problems. Over time, children raised by lawnmower parents may come to perceive challenges as personal shortcomings, placing blame on themselves for setbacks. This, in turn, can result in heightened anxiety, a diminished capacity to handle distress, and a sense of helplessness[20].

While it is important to note that the association between parental intervention and anxiety is not necessarily causal, incessant rescuing can undermine one's self-assurance. These early interactions with overbearing parents can have significant and lasting impacts. Extensive research conducted with college students has highlighted the correlation between high levels of parental "helicoptering" and increased risk of student depression and anxiety. It has been observed that when parents excessively intervene and control every aspect of their children's lives, it can hinder their ability to develop independence and resilience. On the flip side, students who grow up with parents who enable their every move may display traits of narcissism and entitlement as they become accustomed to always getting what they want. While anxiety can be detrimental to one's well-being, it is equally problematic to foster overconfidence and the unrealistic expectation that life should always be easy[21].

According to Professor Graham Davey, a renowned psychologist from the University of Sussex in the United Kingdom, there is evidence to suggest that children who grow up with overprotective parents may be more susceptible to anxiety. However, it is crucial to acknowledge that parental involvement, especially from caring and firm parents, can have positive effects. When children have faith in their own capabilities and receive support from their parents, it fosters a sense of security.

Striking the right balance may seem complicated, but over 50 years ago, pediatrician and psychoanalyst Donald Woods Winnicott introduced the concept of "good enough parenting." This concept highlights the idea that parents who are both loving and provide a stimulating environment while also setting boundaries and not obsessing over doing everything perfectly tend to have children with the best outcomes[22].

Winnicott's theory emphasizes the importance of finding a middle ground between being overly permissive and being overly strict. It recognizes that perfection is not attainable, and that parents who strive for perfection may inadvertently put too much pressure on themselves and their children. By adopting a "good enough" attitude, parents can alleviate some of this pressure and focus on providing their children with a nurturing and supportive environment.

So, what does "good enough parenting" look like in practice? It means recognizing that mistakes are inevitable and that it is okay to make them. It means acknowledging that children need both love and structure to thrive. It means finding a balance between meeting their needs and allowing them to develop independence. It means being responsive to their emotions and providing a safe space for them to express themselves[23].

The most valuable parenting advice I have ever received is to empower my kids to solve their own problems instead of fixing everything for them. By encouraging them to think through and discuss potential solutions, I have witnessed tremendous success in my own household. Additionally, it is important not to shield my children from the consequences of their actions, but rather to hold them accountable and encourage them to take responsibility for their role in creating the situation.

I firmly believe that the most effective teachers are those who maintain a balance between strictness and fairness. While one might assume that students would dislike such a teacher, I have found that children recognize the teacher's actions as expressions of concern and an establishment of structure. This structure, in turn, fosters a sense of equilibrium between the students and the teacher, ultimately creating a positive learning environment.

In 2020, Business Insider published a thought-provoking article titled "11 science-backed ways your parents' behaviors shaped who you are today." This insightful piece sheds light on the profound impact parents' behavior during childhood has on individuals' behavior as adults. Through countless studies and extensive clinical research, it has become evident that there are strong connections between parental influence and our development as individuals[24]. For example:

- If your parents made you do chores, you are likely to take on tasks independently.
- If your parents taught you social skills, you are more likely to obtain a college degree and a high-paying job.
- If your parents told you white lies, it may have led to trust issues in adulthood.
- If your parents spoke negatively about their bodies, you are more likely to have low self-confidence.
- If your parents set high expectations for you, you probably performed better in school.

- If your mother attended high school or college, you were more likely to do the same.
- If your mother was constantly stressed, you were more likely to struggle with math.
- If you're a girl and your mother worked outside the house, you are more likely to earn a higher income than other women.
- If your mother was loving and attentive when you were a baby, you were more likely to excel in school.
- If your parents taught you to verbalize your feelings, you are less likely to get divorced.
- If your parents sheltered you, you are more likely to experience anxiety.

Developing Work Ethic in Your Kids

Maybe the title of this section should be "Developing Work Ethic in Your Kids Starts at Home." I strongly agree that there has been a noticeable increase in the number of spoiled children over the past decade. This observation is supported by conversations with teachers, employers, and business managers who have noticed that the younger generation is more likely to quit their jobs when faced with discipline, show little initiative or work ethic, or even fail to show up at all. Considering their abundance compared to past youth, it is challenging for our kids not to be more spoiled than previous generations. However, previous generations were less likely to quit a job because, in most cases, they did not have parents who would bail them out, pay their bills, or allow them to live at home indefinitely for free.

As a parent and business owner, I have had the opportunity to meet and speak with many other parents through my everyday life, whether through my own kids' involvement in sports or dance or through conversations with people I meet through our business. I am often dumbfounded by some parents' attitudes towards their kids working. Many parents have rationalized that their children should not have a job while in school. I have listened to their reasoning in silence, with a crinkled brow, and their reasons seem to fall into the following categories:

1. My kids shouldn't have to work because it would reflect poorly on my ability as a parent to take care of them.
2. I want them to enjoy their childhood years without any stress.
3. I had to work when I was a teenager, but that was because my parents couldn't afford to help me buy a car.
4. (My personal favorite) I want my kids to get jobs, but they refuse.

I won't spend much time on number 4 except to say that parents may need to reevaluate who is in charge at home. I can address points 1 through 3 together because, in each case, the parent is missing the more significant issue.

When I was a teenager in high school and college, my parents couldn't provide much financial assistance, so I worked to ensure that I could afford the things I needed beyond basic necessities like clothes and food, which my parents did provide. Working for my own money instilled in me a strong work ethic, taught me the value of money, and gave me a sense of responsibility. In my own home today, our teenagers started working part-time jobs as early as 15. This decision was not because we couldn't afford to care for them or meet their basic needs but because we wanted them to learn how to handle their money and develop essential life skills. We also wanted them to know how to balance school, work, and recreational activities. Why should they take a college time management course when they can learn it through real-life experiences at home? We helped them with 50percent of the cost of their cars, and now they pay us a flat fee for their insurance each month. We do this to prepare them for the real world, not because we are evil or uncaring parents who want to take their money for ourselves.

Work ethic starts at home, with chores and observing how parents work around the house. The lesson continues as they apply it to their part-time jobs. It astounds me that some parents believe it is a good idea for their kids to have their first job after they graduate from college and start their careers. As someone who has run my own business for over 25 years, including a production company, education resource company, restaurant, and gyms, I can confidently say that employees with a strong work ethic stand out quickly from those who lack it. I have had to let go of many employees because they lacked the initiative, attitude, drive, or respect required to succeed in a job. Wouldn't it be better for them to learn these attributes before they start their careers rather than experience the harsh reality of being let go by an employer at the start of their career?

When I was 19, a friend of my dad's who owned a painting business hired me for the summer. It wasn't my first job; I had previously worked in fast food. Although I was a hard worker, I also enjoyed going out with friends late at night, sometimes making arriving at work on time diffi-

cult. One day, my boss warned me that I would be terminated if I were even 5 minutes late again. Unfortunately, a
week later, I was fifteen minutes late, and when I arrived, I
was handed my final paycheck without even having the
chance to defend myself. This experience was embarrassing
but also a valuable life lesson. Since then, I have made it a
point to be early to almost every appointment and always
try to be punctual for all my employers. Imagine if that had
been the job that marked the beginning of my career.

Our teenagers started working part-time jobs when they
turned 15. From my perspective, it is a simple decision. We
want to gradually introduce our children to life's responsibilities rather than throwing them into the deep end the day
they graduate. By doing so, we can help them understand
the value of jobs and money. So, when your teenager wants
to call out of work because something more exciting is
happening, you can talk with them about responsibility.
When your teenagers do not have jobs, you miss out on the
funny conversations about how "my job sucks; all I do is wait
on or clean up after people." To which you can respond, "If
you don't improve your grades, you'll be doing that for the
rest of your life." This is not to say we were perfect parents
who did everything right, far from it. Like many parents, we
learned as we went along.

Our country faces an epidemic of young men who have
dropped out of the workforce. While pundits may come up
with various reasons, perhaps one reason we overlook is
that they have been spoiled. I personally know several
people whose sons have graduated from college and are
now in their mid-20s, living at home without a job because
they haven't found the right career or realized they don't
enjoy the field they majored in. In both cases, the parents
provide them with spending money and require nothing in

return for them to live at home. With free food and some spending money, why wouldn't they stay at home, playing video games in their basement apartment?

Teaching your kids to pay for things themselves gives them an understanding of the value of money and how it applies to their own lives. It helps them appreciate what they have because they earned the money and made the purchase.

This gets back to education because a strong work ethic translates to school and the balance that work and academics play in their development as young adults.

Living Through Your Kids

If you have ever coached a kids' sport, you have undoubtedly encountered parents who are overly enthusiastic about their children's athletic endeavors. These parents seem to be living vicariously through their kids, perhaps because they didn't have the opportunity to participate in sports themselves beyond middle school. You might be wondering why I am discussing this topic in a book about education. It's because many parents have convinced themselves that sports should take precedence over education. As a result, teachers often receive notes from parents explaining that their child couldn't complete homework due to late-night sports activities or that they were away all weekend playing sports and, therefore, couldn't finish a project. Let me clarify that I am not against sports—I played organized sports until I was 47, and I even coached two of my kids for over 15 seasons. I genuinely love sports. However, as a parent, your primary responsibility is to prepare your children for the real world once they leave the nest. I cannot count the number of times parents approached me, as early as their child was ten years old, asking if their kid had what it takes to make it to college sports. Trust me when I say that if you need to ask, then the answer is probably no! The kids who make it to the highest levels of sports outshine everyone around them, and the difference in talent compared to their peers is glaringly obvious.

Parents are inadvertently teaching their children that education is not a top priority. Very few parents would openly admit this, but their actions speak louder than words. When it comes to sports activities, parents often live vicariously through their children, hoping that their kids will achieve what they never could. In my experience, I have coached four different kids whose parents were former professional ball players. Surprisingly, I never heard a single complaint or objection from any of these parents, regardless of the decisions I made as a coach. These parents remained silent even when I benched their kids or disciplined them. In fact, they went out of their way to avoid interfering with my coaching. I vividly recall two instances where these kids missed practice because they hadn't completed schoolwork.

Perhaps, and most likely, the work ethic and drive that propelled these parents to the highest levels of sports are the same qualities they are passing on to their children. It's possible that they want their kids to develop the same determination and always strive to do their best. Lastly, I want to offer a dose of reality to parents. No matter what sport your child is playing, millions of kids across the country participate in the same sport. However, only a limited number of opportunities are available for the very best. The odds of your child making a career out of athletics as a player are incredibly low. That's why it is crucial to emphasize the importance of graduating with decent grades. After all, what will they do once their sports career ends? Even if they make it to the highest level of sports, the average player's lifespan in all professional sports is only 3.3 years. While there are outliers like Tom Brady, most athletes have a limited time in the spotlight. So, it's essential to have a plan B, whether pursuing higher education or a vocational path.

What I find ironic is that many parents push work ethic on them for sports but do not see that the same drive to succeed in sports would go a long way towards shaping them as students if applied correctly.

It's also worth noting that, except for football, which receives the most scholarship money from big schools, the chances of receiving a scholarship or partial scholarship are pretty slim. This means your child needs to have the grades to gain admission to a school if a coach wants to offer them a non-scholarship spot on the team.

Below are the odds of your kids making it to the next level in sports:

Let's explore the comprehensive data compiled in 2017 by the National College Athletic Association (NCAA) to gain insight into the practical prospects of your child or any individual's child achieving professional success. In order to provide a framework, we will specifically examine those who have participated in a sport during their high school years.

For male high-school basketball players, the chances of transitioning to college are a mere 3.3 percent. This means that out of 100 players, only about three will have the opportunity to continue their basketball careers at the college level. The odds of making it to the professional level are even slimmer, with only a minuscule 0.03 percent chance of success. This means that out of 1000 high-school basketball players, only three will have the chance to see their dreams of playing professionally come true.

Similarly, for female high-school basketball players, the odds of going to college are slightly better at 3.9 percent. However, this still means that less than 4 out of every 100 female players will have the opportunity to play basketball at the college level. The chances of reaching the professional level remain the same for both genders, with a mere 0.03 percent chance of success. This shows just how competitive and challenging it is for aspiring basketball players to make it to the top.

It is important to recognize that basketball players encounter some of the most difficult challenges in pursuing a professional career because of the smaller number of players for each team. Nevertheless, it is worth noting that other sports do not provide significantly better chances. To illustrate, male high-school football players have a mere 0.08 percent probability of reaching the professional level. On the other hand, male high-school hockey players face odds of just 0.07 percent, while male high-school soccer players have a slightly higher chance of 0.09 percent.

While these statistics may be disheartening, the truth is that the situation is even more challenging than it seems. One factor that contributes to the seemingly more favorable statistics in baseball compared to basketball is the presence of farm teams. Unfortunately, basketball lacks a similar system, which greatly limits the opportunities for high-school players to pursue their dreams in the sport. Moreover, even in baseball, many high-school players who manage to make it to the professional level make it to the pros in name only and often find themselves earning a meager income while playing in farm clubs. In fact, a lawsuit filed against Major League Baseball in 2016 revealed that the average player in a farm club earns a mere $4 per hour. In March of 2023 the Players Association ratified pay in benefits increase for minor league players that nearly doubles their pay. This is good news for minor league baseball ball players, however, their salaries are still meager and below the median income level in the United States. For instance, Low-A: $11,000 to $26,200, High-A: $11,000 to $27,300, AA: $13,800 to $30,250, and AAA: $17,500 to $35,800.

Now, let's delve into the possibilities of a high school athlete making the transition to the college level. By examining the participation of athletes in varsity sports at high schools in the United States and comparing it to the number of college student-athletes, we can gain valuable insights. On the whole, just over 7percent of high school athletes (approximately 1 in 13) manage to pursue a varsity sport at the college level. However, when it comes to NCAA Division I schools, the odds decrease significantly, with less than 2percent of high school athletes (1 in 57) achieving that feat. It should be noted that about 70percent of college athletes are not on scholarships.

In almost every college, the number of scholarships available for football is higher, and because there are more scholarships available for the football team, it limits the number of scholarships available for other sports. NCAA Division I baseball teams have an average roster of 40 players but only a maximum of 11.7 athletic scholarships available. This means the average award covers only about 30percent of annual college costs, and this assumes the sport is fully funded at the sponsoring school. Full rides are rare in college baseball. As a comparison, Division I Football has a max of 85 scholarships available, and Division II schools have around 36 scholarships available for football[25].

Odds of a US High School Student Athlete playing College

Boys playing High School:	Baseball	Basketball	Football	Soccer	Tennis
Odds of making any College roster:	8:1	17:1	11:1	12:1	25:1
Odds of making an NCAA I Roster:	43:1	110:1	33:1	108:1	155:1

Girls playing High School:	Softball	Basketball	Volleyball	Soccer	Tennis
Odds of making any College roster:	10:1	14:1	16:1	10:1	28:1
Odds of making an NCAA I Roster:	51:1	81:1	83:1	41:1	182:1

Odds of a US High School Player:	MLB	NBA	NFL	MLS	WNBA	NWSL
Making any College roster:	8:1	17:1	11:1	12:1	14:1	10:1
Making an NCAA I roster:	43:1	110:1	33:1	108:1	81:1	14:1
Making a Pro Roster:	829:1	1920:1	554:1	1344:1	3086:1	1435:1

Odds of a US High School Athlete playing Pro Sports

Special Education

I am putting this information in the parents section because I am aware that this topic can cause a lot of stress and concern for parents. Nevertheless, I want to provide reassurance to any parent who may come across this and whose child has been placed in special education. I want to assure you that there is no need to excessively worry about your child's future outcome. It is simply a temporary obstacle that can be overcome. Rather than viewing it as a setback, it is crucial to see it as an opportunity for growth and development.

Enacted in 1975, the Individuals with Disabilities Education Act (IDEA) is a federal law that ensures eligible students between the ages of 3 and 21 receive a free and appropriate public school education. These eligible students are identified by a team of professionals as having a disability that negatively impacts their academic performance and requires special education and/or related services.

Under IDEA, schools are required to provide individualized educational plans (IEPs) for students with disabilities. These plans outline the specific educational goals, services, and accommodations necessary to support the student's unique needs. The goal is to provide students with the necessary tools and resources to succeed academically and prepare for life beyond school.

By placing a child in special education, parents are ensuring that their child has access to the necessary resources, services, and accommodations to thrive academically and socially. It is a decision made with their best interests in mind[26].

The number of students receiving special education in public schools is on the rise. According to a report entitled "The Condition of Education 2018" by the Department of Education, there was an increase in the number of students aged 3 to 21 receiving special education services from 6.6

million to 6.7 million between the 2014-2015 and 2015-2016 school years. Of these students, 34 percent had specific learning disabilities, 20 percent had speech or language impairments, and 14 percent had other health impairments[27]. During the 2019–2020 school year, there was a significant increase in the number of students receiving special education services, reaching a total of 7.3 million students[28].

In 2018, Joel McFarland, a researcher, gathered federal-level data by examining students served under the Individuals with Disabilities Education Act, which necessitates that schools provide special education services to students in need. Students with autism, intellectual disabilities, developmental delays, and emotional disturbances accounted for 5 and 9 percent of students served under the act[29].

First and foremost, it is crucial to understand that the discussion surrounding the increase in the number of children in special education is a topic of debate. Different sources and studies seem to suggest varying perspectives on this matter.

However, it has been observed through research that there are several factors that could potentially contribute to the observed increases. One crucial factor is the improvement in awareness and understanding of developmental disabilities. Greater knowledge and recognition of these conditions have likely led to more accurate screening and diagnosis.

Furthermore, advancements in accessibility to services have played a significant role in the rise of children receiving special education. With improved resources and support systems, families and individuals have better access to the necessary assistance for developmental disabilities.

A notable study conducted by the Centers for Disease

Control and Prevention (CDC) and the Health Resources and Services Administration (HRSA) revealed some compelling findings. The study discovered that approximately 17 percent of children aged 3–17 years had a developmental disability. Importantly, this percentage exhibited an increase when comparing two time periods: 2009–2011 and 2015–2017. Moreover, specific developmental disabilities within the same age group also displayed noticeable increases[30].

Now that we have covered all the statistical data let's move on to what it means for each family. At the time of writing this, I am 55 years old. I have known several parents who have had children placed in special education due to poor academic performance or learning disabilities that were discovered during testing. In every case, these children grew up to lead fulfilling lives and have successful families. Most teachers have told me that every child develops at their own pace. Kids grow up and mature at different rates. Girls, in general, often mature faster than boys. It is essential to recognize that not everyone's brain develops at the same speed, which is an inconvenient truth for academics who are searching for a one-size-fits-all solution to learning. If you reflect on your friends and classmates from your childhood, you probably remember kids you thought would still be living at home with their parents, being taken care of until they were in their 30s. However, when you attended your class reunion, you likely realized that most people find their path to a career and adult life.

Knowing there is no need to panic if your child has been placed in special education is important. It might mean that your child will face additional challenges initially. However, most studies indicate that children growing up in homes where no one engages in conversation with them, attempts to teach them basic language skills, or where parents are not involved are ten times more likely to require special education services. Additionally, children from challenging home environments are six times more likely to be placed in special education.

More than 20 years ago, psychologists Betty Hart and Todd Risley made a significant finding known as the "30 million word gap". During their research, they conducted family visits and estimated that children under four years old from lower-income families were exposed to 30 million fewer words compared to children from higher-income families. This discovery sheds light on the disparities in language exposure and its potential impact on early childhood development[31].

In a 2018 study conducted by a team of scientists from Harvard, the Massachusetts Institute of Technology, and the University of Pennsylvania, it was shown that it is not just hearing words from parents that is important but engaging in conversation with children. The study found that the benefits of conversation were just as significant for low-income children as they were for high-income children. Children who experienced high levels of conversation scored 12 percent higher on standardized language assessments[32].

However, low-income children tended to experience far less conversation at home, as documented by the study. Researchers compared the peak hour of dialogue for each child and found that a child in a high-income household had 50 more conversational turns in a single hour than a child in a low-income household. A conversational turn is when an adult speaks, and the child responds, or vice versa. A single turn could be as short as this: "Eat." "No!"

Finally, the researchers compared the children's test

scores and brain images in the laboratory with the audio patterns at home. They discovered that for every 11 conversational turns, a child's verbal test score increased by one point. They also observed that the part of the brain involved in language processing was more active in children who had experienced more conversation at home. Furthermore, research has shown that hearing words, such as having the television or tablet videos babysitting, is not the same as hearing conversation and learning how to use language for conversation[33].

_____

1. https://people.com/las-vegas-teen-killed-beating-15-attackers-outside-high-school-8400919

2. https://www.pewresearch.org/internet/2018/09/27/a-majority-of-teens-have-experienced-some-form-of-cyberbullying/
   https://techjury.net/blog/cyberbullying-statistics/

3. https://www.cdc.gov/violenceprevention/youthviolence/bullyingre search/fastfact.html

4. https://www.cdc.gov/violenceprevention/youthviolence/bullyingre search/fastfact.html

5. https://www.pandasecurity.com/en/mediacenter/cyberbullying-statistics/

6. https://techjury.net/blog/cyberbullying-statistics/

7. https://newscenter.sdsu.edu/sdsu_newscenter/news_story.aspx?sid= 71136
   https://www.psychologytoday.com/us/blog/the-narcissism-epidemic/200905/is-there-epidemic-narcissism-today

8. https://www.psychologytoday.com/us/blog/the-legacy-of-distorted-love/201802/how-narcissistic-parenting-can-affect-children

9. https://www.goodreads.com/book/show/256004.Between_Paren t_and_Child

10. https://www.forbes.com/sites/traversmark/2022/11/30/a-psychologist-calls-out-the-many-dangers-of-helicopter-parenting/?sh=3d7f4ffc20d0
    https://www.apa.org/news/press/releases/2018/06/helicopter-parenting
    https://www.parents.com/parenting/better-parenting/what-is-heli copter-parenting/
    https://www.ncbi.nlm.nih.gov/pmc/articles/PMC9532949/

11. https://www.huffpost.com/archive/ca/entry/helicopter-parenting-leads-to-serious-workplace-setbacks_b_10162210

12. https://www.law.uh.edu/ihelg/monograph/11-12.pdf
13. https://www.psychologytoday.com/us/blog/what-mentally-strong-people-dont-do/201708/were-raising-generation-wimpy-kids
14. https://journals.lww.com/jfmpc/fulltext/2022/08000/helicopter_parenting,_from_good_intentions_to_poor.97.aspx
15. https://www.forbes.com/sites/tarahaelle/2016/06/30/want-a-well-adjusted-college-student-stop-helicopter-parenting/?sh=71c8ab477b35
    https://link.springer.com/article/10.1007/s10826-016-0466-x
16. https://www.researchgate.net/publication/303826945_Helicopter_Parenting_and_Emerging_Adult_Self-Efficacy_Implications_for_Mental_and_Physical_Health
17. https://psycnet.apa.org/doiLanding?doi=10.1037percent2Ft47412-000
    https://ir.library.illinoisstate.edu/cgi/viewcontent.cgi?article=1583&context=etd#:~:text=Thepercent20measurepercent20ofpercent20helicopterpercent20parenting,ofpercent20theirpercent20offspringpercent20topercent20handle
18. https://slate.com/human-interest/2015/07/helicopter-parenting-is-increasingly-correlated-with-college-age-depression-and-anxiety.html
    https://www.forbes.com/sites/tarahaelle/2016/06/30/want-a-well-adjusted-college-student-stop-helicopter-parenting/?sh=36ac486077b3
19. https://www.businessinsider.com/parents-hire-professional-moms-for-college-students-on-campus-2023-9?op=1
    https://www.parents.com/parents-hiring-stand-in-moms-for-college-students-8304174
    https://www.simplemost.com/you-can-now-hire-a-parent-by-proxy-for-your-faraway-college-kid/
20. https://www.nbcnews.com/better/lifestyle/why-lawnmower-parenting-robbing-your-kids-how-actually-help-them-ncna987526
    https://www.goodhousekeeping.com/life/parenting/a27044862/what-is-lawnmower-parenting/
    https://learningliftoff.com/family/parenting/signs-lawnmower-parent/
21. https://www.insider.com/lawnmower-parents-helicopter-parents-entitled-kids-2018-9
    https://www.safesearchkids.com/what-is-lawnmower-parenting-and-why-is-it-so-detrimental-to-your-children/
22. https://www.ncbi.nlm.nih.gov/pmc/articles/PMC2654842/
    https://www.centreforperinatalpsychology.com.au/good-enough-parent/
23. https://www.psychologytoday.com/intl/blog/freedom-learn/201512/the-good-enough-parent-is-the-best-parent
24. https://www.businessinsider.com/how-your-parents-behaviors-shape-who-you-are-today-2019-7
25. https://scholarshipstats.com/varsityodds
    https://scholarshipstats.com/pro-odds

26. https://www.cde.ca.gov/sp/se/
27. https://eric.ed.gov/?id=ED583502
28. https://nces.ed.gov/fastfacts/display.asp?id=64
29. https://www.usnews.com/news/education-news/articles/2018-06-06/special-education-students-on-the-rise
30. https://www.cdc.gov/ncbddd/developmentaldisabilities/about.html
31. https://www.brookings.edu/articles/defending-the-30-million-word-gap-disadvantaged-children-dont-hear-enough-child-directed-words/
32. https://journals.sagepub.com/doi/abs/10.1177/0956797617742725?journalCode=pssa
    https://hechingerreport.org/why-talking-and-listening-to-your-child-could-be-key-to-brain-development/
33. https://jamanetwork.com/journals/jamapediatrics/fullarticle/381618?resultClick=1

9

ADMINISTRATION

"Small class sizes, high expectations for student academic performance and behavior, and diligent, invested highly respected educators backed up by an administration who supports teachers over parents and students would fix so many of these problems."

    Elizabeth Emery - Quillette

If you are like me, you may have shared the belief that individuals in positions of power, particularly those who have climbed the career ladder, are the most competent and qualified. Nonetheless, upon closer examination, it becomes evident that numerous higher-level officials in school districts fail to live up to this expectation, with some being hired in districts without any substantial experience in education.

When it comes to the individuals responsible for making decisions in school districts and educational institutions, it is often a source of confusion and perplexity. This issue is prevalent in many local school districts and can also be observed among local politicians. The decision-makers often lack the requisite experience to effectively manage organizations of such magnitude, leading to a trial-and-error approach when it comes to decision-making. For instance, there is a tendency to repeatedly change the curriculum in an attempt to improve the performance and scores of the district. Unfortunately, the unintended consequences of these actions are frequently overlooked or not addressed in a timely manner, thereby exacerbating the very problems that were intended to be resolved.

Regrettably, the primary concern for many district administrations lies in the perception of their decisions. This is why numerous school districts waited to observe how neighboring counties would respond during the COVID-19 pandemic. I have heard that county superintendents engaged in discussions with one another to ensure a unified approach, thereby avoiding sole responsibility for unpopular decisions. By pointing out that other counties had made similar choices, they could deflect criticism.

In recent times, there has been a noticeable surge in the number of parents attending school board meetings across the country. These parents are seeking answers and clarification regarding the decisions being made by the districts. However, it is disheartening to observe that instead of providing satisfactory responses to their inquiries and concerns, some board members are inclined to exclude these parents from the decision-making process altogether. It appears that in many cases, board members lack the necessary answers to address the "why" questions raised by these parents. This has led some school boards to have parents physically removed from the meetings.

An incident during a recent board meeting in New Jersey exemplifies this dismissive attitude. A lawyer representing the school board confidently asserted that parents do not possess the right to determine the curriculum taught in schools. Although this statement may be grounded in legal interpretation, it raises concerns about the level of parental involvement in educational decision-making. It begs the question: should New Jersey residents consider exploring alternative schooling options to ensure greater agency in their children's education? This highlights the significance of school choice and the need for parents to have a voice in shaping their children's educational experiences.

Another issue that plagues many government institutions, including district administrations, is the lack of coordination and communication among different departments. This deficiency hinders the efficiency of processes such as course changes, technology upgrades, community engagement, and problem-solving. Often, the response to challenges is slow and arrives too late to make a meaningful impact.

Through my conversations with various district leaders, I have noticed a troubling absence of urgency.

It appears that many leaders are complacent, believing that they are already doing enough to address the concerns in their education systems. What truly alarms me is encountering district leaders who refuse to accept any responsibility for the issues within their schools. They tend to shift blame onto individual schools, teachers, and students, claiming that they have provided clear guidance and direction, but these parties have failed to implement the necessary measures.

For any meaningful improvement to occur, it is essential for administrators to take ownership of their failures. Unfortunately, this willingness to accept responsibility seems elusive at present. In order to effectively lead and inspire their subordinates, leaders must provide clear and compelling justifications for their decisions. It is crucial to communicate the thought process and rationale behind the decision-making process in order to instill confidence and motivate others to carry out directives. By presenting a well-defined set of reasons or bullet points that support the "why" behind the decisions, leaders can establish a sense of transparency and demonstrate that careful consideration was given to the chosen course of action.

The Arms Don't Know What the Feet or the Toes are Doing

Technology

Are you puzzled by the heading? It reflects the lack of communication and understanding between departments in districts and their individual schools, leading to failures. During my travels and conversations with schools and districts, I was astonished by how little communication there is between the two.

Most districts will vehemently disagree with this, but the devil is in the details. Sure, the districts are communicating with the schools on a regular basis because they are in the new business of micro-managing their teaching staff. When it comes to knowing what schools have and don't have in the way of resources, there is a big gap.

Some school districts are investing millions of dollars in online resources to reduce paperwork and achieve cost savings. However, I have personally witnessed situations where teachers were frustrated because the effectiveness of computer-based lessons and assessments depends on having enough computers or tablets for each student. Unfortunately, most schools in our country do not have sufficient computer resources to accommodate every student. And the ones that have enough computers and tablets do not have functional computers and tablets.

For example, in a school in my state, teachers were instructed to take their students to another room for lessons and assessments because the laptops and tablets meant for their classes were not all working. This setup would lead to a continuous stream of classes utilizing the computers in another teacher's room, rendering it impractical for the teacher whose room is now occupied by another class to conduct her own lessons effectively. The absurdity of relocating an entire class to another room daily to teach and test for one subject on computers is far from a reasonable solution.

Teachers have expressed their frustration with the lack of support from school administrators, who tell them to "figure it out." It is baffling how district administrators can allocate millions of dollars to programs that the schools in their district have no means of implementing. One would expect a district administration to be well-informed about the available technology resources in the schools they manage.

School districts must have a comprehensive understanding of their schools' technological capabilities before investing in expensive programs. This would ensure that the allocated funds are used effectively and that teachers are provided with the necessary resources to deliver quality education to their students. It's even more problematic when the resources that aren't working are the only options for getting lessons or assessments done.

Now, let's delve deeper into the issue of computers in public schools. I soon came to realize while meeting with teachers that a significant number of computers and tablets are not functioning properly. If the general public were aware of this, they would undoubtedly question why funds are allocated to other projects instead of ensuring that essential technology is kept up-to-date and operational. Regrettably, many schools do not allocate sufficient resources to employ dedicated technology personnel, often relying on individuals without degrees in IT or retiring teachers seeking temporary positions until retirement. Unfortunately, due to limited resources and qualifications, these in-school individuals cannot efficiently address technology-related issues and are often limited to basic tasks like reinstalling software.

Our product/services primarily operate online and require a computer or tablet. While our technology primarily served as a supplemental study resource for parents and students at home, it was necessary for us to collaborate with school staff and teachers to provide training. This necessitated our presence in the schools, working closely with the staff and occasionally assisting the teachers.

Based on my experience and conversations, I would guess that approximately one-third of the tablets and computers in schools today are not functioning correctly and are essentially useless. In some schools, the percentage is even higher than 30 percent. On numerous occasions, I found myself in classrooms engaging in discussions with teachers, only to discover that not all the computers in the room were operational. Even more concerning, some teachers informed me that these same computers had been non-functional for over a year. It is truly perplexing to contemplate how teachers are expected to effectively educate students when not all the necessary resources are functional.

District administration needs to prioritize the maintenance and functionality of their in-school technology. By investing in qualified technology personnel and ensuring regular maintenance and repairs, administrators can ensure that the technology functions properly.

Administrators also need qualified individuals who can promptly address technical problems. It is unforgivable that about a third of the technology in your kids' schools is nothing more than paperweights, often sitting idle for a year or more.

This situation poses several challenges for the schools. Firstly, relying on a single technology expert at the district level can delay resolving issues at individual schools. With numerous schools to oversee, the district expert will struggle to provide timely support to each school. This can result in prolonged downtime for teachers and students, hindering the smooth operation of educational activities.

I have consulted with several large corporations, and when computers or tablets used by their employees break down, they have a team that promptly addresses the issue to avoid delaying the employees' work progress. Why shouldn't it be the same for the teachers and the students?

Managing Class Sizes

Every year, I have observed a recurring issue in schools that never seems to be resolved or improved upon. At the end of each school year, district administrations typically have a relatively accurate estimate of the number of students moving up to each grade level based on the progression from lower grade levels. While it may not be an exact science due to students moving in and out of the district, there is a certain level of predictability. Additionally, new student registrations are also taken into account by the district administration.

However, despite having this information, there are numerous instances where the number of teachers assigned to a particular grade level does not align with the number of students moving up. In some cases, there are too many teachers for a grade level, leading to a surplus of staff. On the other hand, there are also situations where there aren't enough teachers assigned to a grade level, resulting in over-crowded classrooms.

Surprisingly, year after year, schools across the country seem to delay hiring additional teachers until a few weeks into the school year, long after classes have already begun. This delay in hiring temporarily leads to overcrowded classes. That assumes the school can find another teacher or that the school has a classroom open to be used for another grade-level class. It puts immense pressure on teachers, who are then left to plead for additional staff to reduce the student population in their classrooms. Naturally, this situation frustrates the teachers and leaves parents upset and disappointed. After all, they have already formed a connection with their child's teacher, only to have their child later moved to a new class.

The same issue arises when it comes to removing teachers. I have witnessed schools informing teachers, who have put in significant effort to prepare for the new school year, that their services will no longer be required because there aren't enough students for their grade level. What is truly disheartening is that this often happens after the school year has already commenced, leaving the dismissed teacher with the urgent task of finding another school to work at or facing unemployment. If the teacher is lucky, another grade level in her school will need additional teachers, and the teacher will be allowed to fill that spot in a grade level they probably haven't taught before. This kind of uncertainty and instability can be incredibly stressful and demoralizing for educators, especially for those with less seniority.

One cannot help but wonder why the district administration does not have these staffing issues sorted out well before the school year begins. This problem first came to my attention in 2013, but it seems to have plagued the education system for much longer. I vividly recall a specific incident where I was working with a teacher to provide training on our product/service, only to have her abruptly informed that she would no longer be needed. This unexpected change left her without work for the remainder of the school year, except for occasional substitute teaching opportunities.

Lets Try this Academic Program

One of the most common challenges teachers face is the constant fluctuation in curriculum or teaching programs. As discussed in previous chapters, this issue often comes hand in hand with another obstacle: the delayed update of end-of-year assessments to match the new program or curriculum. I have had teachers vent their frustrations about this predicament. They diligently teach what they have been instructed, only to discover that the previous curriculum or standards are still being assessed at the end of the year. One teacher eloquently expressed her exasperation, stating, "There are questions on the assessment that we didn't work on all year because it's not part of the new way of doing things, but here it is for my students to get wrong." Instead of hastily implementing changes, it would be prudent for district administrators to take the necessary time to ensure that everything is properly synchronized. One can understand the reluctance of teachers to be evaluated under such circumstances. Often, district administrations hastily purchase new math or reading programs and expect immediate implementation within the same academic year. However, this leaves no room for the county to make corresponding adjustments to the assessments, resulting in assessments lagging behind by a year or sometimes more. Just as changes are made, a new program is purchased, and the cycle starts all over again.

Federal Funding

Let's dive deeper into the Department of Education and its funding process. Each year, the federal government collects tax dollars from the states to provide financial support for education. As discussed in previous sections, these funds are distributed based on various criteria, such as Title One and free and reduced lunch programs. However, there is a significant delay in the allocation of these funds.

Traditionally, the federal government waits until late September or early October to divide the funds and send them to the states. Unfortunately, it takes a few more weeks for the funds to reach the districts and eventually be dispersed to the schools. This posed a challenge for us and other vendors as every school we approach to offer our product/services required the resources to be available in August. However, the school districts could not pay us until the first or second week of December.

This issue was not unique to us; many other resource providers faced the same dilemma. As a result, schools that rely on purchasing these resources cannot do so until halfway through the school year. This recurring problem in the education sector has not received adequate attention. Despite educators expressing their concerns, school administrators often express resignation, stating, "This is just how it is."

The timing of resource allocation is even more critical now that nearly half of the country follows a balanced school year schedule, with students returning to the classroom in the first weeks of August. Even under the traditional school schedule, which usually begins in the first week of September, the delay presents significant challenges.

It is not uncommon for people to joke about the government's inefficiency and illogical operations. One can't help but question whether the federal bureaucrats are unaware of when the school year starts or if they truly comprehend the urgency for schools to have all their resources in place from the beginning. After all, it isn't easy to imagine a business operating without essential resources until halfway through the year.

Every principal and school administrator expresses frustration with the current timeline but reluctantly accepts it because they feel powerless to instigate change. This situation highlights the pressing need for reform and a more efficient process of allocating education funds.

They Don't Know What Works

In many school districts, there is a growing concern about the practice of lowering grading standards to create an illusion of success. This trend is often justified by administrators using explanations that can be convoluted and require a suspension of logic to accept. One of the main reasons behind this trend is the pressure schools face to demonstrate positive outcomes and high success rates. Lowering grading standards can make it appear that more students are achieving high grades and meeting academic requirements. However, this approach ultimately undermines the integrity of the education system.

When grading standards are lowered, it diminishes the value of a student's achievements. It fails to reflect their true abilities accurately. It also hampers the ability to identify areas where students may be struggling and in need of additional support. This not only harms the students in the long run but also compromises the overall quality of education being provided.

Moreover, lowering grading standards creates a false sense of accomplishment for students. When they receive high grades without truly earning them, they are deprived of the opportunity to learn from their mistakes and develop the necessary skills for future success. In 2021, the state of Oregon made changes to academic standards in an effort to promote equity and antiracism. Oregon lowered the standards and did away with many grading standards making it almost impossible to fail. Some individuals argue that this decision reflects a lack of confidence in minority students' abilities to succeed academically. Concerns have been raised that removing these standards might hinder their academic progress and potentially affect their readiness for college.

How college admissions boards will evaluate students from districts with adjusted academic requirements remains to be seen. This is essentially a new kind of racism. One of low confidence in the abilities of the people you propose to help[1].

In 2011, my stepson played in a church basketball league. The league decided not to keep score so that no ones feelings would be hurt. If you think that works, you are fooling yourself. The kids who were playing, and the parents still knew who won. They weren't blind to who was better and who scored more points. The administration of the church league, much like the administrations of states that implement these rules, is driven by the objective of improving their own sense of righteousness. Now, they can feel virtuous and signal to everyone that they care. But everyone who has raised kids the right way knows that sometimes your kids have to struggle or fail to truly learn. This is why all data surrounding helicopters or lawnmower parenting shows negative long-term results.

The Reasoning behind lowering grading standards typically falls into three categories:

1. The claim that the old grading standards are systemically racist.
2. The belief is that higher, easily attainable grades benefit student self-esteem.
3. The argument is that some students experience test anxiety, leading to the decision to disregard test scores.

Regrettably, rather than investing efforts in achieving authentic triumph in the educational realm, many school authorities tend to opt for the more straightforward route of altering grading standards. This approach, unfortunately, emanates from a discernible lack of clarity concerning effective strategies for ameliorating the education system[2].

Lower Standards

Numerous administrators are perpetually enacting annual modifications to both curriculum and pedagogical standards, creating a challenging navigational course for educators to stay up-to-date with. Though purposed to enhance academic performance, these alterations appear to have not borne the desired outcomes. On the contrary, an examination of school assessment data reveals a disturbing trend - student performance is deteriorating yearly[3].

This unsettling trend mirrors the corporate sphere, where it's not unusual to find individuals at the helm of various departments and committees initiating unfeasible changes, primarily to earn recognition. However, there is a stark difference in the two scenarios. Corporations, unlike their educational counterparts, are relatively swift in assessing the efficacy of their changes and reverting to proven strategies when necessary. In contrast, educational administrators tend to demonstrate a propensity towards total overhauls, even when the existing trajectory may be working.

Rather than revisiting and fine-tuning previously successful practices, they often plow ahead with unproven sweeping alterations. This tendency is especially prominent when faced with the challenge of boosting test scores. Administrators, seemingly at a loss for effective strategies to enrich academic performance, often resort to diluting the curriculum or revising the grading criteria used to assess student outcomes.

According to the nonprofit organization that administers the ACT college admissions test, high school students' scores on the exam have reached their lowest point in over three decades, indicating a concerning lack of preparedness for college-level coursework. This downward trend in scores has persisted for six consecutive years, but the COVID-19 pandemic has expedited the decline. The class of 2023, whose scores were recently reported, began their high school journey when the virus first arrived in the United States.

Janet Godwin, the CEO of the nonprofit ACT, expressed a sobering reality, stating, "The hard truth is that we are not doing enough to ensure that graduates are truly ready for postsecondary success in college and career.[4]"

In terms of specific figures, the average composite ACT score for U.S. students fell to 19.5 out of 36. This represents a slight drop from the previous year's average score of 19.8[5].

One head-scratcher is the push for more rigor in education. Then, they wonder why their scores and grades continue to fall. That's when schools choose to lower the grading standards. They have often made it so much more challenging for the kids academically that they must fudge the results to prove that their rigorous standards are succeeding.

Many schools have already transitioned to Standards-Based Grading, also known as proficiency-based or competency-based learning. This approach requires teachers to grade students separately on each standard in the curriculum map, which outlines the specific standards students must master throughout the school year[6]. For example, an elementary teacher may assign approximately

21 different grades for math alone. While this approach has merits, the problem arises when administrators change the definition of passing or failing grades.

Unfortunately, in some districts, the number of standards a student must pass to move on to the next grade continues to decrease. For instance, in districts I have worked with, students were initially required to pass at least 70 percent of the standards to pass a subject or grade level. However, administrators faced scrutiny when a significant number of students failed to meet the standards. As a result, they changed the passing requirement to mastering only 60 percent of the standards. This is not an isolated incident. Many inner-city schools boast high graduation rates even though a majority of their students are not proficient in math or English. It is concerning to see administrators celebrating the ability to move students forward without equipping them with the necessary skills for success in the real world. The administrators have clearly lost sight of their goals. Their goals are not to cheat to produce high graduate numbers, but to achieve well educated students.

This trend raises questions about the purpose of education. Are schools prioritizing high graduation rates over ensuring students are truly prepared for the challenges they will face beyond the classroom? Students mustn't be passed along without a solid foundation of knowledge and skills. By lowering the passing requirements, administrators are sending the message that mediocrity is acceptable. It is indeed true that we have emphasized the ineffectiveness of holding students back as a means of helping them. However, the underlying issue lies in the continuous decline of their academic performance over several years, which can be attributed to the policies and decisions implemented by district administrators. Additionally, the sheer magnitude of students struggling in certain districts is cause for concern, as it poses a significant threat to the future.

Furthermore, altering the definition or requirements for passing undermines the credibility of the grading system. Grades are meant to reflect a student's level of proficiency in each subject, providing an accurate measure of their knowledge and abilities. When the standards for passing are manipulated, it becomes difficult to determine whether a student has truly mastered the material. This can have long-term consequences for students, as they may enter higher grade levels or college without the necessary skills to succeed.

When we were young, students received grades ranging from A to F. The grading system was simple: any grade of A, B, or C was considered a passing grade, while a D or an F indicated that a student was failing and needed to put in more effort to improve their grade or risk repeating the course.

However, in recent years, several school districts, including Los Angeles, Oakland, Sacramento, and Santa Ana, have made the decision to gradually eliminate grades D and F, leaving only passing grades. This significant change in the grading system has sparked a heated debate among educators, parents, and students alike[7].

Supporters of this modification argue that removing failing grades will have several positive effects. They believe that by eliminating the stigma associated with academic failure, students will feel more encouraged to take risks and explore their full potential. This shift in perspective aims to promote a growth mindset and emphasize the importance of effort and improvement rather than solely focusing on the final grade. Moreover, supporters of this grading system change argue that by providing additional support and resources to struggling students, they can address the underlying issues hindering their academic progress, leading to better outcomes and higher levels of achievement.

On the other hand, critics express concerns about the potential consequences of eliminating failing grades. They worry that without the possibility of failure, students will become complacent and lack the motivation to strive for excellence. Critics argue that failing grades can serve as a wake-up call for students, encouraging them to reflect on their performance and make necessary adjustments to improve. Additionally, they emphasize that grades serve as an evaluative tool that accurately reflects a student's academic abilities for future challenges and college admissions. They contend that an inflated sense of confidence built upon false positives may ultimately hinder a student's development and preparedness for real-world situations.

It seems to my common sense perspective that students who never fail or know they didn't truly succeed will find it difficult in the real world where winners and losers are picked by how well you do in life, whether you want it that way or not. We've already reviewed the harm that lawnmower and helicopter parents do to their kids by not letting them fail and solving how not to fail, plus learning to cope with failure by brushing themselves off and trying again. Now, the state or the city is going to be the lawnmower parent?

The ridiculous notion that it will encourage students to take risks and explore their full potential is baffling. Who believes that some of the kids who are failing school are failing because they are afraid to take risks and explore their full potential?

While it is true that not all challenges in education can

be solely attributed to the school or district, administrators hold a significant responsibility in navigating the difficulties of student education. However, as the district leader, the buck stops with your management or decision-making. The actions taken or lack thereof by administrators often demonstrate a preference for the path of least resistance. One example that highlights this issue is implementing a rule in certain school districts, such as in Washington DC, where students are prevented from receiving a grade below 50 on tests, even if they have answered no questions correctly or even if they didn't try to answer one question[8]. This practice is a clear manifestation of what is commonly referred to as the "Soft Bigotry of Low Expectations." By setting such low standards, administrators perpetuate the notion that students are not capable of achieving higher levels of success.

Author and political commentator Kira Davis writes "The move to lower education standards to accommodate minority students feels like justice to people who believe it is their job to be saviors. To the rest of us, it feels like a slap in the face. What could be more insulting than someone you consider your moral and societal equal — someone you may even look up to — telling you that, in effect, your hard work will never be of equal worth to their hard work[9]?"

A report by economist Seth Gershenson titled "Great Expectations: The Impact of Rigorous Grading Practices on Student Achievement" conducted a comprehensive analysis of the grading practices of Algebra I teachers in North Carolina. Gershenson's study, which encompassed 350,000 students and 8,000 teachers, yielded fascinating insights into the issue of grade inflation. Surprisingly, the findings revealed that students benefited more from teachers who maintained higher grading standards.

Intriguingly, Gershenson's research highlighted that these more rigorous standards had a positive impact on learning outcomes for students across all major ethnic groups, regardless of their socioeconomic background. Such a discovery underscores the importance of maintaining high grading standards to foster academic growth and equity within our educational system[10].

However, it is disheartening to observe that district administrators often overlook the potential dangers posed by lenient grading practices. The reason behind their negligence is relatively straightforward—they have chosen to turn a blind eye to this pressing issue. Instead, their attention is fixated on data manipulation, which allows them to create a distorted image of the educational landscape. Yet, Gershenson's research serves as a cautionary tale, warning us about the detrimental consequences of allowing grading standards to plummet within public schools in the United States.

One of the most alarming outcomes of low grading standards is the message it sends to students—that mediocrity is acceptable and excellence is unattainable. By assigning inflated grades for subpar work, students are robbed of the opportunity to strive for greatness. This lax grading culture instills a false sense of security and accomplishment, impeding students from realizing their full potential. Furthermore, there is a lack of research studies that present empirical data demonstrating the positive outcomes of reducing grading standards. [11]. Is it any wonder people call kids today soft or snowflakes?

The decision to lower grading standards clearly indicates that the constant tinkering with education has failed, and the administrations at all levels have no idea how to solve the problems.

Behavior

As we've discussed earlier in multiple chapters, behavior is a problem. Administrations often take the same ridiculous direction with behavior. They are choosing to believe that discipline is always negative or self-esteem lowering and must be pared back or eliminated altogether. In two districts that I know of, teachers have been told that only positive reinforcement is allowed. Positive reinforcement for negative behavior rarely works on a full-time basis. Giving positive feedback for negative behavior means that you are rewarding the person who has broken the rules or is misbehaving.

I was taught in school that you use positive reinforcement to reinforce the behavior you want to see replicated and promoted. The kid or person wants the positive reinforcement, not the negative reinforcement, which is often associated with loss of privileges, so they change to the behavior that gets them the positive reinforcement. Sounds like common sense to me. But now, some district administrations have outright decreed that there will be no more negative consequences.

A story was recently told to me by a teacher about a school where she would routinely give points to the students who did well in class each day and who had overall good behavior. Students who got into trouble or were disruptive had points taken away—essentially a merit/demerit system. At the end of the week, the students with the most points got to eat lunch in the classroom on Fridays and watch an educational video. This worked well for the teacher, and she had been using this method for years. But then she was told she could only give points, not take them away, because it might hurt the student's self-esteem.

As I mentioned previously, one of the challenges that teachers face is the gradual erosion of their disciplinary power. This lack of meaningful leverage is resulting in a growing number of teachers opting to leave the profession. When educators find themselves unable to effectively manage their classrooms, it creates an almost insurmountable obstacle to achieving positive educational outcomes. It becomes a lose-lose situation for both the teacher and the students. The disruptive behavior of a few students not only impedes their own progress but also has a detrimental impact on the learning environment for the entire class. This, in turn, consumes precious time and energy that should be dedicated to the actual instruction and educational development of the students[12].

The Nutrition Equation

In 2014, Michelle Obama spearheaded a campaign for healthier school lunches, which sparked a strong reaction from many parents. The question arises: why were they so angry? Were they advocating for schools to continue serving nutritionally deficient junk food? The unfortunate truth is that most school lunches are not much better than fast food meals. Due to budget constraints, the allocation of funds for school lunches often prioritizes quantity over quality, resulting in meals that lack significant nutritional value. To exacerbate matters, many school districts attempt to generate additional revenue by selling unhealthy snacks to students without any restrictions or limitations. Teachers have expressed their concerns, revealing that school cafeterias sell extra cookies, chips, ice cream, and candy to students, allowing them to opt for these indulgences instead of consuming a balanced meal[13].

Although it may seem like a minor issue, consider this scenario: a classroom filled with 20 elementary students, hyped up on sugar and empty carbohydrates, expected to remain focused at their desks. Inevitably, their energy levels will crash, adversely affecting their ability to concentrate and learn. Clearly, this is not conducive to a quality education. Schools selling junk food devoid of nutritional value should feel a sense of shame. Our nation already faces an obesity epidemic, and schools should be leading the charge in teaching children about healthy eating habits and promoting their overall well-being. Unfortunately, even the free breakfast provided to students often consists of sugary cereals or worse.

While most schools offer health classes that touch on the basics of nutrition, the decision to prioritize cost-cutting over providing nutritious food undermines the education these students receive about what a healthy diet entails. It stands to reason that poor nutrition in schools leads to a variety of unintended consequences, one of which is the decline in students' academic performance. Studies have shown that the average child under 12 consumes a staggering 49 pounds of sugar per year, only three pounds less than the average adult.[14] Sugar is known to activate the brain's pleasure response, but recent research has demonstrated that it affects the brain in various other ways as well.

When individuals consume excessive amounts of sugar and then engage in challenging tasks, such as math problems, their brains release large amounts of cortisol—a stress hormone—which impairs memory. Consequently, when children's bodies are flooded with cortisol at school, they struggle to pay attention to their lessons and find it difficult to remain still. When their attention is diverted, their ability to absorb and retain information is compromised[15]. Researchers from the University of Southern California conducted an experiment in which adult and adolescent rats were fed beverages with sugar levels equivalent to those found in ordinary sodas[16]. While the adults displayed normal brain function after a month, the adolescent rats exhibited reduced memory and learning capacity. Furthermore, these adolescent rats had inflamed hippocampi, a region of the brain crucial for memory formation, organization, and storage. Essentially, sugar decreases attention span and memory, and chronic sugar consumption might permanently impair memory functions[17].

I t is worth noting that sugar seems to be present in almost all processed foods. Fast food establishments often add sugar to meat products and buns, and even seemingly healthy items like white bread, yogurt, sauces, salad dressings, oatmeal, canned fruit, cereal, granola bars, cheese spreads, pretzels, and nutrition drinks contain added sugar. This is just a small sample of the many sugar-laden products that children, as well as adults, consume. Consequently, processed foods have lower nutritional value compared to whole foods, such as fruits, vegetables, and whole grains. High-fructose corn syrup, a common sweetener found in many U.S. food products, has been associated with increased body fat and is commonly found in sodas and baked goods like muffins and donuts[18].

When children fill up on empty calories, they miss out on essential nutrients that support optimal serotonin levels, a balanced microbiome, and healthy brain function. Unfortunately, processed and sugar-laden foods lack these vital nutrients. School systems are comprised of intelligent individuals who are undoubtedly aware of the information presented thus far. It is worth noting that several dozen studies support the notion that poor nutrition negatively impacts learning outcomes. It is no secret that the foods served in our schools are subpar in terms of nutrition and overall value[19].

In many cases, people expressed dissatisfaction with Michelle Obama's efforts because they believed that the healthier choices offered were unappetizing. However, it is possible to address this concern by improving the taste of healthy food options. Not all healthy, nutritious food is a vegetable. School districts often opt for the most cost-effective solution when it comes to providing meals for students. However, it is important to remember that, as mentioned earlier in this book, there is ample funding available for education; it simply doesn't reach the schools. This situation serves as a prime illustration of that issue. By not prioritizing the quality of food served to students, schools are inadvertently affecting their academic performance and achieving subpar outcomes.

Hopefully, the resistance was not due to a collective aversion to eating healthier. Given the current eating habits of many Americans, discerning their true stance may be challenging. Nevertheless, it is common sense that if we want our children to receive the best education possible and retain what they have learned, we must provide them with the proper fuel to nourish their bodies and minds.

Somethings Not Right About the Answers

There could be no more absurd mandates from administrators than what is going on in several states and districts. It is disheartening to see that some districts have labeled getting the right answer on a math problem as systemically racist. As my teenage alter ego would say, "WTF." It is clear that these district and state leaders have lost sight of clarity and are pushing their own agenda. Other states, such as Vermont, Washington, and California, have already taken the initiative to develop K-12 educational materials that place a strong emphasis on valuing and reflecting the experiences of communities of color.

However, there is an evolving perspective in education that aims to explore the broader implications of mathematical principles and their impact on society. Take, for example, Seattle's recently released proposal on math education. This proposal introduces questions such as, "Where does power and oppression show up in our math experiences?" and "How is math manipulated to allow inequality and oppression to persist[20]?"

This misguided ideology has gained momentum in many progressive districts and is now being mandated by some district administrations, including the idea that 2+2 doesn't always equal 4[21]. The notion that 2+2 can equal something other than 4 is not only absurd but also shameful[22]. Math, as I will explain later, is anything but racist. It is the most pure and straightforward subject, where the answer is either right or wrong. One can argue the results of history or a science experiment, but when it comes to math, anyone who has spent time with an architect or an engineer knows that correctness is crucial.

Imagine the consequences if a builder got close to all

their measurements and calculations when constructing your house. Precision is paramount in ensuring a sturdy and safe structure. Yet, these administrators want us to believe that the student's feelings matter more than being honest or right. They want us to accept the idea that as long as students get close to the correct answer, it is acceptable and even praiseworthy. Their effort to get the right answer is more important. So now we're giving trophies for wrong answers.

This approach seems like a lazy way of administrating. Instead of focusing on improving grades and test scores, they choose to downplay the importance of getting the right answers. They want to create an illusion of virtue by making students feel better about getting the answers wrong. And to make matters worse, if you happen to insist on students getting the correct answer, you are somehow labeled as a white supremacist.

Some school districts are now promoting additional alternative approaches, arguing that students who frequently get the answers wrong may become discouraged or develop low self-esteem. They claim that focusing on finding the correct answer perpetuates a racist ideology and that grading systems that track students' performance throughout the year only perpetuate inequality. Their proposed solution is to adopt an "everyone gets a trophy" approach, which undermines the importance of accuracy and critical thinking.

Is it any wonder that our children are being called snowflakes?

Several school districts across the country have recently adopted a concept known as "equitable grading," which has sparked both support and criticism. In this new approach, the focus is placed on students' understanding of the mate-

BRYAN THOMAS WETZEL

rial rather than on rewards or penalties. Homework is assigned but carries minimal weight, and tests often come with multiple retake opportunities or may be eliminated altogether. Additionally, behavior, including attendance, is no longer considered in a student's final grade, as it is deemed unrelated to their ability to excel in academic tasks such as writing a competent, argumentative essay[23].

Advocates for equitable grading argue that this approach recognizes the diverse challenges students face and aims to create a more inclusive learning environment. Removing external factors that may hinder a student's performance allows for a fairer assessment of their actual understanding and knowledge. However, there are concerns about the potential lack of accountability and the decreasing value placed on academic achievement. Critics argue that by eliminating consequences for incomplete or subpar work, students may not be adequately prepared for the demands of the real world[24].

Here are some examples of practices many schools have adopted in moving toward grading equity:

- Avoiding zeros on the 0-100-point scale and implementing a 50 in place as the minimum grade
- Standards-based grading practices
- Letting a student's most recent retake grades replace former grades as new evidence of learning
- No late points taken off—work is graded on standards
- Giving non-grade consequences for cheating and excluding participation and effort from the grade

- And giving feedback remarks as grades as opposed to any points or letter scales

It is important to consider that in the adult world, punctuality, attendance, and accountability are essential attributes for success. In professional settings, individuals are expected to meet deadlines, attend meetings promptly, and take responsibility for their work. By removing these elements from the grading system, some argue that an equitable grading approach may not adequately prepare students for future challenges. Proponents say that this idea increases rigor. Anyone with common sense can see from the list above that it doesn't make sense. Furthermore, in many professional settings, there are no opportunities to redo work repeatedly until a satisfactory result is achieved. In the real world, individuals often have just one chance to deliver quality work or face consequences. By allowing multiple retake opportunities, an equitable grading system may not accurately reflect the realities of adult life and may diminish students' understanding of the importance of effort, perseverance, and work ethic.

How about teachers who have been in districts where equitable grading has been implemented?

On a website called We Are Teachers, Ms. Penrod wrote the following: "One of the biggest challenges was allowing students to turn in late work for extended periods, leading to apathy and a lack of urgency. With such a heavy weight placed on summative assessments, the policy also caused an unexpected increase in student testing anxiety. Students didn't find any value in doing assignments that only weighted 10 percent of their final grade. Some students wouldn't complete homework or daily work and then wonder why they didn't do well on assessments or timed writing. Since they weren't practicing on their formative assessments, they weren't prepared for their summative assessments. Additionally, students started gaming the system when they learned they could earn 50percent for no work done, fostering a lack of motivation. Finally, students who actually needed the extensions and retakes weren't taking advantage of them[25]."

Social and Emotional Learning

Many school districts are now heavily influenced by a social justice perspective, which seems to be gaining prominence yearly. The COVID-19 pandemic has brought to light what is taught in classrooms, going beyond the usual school curriculum. It is essential to acknowledge that not all blame can be placed solely on educational leaders, as some teachers have incorporated their own ideological leanings into their lessons. However, it is evident that social justice is permeating much of the curriculum, including mathematics. This is often done under the guise of Social and Emotional Learning (SEL), an approach that has garnered support from local and state politicians.

How does math blend into social justice, you ask? Dr. James Lindsey describes it like this;

"Johnny is riding with his mom and dad in the car on the way to the amusement park. The amusement park is 50 miles away; they've already driven 30 miles. How much further do they have to drive? Imagine seeing that in your children's homework. Who's going to object to this? Teachers are taught to pick certain words and use them as generative themes to generate political conversations from that math question. A teacher trained in the SEL,

cultural competence, or culturally relevant teaching method will look at that and give it to the class and say, before we answer the question, let's do this: who's been to an amusement park before? Now, you're just getting the students engaged. Some kids raise their hands, and some kids don't. The teacher asks why some of you have gotten to go to an amusement park and some of you haven't. What are some reasons why kids wouldn't get to go to an amusement park? The teacher is trained to keep pressing until somebody says maybe not everybody can afford it, or my parents won't let me. Now you're ready to have a political conversation you've generated out of the word amusement park. You've generated a political conversation about socialism and redistribution or parental authority, a major theme we're seeing now. Maybe some parents shouldn't make the decision. Maybe the school should make some of these decisions instead. Don't you think you should be making decisions instead of your parents? Or you could go riding in a car, now you're having an environmental conversation. Mom and Dad can be a trigger. Do all families look like that class? Does everybody have a mom and dad? No, I only have a mom; now you're discussing feminism. No, I have two moms; now you're conversing about all the sexuality or LGBTQIA+. The class is LED into this Equity framing or sustainability framing dialogue. The math lesson just got set to the side and forgotten about. It's supposed to make the kids more interested in learning math[26]."

There is a growing concern among parents and the community regarding the decision-making process of school boards when it comes to curriculum development, especially when it involves the teaching of social issues. Recent revelations have shed light on audio and video recordings capturing discussions between school board members and teachers, where they deliberate on ways to keep these controversial ideologies hidden from parents.

Needless to say, this raises serious ethical questions about the transparency and integrity of those entrusted with shaping our children's education[27].

It is crucial to question why school boards and teachers fail to acknowledge the inherent ethical issues surrounding the deliberate concealment and deception of parents regarding the subjects being taught to their children. If transparency is lacking in these matters, it begs the question of whether these contentious topics should even be included in the school curriculum. As parents, we tirelessly instill in our children the values of honesty and integrity, teaching them that lying and hiding actions are morally wrong. It is only fair to expect the adults entrusted with their education to adhere to the same principles.

It is essential to recognize that social issues can vary in terms of acceptability among different individuals, groups, and parents. What may be considered socially acceptable for one group may not be acceptable to others. This under-scores the need to carefully consider whether such topics should be included in the school curriculum.

On the other hand, it may be valuable to remind school boards and teachers of their role as public servants, as their salaries are funded by the parents who entrust their children's education to them. This highlights the importance of engaging in a national discourse to address this matter and determine the appropriate inclusion of social issues in schools.

Furthermore, it is crucial to understand that the decision to include or exclude specific social issues from the curriculum should be based on a comprehensive evaluation of their educational value, potential impact on students, and alignment with the overall educational goals and values of the community.

After engaging in conversations with numerous parents, it has become apparent that there is a widespread desire for the school system to prioritize the teaching of core subjects such as math, English, writing, and science over focusing on social issues. Many individuals argue that it is the responsibility of parents, not the government, to instill moral values and acceptable behavior in their children. By relying solely on the government to fulfill this duty, some view it as a form of negligent parenting. To ensure that our children acquire these crucial life lessons, we must take control by either teaching them at home or seeking out a church community that aligns with our values.

The idea that parents would rely solely on the government to educate their children on social and moral issues is genuinely astonishing. When examining the government's track record at both the local and federal levels, it becomes clear that their successes in this particular domain are limited. Entrusting the teaching of our moral values to a system that is prone to frequent leadership changes poses significant risks. It is entirely plausible that future leaders may possess different perspectives on what is right and wrong, which could contradict the values we hold dear. This appears to be the situation we have now.

It is precisely this realization that has led to a growing number of parents opting for homeschooling[28]. Homeschool families can be categorized into two groups. First, some parents choose to homeschool to ensure their children are taught a curriculum that aligns with their religious values. These parents recognize the significance of providing a learning environment that nurtures academic growth and spiritual development. These are parents who are willing to sacrifice one income to protect their children from these prevailing social ideologies.

In today's digital age, the visibility of alternative lifestyles has increased, thanks to teachers who openly share their personal beliefs on social media platforms. Some educators go a step further by incorporating these beliefs into their teaching practices, which may not resonate with all students or their families. As someone who values freedom of choice and expression in my personal life, I don't pass judgment on what teachers do privately. However, the situation becomes concerning and disconcerting when these teachers use platforms like TikTok to express their intentions of teaching alternative lifestyles and sexuality to children while implying that parents have no control over it. This kind of statement is likely to prompt parents to take action.

It is concerning that the administration does not reprimand these teachers and seems to view their role as an opportunity to indoctrinate their students, who are someone else's children[29]. It is vital to convey a simple truth to these teachers and the administration: acting as prophetic authorities on social and moral issues is not their role. Instead, too many schools treat families as adversaries, denying them basic information about their children's education.

Over a thousand school districts across our country have parental exclusion policies that deny families the right to know their child's gender identity in taxpayer-funded schools. Teacher training sessions state that parents are not entitled to know their children's gender identities, and such knowledge must be earned. Earned? How has the school system earned that right and not the parents who birthed and are raising the children?

This situation underscores the need to refocus on teaching the fundamental aspects of education. Like many parents, I believe that education's core purpose is to equip students with the necessary knowledge, skills, and critical thinking abilities to thrive in an ever-changing world. While social issues undoubtedly play a role in shaping society, it is essential to strike a balance between addressing these topics and respecting the autonomy of families to guide these discussions at home. It still surprises me that the last sentence would be controversial in any way.

The Book Banning Argument

There has been considerable debate surrounding the presence of sexually explicit books in K-12 schools, with various activist organizations and teachers' unions adding to the confusion by making inaccurate comparisons to historical book-banning practices in the early 20th century. It is important to clarify that the concerns expressed by families regarding books in schools do not aim to ban books altogether. Rather, the issue revolves around the careful selection of age-appropriate content for educational environments.

In this regard, it is widely agreed upon that there are no educational contexts in which it is appropriate for elementary and middle school students to be exposed to explicit content, such as discussions of anal sex and blow jobs. Some may argue that such content also does not belong in high school. This raises the question of the purpose of K-12 education and what parents deem appropriate at this level.

When asked, the majority of parents would likely express that exploring sexual positions, toys, or devices is not appropriate for K-12 schools.

There is a significant amount of research that highlights the negative impact of early exposure to pornography on young children. This evidence is overwhelming, and it raises concerns about certain school leaders advocating for including such material in school libraries. This is a development that requires careful consideration[30].

Regrettably, there are individuals in the field of education who defend the presence of these materials in K-12 schools. They argue that what they are introducing is not pornography but rather educational resources designed to enhance body awareness. They claim that "kids of all ages have questions about sex." This statement was quoted from Parent.com, a platform that is supportive of books that have a comic book appearance but show sexual acts[31]. However, this claim lacks credibility. If you speak to an elementary school teacher with enough experience, they will confirm that children between kindergarten and 5th grade are typically not preoccupied with thoughts of sex and sexuality unless it is explicitly presented to them. In essence, these books are inadvertently encouraging children to explore sexuality at an earlier age, which is concerning. Let's be realistic, you do not need to show blow jobs or anal sex to promote positive body awareness. Keeping your kids off of social media would be a good start towards that goal.

While some proponents of early childhood sexual exploration point to a few individuals with PhDs who support their argument, there is a significant number of other experts with PhDs who strongly disagree. These experts assert that the books in question are not promoting healthy sexual exploration but rather engaging in grooming behavior. It is important to consider the perspectives of these dissenting voices, as they provide valuable insights into the potential dangers associated with such materials. I would like to emphasize that there is a lack of studies supporting the inclusion of sexually explicit books with pictures for young children to see and read.

Proponents of these books often emphasize that they are tastefully illustrated and not pornographic. However, a closer examination of the specific books in question reveals a different reality. Many of these books contain explicit content that resembles the explicit nature of adult magazines. The explicit illustrations and content, which include references to kink, bondage, and domination, raise legitimate concerns about the appropriateness of these materials for young children.

The detrimental effects of early exposure to sexually explicit content on children have been extensively studied and consistently highlighted in research. Numerous studies have shown that children who are exposed to such content at a young age are more likely to engage in sexual activities earlier than their peers. It is alarming that these children often lack a full understanding of the implications and risks involved in such behavior.

It is worth highlighting the work of Dr. James Schroeder, a renowned pediatric psychologist, whose article on the harmful impact of pornography gained significant attention when it was featured on Yahoo! News. Schroeder's expertise and experiences in working with young individuals have led him to underscore the negative consequences of sexually explicit material on the well-being of children, even at a tender age. His valuable insights shed light on the detrimental effects that exposure to pornography can have on the lives of young individuals[32].

The National Library of Medicine further corroborates these concerns, emphasizing the critical need to address the issue of early exposure to sexually explicit media and implement appropriate measures to safeguard our children from potential harm. Their research reveals a strong association between exposure to sexually explicit content during early adolescence and engaging in risky sexual behavior during emerging adulthood[33].

It is crucial to acknowledge the already significant challenges our society faces regarding child sex trafficking and sexual abuse[34]. Introducing sexually explicit images and text to children who are too young to fully comprehend the complexities of sexual relationships can only exacerbate these problems.

In the past, there was a widely held belief that exposing young children to any form of sexual content could have negative effects on their well-being, and it was even considered a criminal offense. This perspective was based on the understanding that children need a safe and nurturing environment to grow and develop, free from exposure to adult themes. As a result, measures such as movie ratings were implemented to protect children. It is important for us to acknowledge the potential dangers of early exposure to sexually explicit content and to take proactive measures to safeguard children from these harmful influences.

The administrators of the school districts that advocate for the inclusion of sexually explicit materials in library collections may argue that such materials can contribute to comprehensive sex education and promote healthy adult sexual relationships. However, it is essential to critically examine the track record of school boards, administrators, and government entities, as highlighted in this book. Many parents I know believe that allowing children to grow up without the complexities of sex and instead teaching them about healthy sexual relationships when they are mature enough is the preferred approach. They prioritize preserving their children's innocence and ensuring they have the emotional and intellectual readiness to navigate the subject matter. This approach recognizes the importance of respecting the developmental stages and emotional well-being of these young individuals. Pushing elementary school children towards sexual activity can be seen as a distressing element, bordering on sadistic, as it disregards the developmental stages and emotional well-being of these young individuals. It is crucial to provide children with an environment that fosters their growth, curiosity, and overall well-being without exposing them to explicit content prematurely. Furthermore, thorough research should be conducted before implementing any curriculum or materials related to sex education in schools. While proponents of early exposure to explicit content may theorize positive outcomes, it is important to consider the vast amount of existing scientific studies that contradict these claims. To date, no conclusive evidence suggests that introducing young children to sex, sexual devices, kink, etc., is beneficial. On the contrary, years of prior scientific studies emphasize the potential risks and negative impacts that may arise from premature exposure to explicit material. Therefore, it is imperative for educational institutions and policymakers to prioritize the well-being and development of children and base their decisions on evidence-based research. This approach ensures that children receive the appropriate education at the right time, considering their emotional, cognitive, and physical maturity.

What is even more concerning is the behavior of certain administrators who openly ridicule parents for expressing their concerns about inappropriate books being present in their children's schools. Let's consider the case of Karen Smith, a Democrat who was recently re-elected as the new president of the Central Bucks school board in Pennsylvania. During her swearing-in ceremony, Smith's husband accompanied her to the podium, carrying a stack of sexually explicit books that parents have been requesting to be removed from the school libraries. In a rather symbolic gesture, Smith placed her hand on these books while taking the oath of office. This action can be interpreted as a dismissive response to the parents who simply want their children to receive an academic education rather than being exposed to explicit content that may not be age-appropriate[35].

As Nicole Neily, President of Parents Defending Education, said so eloquently at the U.S. Senate Judiciary Committee's hearing on book banning, "suggesting that children who believe in Santa Claus should have unrestricted access to graphic sexual novels is often met with extreme reactions, such as equating it with murder. This was exemplified by a resident in Connecticut who claimed that implementing parental consent rules for certain books deemed obscene and explicit was a matter of life and death, which is clearly an exaggeration."

She went on to say, "When parents share their concerns about books, they often express the importance of age-appropriate content. It is worth noting that school boards across the country have silenced parents who read explicit passages from certain books during board meetings, citing the presence of children in the room. Yet, these same books are being provided to children in schools. This inconsistency is puzzling. The average parent who has little knowledge of the content of some of these books should spend some time looking through them and reflecting on whether you consider such content to be educational. As a society, we do not place Playboy magazines in elementary classrooms, and this is not considered a book ban but rather a matter of common sense."

It is interesting to note that the media tends to sensationalize and exaggerate this issue, presenting any discussion surrounding it as an assault on freedom. This portrayal is not only misleading but also lacks sincerity. Given the limited space and resources available in classrooms, schools, and libraries, there arises a need to prioritize certain materials over others. As a result, the process of decision-making and the individuals responsible for selecting these materials should be held accountable to the public. However, when individuals raise legitimate questions regarding these decisions, they are often met with harsh criticism, as if any concerns regarding minors accessing explicit sexual content are an attack on both liberty and literature. This diversion from genuine concerns about the quality of children's education and their safety within educational institutions only serves as a distraction.

It is not wrong for parents to want to be involved in their child's education. Every time a parent is wrongly accused of trying to ban a book due to valid concerns about the appropriateness of its subject matter, it creates a division among neighbors based on false premises. This deliberate attempt to demonize parents and suppress their freedom of speech and activism is harmful. Two decades ago, if a six-year-old mentioned sex at school, teachers would suspect abuse. In today's world, elementary children are not only learning about sex in school but are also being encouraged to keep secrets from their families. And not so long ago, If an adult were to show a child sexually explicit materials, such as how to use a vibrator, why anal sex can be gratifying, or how to use a butt plug (all actual examples from books that have been found in elementary school libraries), that adult would have been arrested and put on the sex offender list. Yet, school administrators have no issue with allowing them in their school libraries and apparently have no concern about the legalities of such decisions. Being labeled a school administrator is a shield against the laws in their states against subjecting minors to sexually explicit materials[36].

Although I haven't conducted an official survey, it appears that the majority of parents express concern about any form of adult behavior that may sexualize their children, regardless of the individual's position or title. In more progressive districts, there seems to be a tendency among parents to unquestioningly accept the opinions and decisions of school/district administrations and the government, even if they defy logic. It appears that these parents may be disregarding their own critical thinking skills. A notable example of this blind trust in authority was evident during the COVID-19 pandemic, where government officials at both federal and local levels were found to provide misleading information or hide the truth while claiming to act in the best interest of the public. Perhaps it is time for parents to demand that administrations at all levels prioritize common sense over ideological agendas.

One has to question the urgency behind the push for exposing young children to explicit and mature content. Why is it deemed so important to introduce sexual images and themes to elementary school-age students? We would hope that these young kids will not be engaging in sexual activity anytime soon. Why the rush? Apparently, this is the hill progressives want to die on.

In summary, the discussion about the role of books in educational institutions brings up important concerns regarding content appropriateness for different age groups. It is crucial to carefully consider the potential effects of exposing children to explicit material at an early age and to prioritize their emotional and intellectual readiness. It is unfair to silence or criticize parents who express valid concerns, as they are only looking out for the best interests of their children. Therefore, the process of selecting books should be open, transparent, and accountable, taking into account the perspectives of parents and the community. This way, we can ensure that children are exposed to materials that are suitable for their development. And this starts with the administrators of the districts and schools. What proponents of this content want you to believe is that it's not pornographic or explicit, so the research on early exposure doesn't apply. At the end of the chapter "Social & Emotional Learning there are examples, you can be the judge.

Finally

I find it quite perplexing that many of the latest directives being implemented in the field of education seem to contradict solid research findings. It is disheartening to see that these decisions are not aligned with the path that would truly lead to improved education outcomes.

In order to truly elevate the quality of education, it is crucial to base our decisions on sound research and evidence. By veering away from the proven strategies and approaches, we run the risk of hindering the progress we aim to achieve. It is imperative that we take a step back, reevaluate these decisions, and make choices that are firmly grounded in the best interests of students and their educational development.

It's time that administrators at the district level of education be called to answer for their failed decisions and their part in the continued decline in student performance. The responsibility lies with them to take accountability for their actions, just like good leadership should. Instead of accepting blame, they often shift responsibility onto other factors, such as blaming falling grades and scores solely on the impact of COVID-19. However, it is important to note that the decline in academic performance existed before the pandemic.

When will the public hold them accountable for their poor decisions? Why were these decisions made, and what was the logic behind them? What was the ultimate goal? These questions need to be answered, and the public needs to demand transparency and accountability from the education system.

A company or corporation would not hesitate to replace leadership if its decisions were leading to a decline in performance and revenue. They understand that continuing in the wrong direction would be detrimental, and they actively seek out individuals who can rectify the situation and set the organization on the right course.

---

1. https://www.mindingthecampus.org/2021/08/13/oregon-abolishes-acad
    emic-standards-in-the-name-of-equity-and-antiracism/

2.

3. https://www.usnews.com/news/education-news/articles/2023-12-05/
    global-assessment-reveals-historic-setbacks-in-student-learning
        https://www.forbes.com/sites/nataliewexler/2021/05/26/scores-for-
    low-performing-students-get-steadily-worse-and-the-explanations-
    are-muddled/?sh=ed60b6b29f7e
        https://www.silive.com/education/2022/09/data-shows-significant-
    decline-in-student-test-scores-nationwide-since-pandemic.html

4. https://www.pbs.org/newshour/education/act-test-scores-for-u-s-
    students-drop-to-a-new-30-year-low

5. https://apnews.com/article/act-college-admission-test-score-optional-
    99f80b26696a92c78e2680873a3df68c

6. https://www.edutopia.org/article/getting-started-standards-based-grading
    https://knowledgeworks.org/resources/traditional-grading-vs-standards-based-grading/
7. https://fox5sandiego.com/news/california-news/large-california-school-districts-eliminate-d-and-f-grades/
    https://abc7news.com/california-schools-drop-d-f-grades-oakland-unified-phases-out-below-c-competency-learning-mastery-based/11308550/
8. https://www.washingtonpost.com/education/2022/10/23/dc-schools-grading-policy-50-percent-rule/
    https://www.edweek.org/teaching-learning/when-it-comes-to-grading-is-50-the-new-zero/2016/07
9. https://thespectator.com/uncategorized/soft-bigotry-lowering-exam-standards-law-race/
10. https://fordhaminstitute.org/national/research/great-expectations-impact-rigorous-grading-practices-student-achievement
    https://fordhaminstitute.org/national/commentary/students-learn-more-teachers-high-grading-standards
    https://www.k12dive.com/news/study-tough-teachers-get-better-results-from-students/572059/
11. https://fordhaminstitute.org/national/commentary/no-zeroes-grading-policy-worst-all-worlds
12. https://www.theguardian.com/education/2023/oct/14/california-gavin-newsom-student-suspensions-willful-defiance
13. https://www.washingtonpost.com/news/wonk/wp/2014/11/24/students-are-blaming-michelle-obama-for-their-gross-school-lunches/
14. https://www.dvo.com/newsletter/monthly/2017/september/tabletalk2.html
15. https://hms.harvard.edu/news-events/publications-archive/brain/sugar-brain
16. https://futurism.com/neoscope/rats-sugary-soda-stupider
    https://www.theatlantic.com/health/archive/2012/05/study-of-the-day-a-diet-loaded-with-sugar-makes-rats-dumber/257748/
17. https://learningliftoff.com/students/health-and-wellness/the-effects-of-sugar-on-a-childs-academic-performance/
18. https://www.childrens.com/health-wellness/sugar-and-kids-how-much-is-too-much
19. https://www.hopkinsmedicine.org/health/wellness-and-prevention/finding-the-hidden-sugar-in-the-foods-you-eat
20. https://www.seattletimes.com/education-lab/new-course-outlines-prompt-conversations-about-identity-race-in-seattle-classrooms-even-in-math/
21. https://newdiscourses.com/2020/08/2-plus-2-never-equals-5/

22. https://www.washingtonexaminer.com/news/math-professor-claims-equation-2-2-4-reeks-of-white-supremacist-patriarchy

https://mindmatters.ai/2021/02/yes-there-really-is-a-war-on-math-in-our-schools/

https://www.wsj.com/articles/in-california-2-2-4-may-be-thought-racist-11621876555

https://www.hoover.org/research/seattle-schools-propose-teach-math-education-racist-will-california-be-far-behindseattle

23. https://www.gse.harvard.edu/ideas/edcast/19/12/grading-equity

https://www.nsba.org/ASBJ/2020/February/Accurate-Equitable-Grading

https://www.oregon.gov/ode/educator-resources/Pages/Equitable-Grading-Practices.aspx

24. https://fordhaminstitute.org/national/commentary/grading-equity-isnt-grounded-reality

https://www.postandcourier.com/moultrie-news/opinion/teacher-to-parent-weakening-grades-is-not-a-path-to-educational-equity/article_42c93892-f09b-11eb-8741-df90e36f6b73.html

https://www.wsj.com/articles/homework-school-equity-grading-fail-49b64e19

25. https://www.weareteachers.com/equitable-grading/

26. https://youtu.be/cVoXSPbo1CY?si=BtitqNe7CijOfUfs&t=2227

27. https://www.carolinajournal.com/undercover-video-reveals-crt-topics-are-taught-in-nc-public-schools/

https://www.foxnews.com/media/shocking-video-exposes-school-officials-plotting-trick-ohio-parents-teach-crt

https://www.nationalreview.com/news/missouri-teachers-crt-advocate-plotted-to-hide-social-justice-curriculum-from-trump-country-parents/

28. https://www.latimes.com/california/newsletter/2022-01-24/8-to-3-home schooling-on-rise-8-to-3

https://www.discovery.org/education/2022/05/02/why-homeschooling-is-growing/

https://fortune.com/2022/04/14/pandemic-homeschooling-surge-us-school-reopening/

https://www.washingtonpost.com/education/interactive/2023/home schooling-growth-data-by-district/

29. https://www.msn.com/en-us/news/us/thousands-of-us-public-schools-hide-child-s-gender-status-from-parents/ar-AA18nBEU

https://washingtonstand.com/news/thousands-of-schools-wont-tell-parents-about-kids-gender-transition-report

30. https://www.psychologytoday.com/us/blog/family-and-trauma/202308/silent-educator-the-impact-of-porn-on-young-minds

https://www.psychologytoday.com/ca/blog/real-healing/201208/

overexposed-and-under-prepared-the-effects-early-exposure-sexual-content

31. https://www.parents.com/kids/health/best-sex-education-books-for-kids-by-age/

32. https://www.courierpress.com/story/life/columnists/2022/02/15/james-schroeder-porn-can-have-huge-impact-kids-neurological-psychological-development/6722655001/

33. https://pubmed.ncbi.nlm.nih.gov/32275669/

34. https://htcourts.org/

35. https://www.inquirer.com/education/cbsd-new-school-board-karen-smith-president-swearing-in-20231205.html

36. https://defendinged.org/press-releases/testimony-of-nicole-neily-president-of-parents-defending-education-before-the-house-committee-on-education-the-workforce-subcommittee-on-early-childhood-elementary-and-secondary-education/

10

POLITICIANS

"It is hard to imagine a more stupid or more dangerous way of making decisions than by putting those decisions in the hands of people who pay no price for being wrong."
  Dr. Thomas Sowell

When it comes to the issue of politicians meddling with education, it is crucial to address the detrimental effects of their involvement. Unfortunately, it has become a common strategy for politicians to exaggerate minor problems and position themselves as the ultimate solution. They employ carefully crafted talking points and slogans, often centering their focus on education-related issues. However, this approach is deeply flawed and rarely leads to actual problem resolution. Instead, their poorly conceived policies tend to exacerbate existing issues and give rise to unintended consequences. The most troubling aspect is that politicians conveniently ignore these consequences while continuing to champion their policies, completely disregarding the problems they have created. While state and local politicians do the majority of political tinkering with education, even the federal government has imposed mandates like Common Core and other social justice mandates, which have caused frustration among parents and many teachers. There is some disagreement as to whether Common Core was mandated or not, as states were not required to adopt it, but some federal funds were withheld from states that chose not to. You be the judge.

Public trust in our government leaders has reached an all-time low. In June 2022, the findings of a study conducted by Pew Research on "Public Trust in Government" were published. The study revealed that only a small fraction of Americans, specifically two out of ten, have faith in the government in Washington to consistently make the right decisions. This trust is shared by a mere 2 percent who believe that the government always does what is right, and an additional 19 percent who think that it does so most of the time.[1] This continuous decline in trust is a result of numerous scandals and decisions that seem to prioritize the interests of the leaders over those of the public. This decline is certainly not good news, and our current political leaders, as well as past leaders, can only blame themselves for it. The failures of our state, local, and federal leaders are numerous and have been chronicled in various books and videos. However, what is even more alarming is that political decisions and talking points continue to perpetuate the pattern of politicians manipulating the system for their own benefit. They either seem oblivious to the fact that the public is aware of their deception or think they have successfully fooled the public.

Political leaders often try to convince us that they are in public service for the purpose of benefiting the public and their constituents. However, the reality that the public has come to recognize is quite different. Many politicians are primarily concerned with their own personal gain, with the public's well-being ranking third, just behind their biggest donors. In my previous career as a producer/director, I had the opportunity to create numerous political commercials for state candidates. From firsthand experience, I can confidently say that not all political leaders are equal in terms of their intellect or their understanding of the topics they discuss. Sadly, some of the most intelligent individuals do not seek out these positions, and as a result, we often end up voting for the smoothest talkers and the ones who make the most enticing promises. Deep down, we are well aware that these promises are unlikely to be fulfilled and that they will not accomplish what they claim to have on their platform. Oftentimes, they benefit from blaming the opposing side for their failures to complete their to-do list, only to ask us to vote for them again so they can attempt to accomplish what they failed to do the first, second, or even third time around.

Nevertheless, it's important to note that not all politicians lack intelligence. There are some who are highly intelligent and others who are less so. However, all of them have learned how to manipulate the political systems in which they operate for their own advantage. They quickly understand that the most effective way to secure their position is to instill fear in their voters, making them believe that their lives will not improve if they do not vote for them. They create a narrative that suggests that if the voters do not support them, their opponents will have a chance to take away the remaining happiness in their lives. The election of Donald Trump, for example, caused widespread panic among certain groups of people, while the election of Barack Obama brought about a sense of optimism for the same people. However, for the majority of people, their lives remained largely unaffected by the tenures of either president. In reality, the direct factors that impact our lives are high inflation, high taxes, high unemployment, recession, and, apparently, a pandemic. All of these factors are far more influential than any individual in power. Now, let's shift our focus back to discussing how politicians continue to interfere with education.

Politicians are well aware that a hot-button issue for the public is the well-being of children and what is happening to them now and in the future. They often exploit these concerns to ensure they convey emotionally charged messages. They manipulate people's worries about their own issues, and unfortunately, many people fall for it, believing that politicians have identified the real problem with our children's education. To be fair, not all politicians have negatively impacted education, and some have even made positive changes, particularly certain governors. However, whenever a politician does something positive for education, it often faces criticism from the opposing political faction, as if it will harm the disadvantaged children caught in that state. As a result, the public, which has become increasingly divided, takes sides on these decisions, often without any substantial evidence, relying instead on the opinions presented in talk shows such as The View or by commentators like Sean Hannity.

Parents and educators express dissatisfaction with politicians who intervene in the education conversation without relevant expertise, implement illogical changes, and offer little assistance. As mentioned earlier in this book, my knowledge of the inner workings of education was limited until I co-founded an education technology company. Through our interactions with school districts across the country, I have witnessed firsthand the challenges and issues that exist. However, it is unfortunate that very few politicians possess direct experience with K-12 education in our country. Those who claim to have knowledge often rely on information provided by unions or other special interest groups. Essentially, providing talking points, which is why you will hear almost the same comments from politicians on one side of an issue, even using similar phrases to describe their thoughts on the problem.

An article published in News Week in June 2022 sheds light on the fact that parents desire to remove politics from classrooms. With education taking center stage in upcoming elections, political influence in schools has become the primary concern for parents. According to a recent survey, 68 percent of parents express varying levels of worry regarding non-educators making decisions about classroom matters, surpassing their concerns about family finances.

This survey also included responses from teachers and principals, revealing that they share similar concerns. In total, 70 percent of educators worry about non-education professionals influencing school curriculum decisions.

"However, obstacles persist as the system inherently keeps parents and teachers apart," asserts Bibb Hubbard, the founder and president of Learning Heroes, an education research organization dedicated to enhancing parental involvement. This organization conducted the survey and emphasized the importance of listening to parents and educators, as well as implementing the necessary structures and support systems that will yield positive outcomes for students, encourage teacher retention, and foster family engagement.

Interestingly, while parents express a desire to voice their opinions on prevalent issues, the survey reveals that only a minority of parents have actually done so. Specifically, only 19 percent have raised concerns about school curriculum during a school board meeting, 17 percent have provided feedback on recommended books, and 12 percent have requested their child be excused from an assignment this school year due to differences in opinion about the legitimacy of the assignment's content[2].

Everything is Political

One aspect of today's political environment that greatly frustrates me is the constant polarization perpetuated by 24-hour news channels. It seems that every issue is forced into a right vs left argument, leaving no room for nuance or compromise. For example, if someone voices concerns about inappropriate books in their children's school library, they are immediately labeled a "right-winger" and dismissed without any consideration for their valid concerns. On the other hand, speaking up for the expansion of Medicare often results in being labeled a "left-wing loon." It's like watching a room full of kindergarteners shouting insults at each other, accomplishing nothing productive.

Politicians have a unique platform where they can play a significant role in bridging the divide. They have the power to tone down the rhetoric and facilitate discussions that lead to finding common ground. However, it seems that they prefer the spectacle of conflict. Gone are the days of leaders like John F. Kennedy and Ronald Reagan, who understood the importance of uniting the people and reminding us that we are all part of one nation. Nowadays, division seems to be the prevailing order of the day.

What truly astounds me is the arrogance displayed by some politicians when discussing matters of education, parental rights, and what they deem to be in our best interest. It makes me question whether they even hear themselves speak. Their lack of common sense is baffling. Yet, it is this very arrogance that allows them to confidently assert that parents do not need to know what their children are learning in school or that they can make decisions regarding life-altering medications and treatments for children without parental knowledge. Somehow, they believe they know what is best for our children.

Recently, Education Secretary Miguel Cardona made derogatory remarks about parents who voiced concerns about their children's education. He stated, "I respect differences of opinion. I don't respect people who are misbehaving in public and then acting as if they know what's right for kids." This comment was directed at parents who have been attending school board meetings and speaking up for their children's education. It is disheartening to see such disregard for parents who are simply advocating for the well-being and education of their own children. Maybe his only problem with it is that it is people exercising their right to disagree with people like him.[3]

This is just one example of how politicians react when their decisions are challenged. Parents who have been kicked out or even arrested for defending their children against a political and social agenda that goes against their own values and sensibilities are rightfully outraged. If politicians truly considered themselves public servants, they would prioritize the concerns of the people who voted for them instead of dismissing them as individuals behaving poorly. They would never make choices that contradict the beliefs of the parents they claim to serve.

In the past, comedians and pundits ridiculed politicians for their tendency to change their opinions based on public sentiment, often doing so just to secure re-election. However, nowadays, it seems that politicians are indifferent to public opinion altogether. Instead, they fully embrace the demands of their biggest donors, essentially prioritizing their interests over those of the general public. This phenomenon is especially evident when politicians accept political donations from teachers' unions. Even when confronted with solid evidence that supports opposing viewpoints, politicians willingly ignore such data because it contradicts the predetermined talking points and narratives they have chosen to propagate. This lack of concern for objective data and the preference for donor-driven agendas should be a growing concern in the political landscape.

If these politicians genuinely believe that parents don't understand their intentions or goals, then they should take the time to explain themselves and not hide behind their political offices. They should strive to be effective communicators and work towards bringing their communities together instead of driving them further apart.

In a world where some want us to believe that we are nothing more than evolved primates, it is worth noting how primates and other mammals fiercely protect their offspring when they are threatened. Most parents naturally feel the urge to care for and safeguard their children, not just from other animals but from other people as well. While we all worry about the danger of individuals who may groom our children with explicit content or commit heinous acts against them, it should come as no surprise that we view school boards, administrations, and federal authorities as potential threats when they attempt to expose our children to similar harmful content.

Perhaps it is time for politicians at all levels, from local to national, to take a step back and approach the public with a little humility. They should make an effort to explain their actions and decisions to the ordinary citizens they are serving.

For Instance

In the early 2000s, politicians across the country were vocal about the importance of funding for free access to pre-k education. They argued that starting early education would give children a significant advantage in reading and writing skills compared to those who did not attend pre-k. This perspective found support from teachers' unions, and the mainstream media even framed it as a racial issue, shedding light on limited access to pre-k programs for children of color. However, it is crucial to closely examine the research and assess the long-term outcomes.

Contrary to popular belief, the research does not provide clear evidence supporting the claim that attending pre-k leads to long-term learning advantages over those who did not attend. While teachers with early childhood education degrees may acknowledge that children who attend pre-k enter elementary school with a stronger foundation in reading and writing, these advantages tend to diminish over time. By the time students reach 5th grade, their academic levels are generally on par with each other as they learn from the same curriculum. However, if the goal is for kids to enter Kindergarten or 1st grade with a head start over those children whose parents could not take advantage of pre-K or whose parents did very little at home to teach them basic verbal skills, ABCs, etc., then that should be the stated goal. Politicians do not serve their constituents by hyping data outcomes that will never materialize.

Furthermore, extensive research has been conducted to examine the potential impact of attending pre-kindergarten (pre-k) on a child's likelihood of being identified as gifted. This topic has been frequently discussed by politicians seeking re-election. The findings from these studies are clear and unambiguous - attending pre-k does not have any significant bearing on a child's overall IQ. Although pre-k education may provide initial advantages in terms of early literacy skills, it is crucial to acknowledge that these benefits do not result in sustained intellectual superiority.

This further highlights the fact that politicians often advocate for changes that align with their political narrative, even when the evidence for such benefits is questionable at best. In reality, we can assume that most politicians have access to the actual data and research, yet they still push forward with changes to benefit their political agenda. Once the elections are over, the buzz around pre-k funding will fade away, and they move on to new platforms to capture the attention of parents[4].

School Choice

At the forefront of the political landscape, just beneath the incessant call for more funding, lies the contentious issue of school choice and school vouchers. In a nation founded on the principles of "Freedom," it seems contradictory to deny parents the ability to choose the best educational path for their children. Why do politicians place such importance on where parents choose to educate their children, especially when politicians exercise the privilege of selecting private schools for their own kids? Shouldn't the primary goal be to provide a quality education for all children? If all public schools were equal in terms of curriculum and substance, why would politicians be concerned? The reality, however, is that not all public schools are created equal, and parents who have the means or the determination to seek a better education should be allowed to enroll their children in the school of their choice.

School choice has enjoyed massive success in the past few years; 32 states, along with Washington, D.C., have implemented some sort of school choice program[5]. However, in a year that has witnessed numerous successes for the school choice movement, Pennsylvania seemed poised to achieve a historic milestone. It was on the verge of becoming the first state to have a Democratic governor sign a publicly funded school choice policy into law - a policy that the governor had campaigned on during his election. Pennsylvania Governor Josh Shapiro recently made a surprising announcement. He declared his intention to exercise a line-item veto on the budget dedicated to school choice. This decision contradicts his previous promise to champion and uphold the cause of school choice while actively campaigning for the governorship.

The fight to get parents' school choice rights would be made easier if the AFT and other teachers' unions would stop suing states to block such programs. Due to the over-whelming amount of requests by parents, many charter schools located in areas with underperforming public schools have been forced to implement a lottery system to determine which students are granted admission. If you browse through YouTube, you will come across heart-wrenching videos of parents praying, pleading, and emotionally breaking down as they anxiously await the drawing of their name in the lottery, all in the hopes of securing a better educational opportunity for their children. How can politicians deny parents the choices they so desperately need when all they desire is a brighter future for their kids?

While some politicians turn a deaf ear to the school choice argument, they also fail to address the underlying issues plaguing struggling communities, which directly impact the success of schools in those areas. However, even if these communities were revitalized, it may not be enough. If politicians truly wish to champion causes or take a moral high ground, perhaps they should consider mandating that schools cannot promote students who lack basic reading and writing skills. Furthermore, they should focus on implementing regulations that hold school districts accountable when more than half of the student population struggles with fundamental literacy and math.

Politicians must understand the significance of addressing the concerns of average parents when it comes to making decisions about school choice. Regrettably, it appears that politicians frequently overlook this crucial factor and instead prioritize the interests of larger donors, including unions and lobbying corporations. This unfortunate trend perpetuates a cycle where the persistent issues in our education system remain unresolved. When politicians give too much weight to the interests of larger donors, they risk neglecting the voices of those directly impacted by their decisions. It is important for politicians to remember that parents are the ones who truly understand the needs and aspirations of their children, and their input should be valued.

If you think this is divided across party lines. Conservatives for school choice and vouchers and progressives against, you'd be somewhat wrong. It is true that most democratic states do not have school choice, but it's not true that all Republican-led states have school choice. Case in point, In November 2023 the state of Texas voted down a bill for school choice. A minority of Republican legislators refuse to listen to their constituents and support school choice. Eighty-eight percent of Texas Republican primary voters supported a non-binding school choice ballot proposition last year. Numerous polls show widespread support from Texans of nearly all demographics. Polls showed that 60 percent of black voters supported the voucher bill[6].

Eighteen of the twenty-one Republicans who went against the wishes of their constituents were endorsed by the Texas affiliate of the nation's largest teachers' union. I wonder how much the union gave to their campaigns?

While in the same month, the New Hampshire Supreme Court dismissed a teachers union's challenge to the state's voucher program. New Hampshire, typically a conservative state, passed its school voucher program in 2022, because politicians there listened to their constituents and acted accordingly[7].

In August of 2023, USA Today ran this headline: Voters demand school choice for their kids. So why aren't Democrats embracing it[8]? This is an area where politicians can make great strides in satisfying their voters, which is how you get re-elected. Maybe this message is getting through to politicians as eight states put new school choice policies on the books in the first five months of 2023, with some of them expanding to all K-12 students.

Where are the Leaders

This book meticulously examines the myriad of challenges that currently plague the K-12 education system in our country. It acknowledges that opinions may vary regarding the exact nature of these problems, and it recognizes that some individuals may even disagree with the claims made throughout the book. Nevertheless, there is a widely recognized consensus that our education system is not on solid ground, and it is imperative for leaders to step up, take a principled stand, and enact changes that garner consensus in order to propel education in a positive direction.

As highlighted at the outset of this chapter, there is a reluctance among many politicians to take bold measures that could potentially jeopardize their chances of re-election. In fact, some politicians prefer to keep education as a persistent issue, as it provides them with a talking point during election campaigns. The underlying motivation is to maintain relevance by not solving too many problems that might lead people to question their necessity.

At present, idealism often clashes with the reality of the situation. Addressing the deeply-rooted problems in education would inevitably entail making choices that displease some constituents while pleasing others. Unfortunately, our current political climate often lacks the nuance required for both sides of an argument to find common ground and reach a compromise. Instead, people tend to dwell on issues that do not align with their preferences, leading to a sense of catastrophizing.

Perhaps I may come across as cynical, but it has been a while since I have witnessed a true political leader emerge. Being an effective leader entails making tough decisions and prioritizing what is in the best interest of the greater good, even when those decisions may not be popular. Regrettably, determining what is right has become increasingly elusive. The deep political divide between the left and the right exacerbates this challenge, underscoring the need for a strong leader who genuinely prioritizes the well-being of our children. However, this does not mean succumbing to every politically popular opinion or proposal.

If our education system is currently headed for disaster, we urgently require someone who can apply the brakes and steer it back onto the right track. This does not happen in our current environment because each side of the political aisle begins talking with their leadership on how to spin or make the other side's decisions seem cataclysmic.

To commence the process of bringing about change, the following are a few key proposals that deserve consideration:

Firstly, it is imperative to establish and uphold parents' rights across all states. It is absurd to believe that individuals who have given birth to and are raising a child do not have the right to be informed about what their child is being taught or if there are any considerations regarding hormone-blocking drugs. The only individuals who may attempt to justify such limitations are those who perceive children as wards of the state, with the state or federal government superseding parental authority. However, we must unequivocally reject such a notion and prioritize the rights of parents.

Secondly, it is crucial to ensure that topics related to explicit sexual content or the use of sex toys are not included in the school curriculum. The primary purpose of schools is to provide an education that prepares students to become productive members of society. Not productive members of Only Fans. Knowledge about explicit sexual content at an early age does not enhance one's chances of securing a good job or embarking on a successful career. Instead, our guiding principle should be to simplify the curriculum and focus on topics that truly equip students for their future. It is worth noting that the inclusion of such topics is driving some parents to consider private and home-schooling options.

Third, It is important to acknowledge that teaching critical race theory or any similar ideology extends far beyond simply educating students about racism and our history. It can perpetuate a notion of reverse racism, which many black parents have criticized for conveying the message that their children lack the same opportunities as white or Asian individuals solely due to their skin color. This approach implies that black students are inherently less intelligent or less capable of success without assistance from an elite group seeking to manipulate the system. However, this assertion is simply untrue. As Coleman Hughes emphasized in his impactful Ted Talk, our ultimate goal should be to strive for a colorblind society rather than pursuing equity at any cost[9].

Furthermore, the freedom to choose schools should accompany parents' rights, eliminating any barriers that restrict parents from selecting a school outside their designated district.

Implementing these four changes at the federal level will not single-handedly resolve all the issues discussed in this book. However, it is important to recognize that there is much more that needs to change in order to address all the challenges in education. Many of these problems will need to be tackled at the state or district level, where local policies and practices play a significant role. Despite this, it is crucial for politicians to start somewhere, and these proposals can serve as a vital catalyst for initiating change in education. By taking these steps, policymakers can set the wheels in motion and steer education in the right direction. Furthermore, this approach can help ensure that parents feel satisfied and that their voices have been heard in the decision-making process. While these proposed changes may not be the complete solution to all the issues in education, they are an important starting point.

---

1. https://www.pewresearch.org/politics/2022/06/06/public-trust-in-government-2/
2. https://www.usnews.com/news/education-news/articles/2022-06-23/parents-want-politics-out-of-the-classrooms
3. https://washingtonstand.com/news/education-sec-blasts-parents-who-act-like-they-know-whats-right-for-kids
4. https://www.cnn.com/2021/12/05/politics/universal-pre-k-biden-hiring-teachers-build-back-better/index.html
   https://www.factcheck.org/2022/02/biden-stretches-evidence-for-universal-pre-k/
   https://www.educationnext.org/evidence-benefits-government-funded-pre-k-overblown/
   https://manhattan.institute/article/the-drawbacks-of-universal-pre-k-a-review-of-the-evidence
   https://www.brookings.edu/articles/does-state-pre-k-improve-childrens-achievement/
   https://www.brookings.edu/articles/does-pre-k-work-brookings-experts-weigh-in-on-americas-early-childhood-education-debate/
5. https://www.usnews.com/education/k12/articles/what-school-choice-is-and-how-it-works
6. https://www.dallasnews.com/news/politics/2023/11/17/fight-over-school-choice-teacher-pay-bumps-expected-to-roil-texas-house/
   https://www.statesman.com/story/news/politics/state/2023/11/17/school-choice-debate-sparks-heat-among-house-republicans/71585548007/
7. https://foxwilmington.com/headlines/judge-tosses-new-hampshire-teachers-union-bid-to-shoot-down-voucher-program/
8. https://www.usatoday.com/story/opinion/2023/08/15/democrats-embrace-school-choice-education-reform/70587999007/
9. https://www.ted.com/speakers/coleman_hughes

11

A LESS PERFECT UNION

"The teachers' unions that block school reform have done serious damage to the union brand. The public no longer views unions as their champion. They view them as corrupt, intransigent and more interested in protecting their political clout within the Democratic Party than protecting their members or even school children."

Juan Williams

In 1857, the National Education Association (NEA) was founded in Philadelphia. The NEA officially merged with the American Teachers Association, the historically black teachers association founded as the National Association of Teachers in Colored Schools, in 1966.

The American Federation of Teachers is a union founded in 1916 in Chicago. The initial goal of the AFT was to elevate the status of the teaching profession, standardize entry requirements, advocate for better compensation, and empower teachers to have a greater influence over their working conditions, rather than relying on politicians and community leaders for decision-making. Most of them were men, and in many areas, female teachers didn't have equal pay with their male colleagues. All of this sounds good as these missions are noble. Unions were designed to make working conditions for employees better and to fight for the rights of the workers as a whole through collective bargaining. Today, the AFT is the 2nd largest union, boasting over 1.7 million members. That is a brief history, not a detailed one. However, it provides you with some insight into its origins.

In 1998, a tentative merger agreement was reached between NEA and American Federation of Teachers (AFT) negotiators, but ratification failed. However, five NEA state affiliates have merged with their AFT in some states. Mergers occurred in Florida, Minnesota, Montana, New York and North Dakota[1].

Anyone reading the news over the past 20 years has certainly run into articles about the AFT and its leadership that are head-scratchers. Very few teachers in states that do not require union participation join the union. They see it as a fee that comes out of their paycheck every month that does little to change their life or work environment for the better. Would the teachers in the country have it worse off if the union wasn't there? They would emphatically say everything would be worse and that the teachers in the country would be in danger of being used and abused. That's an actual quote from a paper in Baltimore. The funny thing is, most teachers would say they are used and abused, so the unions don't seem to be preventing that sentiment.

With labor laws and equal opportunity and pay laws, it is hard to see where the AFT does much more than make political speeches to show their relevance and collect money from the teachers. The current leader of the AFT continues to speak out and advocate for policies and changes that seem more radical than what socialist countries advocate for. And their policy recommendations are very heavy-handed. Should we follow a group that got the pandemic recommendations so wrong? At times, it seemed to advocate for teachers to stay home for two years and get paid. It appears that the union leadership has conveniently forgotten these details. Today, the union leadership is the most radical it ever had. Randi Weingarten is in her 8th term as of the writing of this book, and her public statements should be considered alarming. However, when I surveyed teachers in very blue states, I did find support. However, it's hard to separate whether they are supporters of the union or supporters of the leadership. While I didn't have the opportunity to speak to a large number of teachers in solid blue states, the few that I did engage in conversations with regarding union leadership often seemed to be unaware of the statements made by their leadership. Others were very supportive. The funny thing was that a few teachers in these blue areas almost didn't want to answer. All of them asked if their name and answer would be used in the book. I wouldn't do that; I've heard about retribution teachers in very pro-union states have had to deal with.

I began the book by stating that I would not take this book into a political discussion. But with a discussion about the AFT its hard to dodge the topic. The AFT in 2008 spent $5,599,540 on campaign contributions with 4.99 percent of that going to Republicans. In 2022, the union donated $55,262,359 to political causes, steered 99.47 percent to Democrat causes – and just 0.38 percent to Republican causes. You start to see the political leanings with very little effort[2].

Terry Moe, a Stanford Professor and author, has often been critical of the AFT and the amount of money they give to the Democratic party. In his 2011 book, Special Interest: Teachers Unions and America's Public Schools. In his book, Terry M. Moe demonstrates that the problems with making education better have a great deal to do with teachers' unions—which are by far the most powerful forces in American education and use their power to promote their own special interests at the expense of what is best for kids or schools[3].

Weingarten is just another politically motivated leader who has found it beneficial and profitable to frame all arguments around racism. She tags pretty much all discussions with a racism framework. She's a big proponent of teaching the 1619 project, which for an EDUCATION-related company seems off base, considering how many prominent historians have panned the project as not based on the facts of history. She's a big proponent of sneaking critical race theory into the curriculum. Proponents want you to believe that anyone against critical race theory is against teaching about racism or the history of blacks and other minorities being discriminated against[4]. This is very far from the truth.

I'm 55 as of writing this book. I grew up in a little town in Georgia, and we were taught the history of racism and the black leaders who moved equality forward. My kids learned about it, too. What alarms many people, including minority families, is the notion that a white person is guilty of the color of their skin. Can you imagine if white people said that about the color of any other color of skin? We don't have to imagine it; that's what was happening in many parts of the country during the early part of the last century. The struggle to move past that kind of bigotry and racial stereotyping has been celebrated for the progress it has made. But now the AFT and many other leaders want to bring it back as a reverse racism solution. My parents taught me it was wrong to judge someone by the color of their skin, and that was the message of Martin Luther King Jr., But now we've decided that it's okay as long as it's aimed at the right shade of skin. I'm pretty sure that was the rationalizing that many racist groups, including the KKK, used to promote their ideology. In his book Cynical Theories, Dr. James Lindsay and Helen Pluckrose, describe critical race theory in this way:

"Critical Race Theory begins from the assumption that racism occurs in all interactions. To see how this works, consider this thought experiment: Imagine you own a shop, and two customers enter at the same time—one white and one black. Who do you help first? If you help the black person first, Critical Race Theory would say you did so because you don't trust black people to be left alone in your store. That's racist. If you helped the white person first instead, Critical Race Theory would say you did so because you think blacks are second-class citizens. That's racist, too. That's Critical Race Theory. It can find racism in anything, even if it has to read your mind to do it[5]."

In a nutshell, critical theory teaches kids to be negative towards every situation or person, believing there are bad motives that can be found everywhere without exception.

The National Education Association has approved a plan to "publicize" critical race theory and dedicate a "team of staffers" to assist union members looking to "fight back against anti-CRT rhetoric[6]."

Randi Weingarten fully believes this and wants this integrated into every school. The influence of critical race theory has become so significant that the American Federation of Teachers (AFT) has started providing guidance to school systems on how to incorporate its principles without explicitly referring to it as "critical race theory." By hiding the red flag so that parents don't get up in arms, she is propagating a lie to the parents in those districts. That's when she's not denying that CRT is being taught at all. I should point out that many black and brown parents are outraged by this, too. A quick search of YouTube and you will see some very passionate speeches at school board meetings in protest of this ideology. Randi Weingarten has taken this to its full conclusion by installing race-based hiring practices and is promoting this in every school district that her influence reaches.

This chapter is mostly about the teachers' union AFT, not necessarily Randi Weingarten. But her constant presence on TV and any other place she can show up to be seen makes her the target for now. The union was always left-leaning, not necessarily a bad thing, but under her watch, she has dragged it farther to the left and made it more progressive than any other leader in the AFT's history. She has made some very controversial statements. Always in claiming outcomes or data that is in favor of union public schools. Although data supporting her many claims is sparse at best, including this:

"Children are better off under the provision of teachers' unions."

In support of this claim, she used research conducted by Eunice Han and Jeffrey Keefe. They found that the effect of teachers' unions was particularly strong for Hispanic and Black students. So, did she get research from non-partisan researchers? Not even close. Eunice Han from her University of Utah page:

Eunice Han is a labor economist, specializing in labor relations and educational policy. Her research focuses on workers' well-being and inequality. Because the goals of labor unions are aligned with these topics, many of her studies examine the relationship between unions and labor market outcomes in both the private and public sectors. She is also interested in understanding gender differences in labor market conditions, as well as identifying tools to close the gender gap[7].

And Jeffrey Keefe:

A Professor Emeritus of Labor and Employment Relations at the School of Management and Labor Relations, Rutgers University, where he has conducted research on labor markets, human resources, and labor-management relations to inform policy. He earned his Ph.D. at Cornell University[8].

It's not exactly an unbiased group of researchers. I looked through several of their published writings and opinions and couldn't find a single criticism of the teacher's unions. Even if you are pro-union, you can understand the misdirection taking place. Not all things about any organization, especially when you are talking about several unions as a whole, are perfect or without problems. Not pointing this out shows a bias that shouldn't be trusted. Randi Weingarten was very happy to use their research, which she knew would be in her favor, but none of the piles of research to the contrary. That is not a trait that is unique to her, but when we're trying to get to a better truth so that we can make something as important as our children's education better, then we need to be able to see all sides and all success and failures of the many different systems and ideas that are available. The union and Randi Weingarten have done all they can to prove that every other system or method of educating children is a failure compared to union-back schools. That couldn't be farther from the truth. As I wrote in the first chapter, private schools, charter schools, and even homeschooling have pros and cons but show better outcomes. And if their research was accurate, then why is it that non-union states have similar and sometimes better outcomes than union-controlled states? I'm sure they'd have a circular answer that makes very little sense.

As a 30-year union executive, with the exception of a brief one-semester experience as a full-time teacher, she has backed and rubbed shoulders with many of the highest Democratic leaders in government. She actually went to Ukraine during the war. What was to gain from that, and how much did it cost the taxpayers[9]? Or did it cost the teachers who fund her organization? It would appear by her actions that she's looking to climb the ladder to a Federal position. Which is why it's easy for her to say things like:

"Florida's new parental-rights law are "the way in which wars start."

The AFTs and Randi Weingarten herself have worked hard to slow or even stymie the expansion of charter schools. She and her union have spoken out against school choice of any kind and often rail against any discussion about charter or private schools. She recently claimed school choice 'undermines democracy'. I'm not sure how she is defending such a statement. For someone who works in the field of education, you would expect her to know the definition of democracy. School choice allows parents to exercise their democratic choice of schools. Having no choice or being told you have no say in where your kids go to school would be the opposite of democracy[10].

However, several members of the union chapters have been outed for putting their children in private schools. Essentially, they are taking their kids out of the public schools that the union members are supposed to be supporting[11].

No greater example of this comes from our bastions of low-performing public schools in Chicago. It is worth noting that even the president of the Chicago Teachers

Union and executive vice president of the American Federation of Teachers, Stacy Davis Gates, has made the decision to send her eldest son to a private school. This revelation may appear contradictory, considering her strong opposition to school choice, particularly for other people's children. In fact, Mrs. Gates has previously stated that "school choice was actually the choice of racists" and decried its "racist origins." Her union, which she represents, has consistently taken a hardline stance against private school choice programs[12].

Interestingly, the Chicago Teachers Union recently opposed the state's Invest in Kids Tax Credit Scholarship Program for low-income students, leading to its demise this year. For the leader of the union to now exercise the same choice that her union and its representatives in the legislature have effectively denied to underprivileged families is unethical and is disheartening and a clear blow to those who lack the financial means that Mrs. Gates possesses[13].

Mrs. Gates attempted to defend this apparent hypocrisy by issuing a statement. In this statement, she acknowledges that "If you are a Black family living in a Black community, high-quality neighborhood schools have been the dream, not the reality." She goes on to argue that the abysmal state of government schools essentially "forced" her to choose a private school for her son.

According to WBEZ Chicago, the union president claimed that her decision to send her son to a private school "represents a stark statement about disinvestment in public schools." However, this defense appears feeble, given that these failing institutions in Chicago spend over $29,000 per student per year, roughly twice the amount of her son's private school tuition.

It is evident that what may be good for Mrs. Gates is not

readily accessible or viable for ordinary families. This stark contrast only serves to underscore the hypocrisy of the unions and their leaders. However, the AFT seems to be able to make an exception for one of its own. The NYC Dept. of Education voted 22-0 to expand space for a charter school co-founded by none other than Randi Weingarten[14]. Think she had politics and friends on her side? Success Academy CEO Eva Moskowitz called out the United Federation of Teachers for hypocrisy after being silent about the expansion of a charter school partly owned by Randi Weingarten. Moscowitz said that Weingarten has opposed every charter co-location that has ever occurred in the city, yet she is awarded a location with a vote of 22 -0 by her union friends.

"Randi Weingarten has not only opposed all of the charter co-location, she's actually sued to prevent us from opening. Success Academy right now at this very moment, is about to have to go to court because the UFT (United Federation of Teachers) has sued to prevent Success Academy from opening a co-location," Moscowitz said.

A co-location is when a Charter School and a Public School reside in the same building.

She went on to say, "We serve 94 percent black and brown children in challenging neighborhoods where there aren't a lot of good educational options, and we've got people preventing us from opening great schools. It's madness[15]."

In "Not Accountable", Philip Howard argues that public employee unions have undermined democratic governance and should be unconstitutional. American voters elect governors and mayors who, under union agreements, have been disempowered from managing schools and other public agencies. This is why schools can't work, bad teachers can't be fired, states struggle under the weight of unaffordable pensions, and frustrated voters reach for extremist solutions. Politicians can't break the union stranglehold because, among other reasons, they've sold their souls for political and monetary union support[16].

Teacher unions, as a political organization, wield more power than is commonly acknowledged. It is important to recognize that they have significant influence over the content, delivery, and framing of curriculum. In fact, if you want to understand the driving force behind the majority of social-emotional learning or critical theory initiatives, look no further than the teachers' unions. These unions function as political organizations with their own specific agendas, much like any other political entity. However, what sets them apart is that they have a direct impact on our children's education in states where they hold control. They are the ones setting the agenda for schools and teachers. And the people of the states they have control didn't elect them.

During the pandemic, the power and influence of teachers' unions became even more evident, especially when it came to school reopening decisions. Randi Weingarten, the president of the American Federation of Teachers, recently claimed that teachers' unions were supportive of reopening schools as soon as possible. However, it is clear that she is trying to protect herself by distorting the truth. In most states where teachers' unions hold sway, public schools took considerably longer to reopen compared to states like Georgia, Florida, and Texas. These delays contradicted the desires of many parents in cities like Chicago, who wanted schools to open sooner. While the unions may attribute the decision to the mayor or governor, it must be understood that these officials were often responding to the teachers' unions' messaging that it was still unsafe to return. As a result, teachers in these cities and states were able to stay home and receive their salaries for an additional year or more, using COVID-19 as a convenient excuse to avoid returning to work[17].

During the Covid closures, there were incidents that sparked public outrage towards the unions. One such incident involved Sarah Chambers, the area vice president of the Chicago Teachers Union. She expressed her opposition to requiring teachers to return to the classroom by posting a photo of herself by a pool in Puerto Rico in January 2021, accompanied by the hashtag "pool life." On Twitter, she also stated, "Hearing of an educator revolution happening. Tons of members are emailing their administration: I'll be asserting my right to continue working in a safe remote environment on January 4th, 2021. I have signed the pledge, along with over 8,000+ union educators, to continue working remotely."[18]

Some incidents during this time, like the embarrassing interpretive dance videos posted by Chicago teachers on YouTube to express their opposition to going back to work, only served to further highlight the resistance of union-controlled public schools to reopening. These actions rightfully drew online ridicule and criticism. It is essential to note that this criticism is not meant to single out Chicago teachers, as many other union-controlled public schools also put up a fight to remain closed despite clear scientific evidence indicating the benefits of reopening and the low risk involved[19].

Recently, the teachers' union in Colorado, passed a resolution that declares that "capitalism inherently exploits children, public schools, land, labor, and resources." Teachers unions spend their vast coffers on political donations and lobbying to make sure they get their way, similar to capitalist corporations. They don't see the problem or the correlation because they believe their mission is altruistic[20].

It is not surprising that the AFT has been labeled as a socialist group, given the perception that they have been promoting anti-American, anti-capitalist, and anti-white rhetoric in state curricula under their control. Furthermore, they have allegedly been involved in aiding school districts to conceal or rebrand critical theory and other divisive ideologies, which they are aware parents from all racial backgrounds would oppose. To exacerbate matters, they have been accused of being against parents' rights, as they believe that the state or federal government is better equipped to determine how children should be raised and what beliefs they should hold, and whether or not a parent has the right to know if their child is changing their gender[21].

Everything is Political and Racist

In 2023, an issue arose in Florida regarding a passage in their history books that discussed the skills slaves acquired while working on plantations. The passage mentioned that slaves developed trades that could be beneficial to them personally. However, this sentence was taken out of context and caused a controversy that made it seem as though Florida was implying that slaves benefited from slavery. The story received extensive coverage in the national media, with many outlets portraying Florida and its governor in a negative light. The American Federation of Teachers (AFT) and the National Education Association (NEA) also voiced their disapproval, as the media frequently sought their input on the matter.

Adding fuel to the fire, Vice-President Kamala Harris commented on the issue without having all the facts straight. The Florida teachers' union and the NAACP even went so far as to issue travel advisories, warning black people about the state allegedly wanting them to return to the plantation. The hyperbolic rhetoric used in these statements was not only ridiculous but also misguided, as proper research into the curriculum would have revealed the following:

It's important to note that the governor of Florida did not write the history lesson or the specific sentence in question. Instead, Florida officials established an African American History Standards Workgroup in 2022 with the purpose of reviewing the state's education standards for African American history. The workgroup consisted of individuals with expertise in teaching K-12 history, particularly African American history, in Florida. The members were chosen based on their knowledge and experience, with no political, ideological, or identity group requirements. Out of the 13 members, six had African heritage. The workgroup's recommendations were accepted without dispute by the State Board of Education and Gov. Ron DeSantis.

It is worth noting that the Florida teachers' union was given the opportunity to be part of the workgroup but declined. Their decision to criticize the curriculum afterwards suggests that they may have been more interested in generating political drama rather than genuinely contributing to the discussion.

One of the members of the workgroup, Dr. William B. Allen, who is an author, professor, and political scientist, dismissed the allegations that DeSantis or Florida intended to portray slavery in a positive light or downplay the atrocities of plantation life. Dr. Allen emphasized the importance of telling the stories of the people who lived through that history in their own words, without altering them to fit modern expectations. He stated, "The stories of the people who lived through the history, they have a right to tell the story in their own words, and what we have provided for is the telling of those stories as they told it."

Baltimore Schools for Example

Want more examples of how unions are not serving the schools they represent? And that money doesn't equal better in education?

A new report reveals that the Maryland State Education Association (MSEA), one of the largest teachers' unions in the state, has experienced significant financial growth over the past decade. However, this growth in revenue has not been reflected in improved test scores across Maryland. In fact, test scores have plummeted during this time, raising concerns about the effectiveness of the union's efforts to elevate the quality of public education for all students.

Denisha Allen, the founder of Black Minds Matter, a Black student advocacy group, expressed her dismay at the situation. She highlighted the alarming reality that students are graduating from high school without basic reading skills, which has dire consequences as they are funneled into the criminal justice system. Allen emphasized that the MSEA, an organization that should be working towards increasing education opportunities, is falling far short of its responsibilities.

Allen further criticized the union, accusing it of profiting off the dismal outcomes experienced by the students. The report from FOX45's Project Baltimore shows that MSEA's revenue has grown by 34percent between 2013 and 2022, reaching a record high of $26.5 million in 2022. Unfortunately, this financial success has not translated into academic success for Maryland students.

Federal test scores have witnessed a decline over the years, with Maryland fourth-graders now performing below the national average in both reading and math. This is a significant departure from 2013, when they were outperforming their peers. The report also highlights the concerning drop in fourth-grade math scores from an average of 245 in 2013 to 229 in 2022, as well as the decline in reading scores from 232 to 212 during the same period. Shockingly, FOX45's Project Baltimore recently reported that 23 local schools had zero students proficient in math.

The disturbing academic results in Baltimore City Public Schools cannot be overlooked. In 2022, they had the lowest graduation rate in Maryland, and a staggering 77percent of students at one high school were reading at only an elementary or kindergarten level. These outcomes are in stark contrast to certain parts of Maryland where education results are relatively better.

The issue goes beyond funding, as Baltimore City Public Schools boast one of the largest education budgets in the country, amounting to $1.62 billion per year. Despite this substantial investment, which equates to approximately $21,600 per student, improved educational outcomes have not materialized. This only proves the point that more money doesn't equal better educational results.

Denisha Allen believes that it is paramount to hold public schools accountable for their role in educating students and to address the systemic failures within the education system. Anirban Basu, an economist and former member of the Baltimore City School Board, supports this view, noting that unions like the MSEA should prioritize the needs of children over the interests of adults[22].

New Jersey Teachers Union

The New Jersey teachers union is advocating for a change in the state's standards for entering the teaching profession. Currently, candidates for teacher certification in New Jersey are required to pass the Praxis Core Academic Skills for Educators, a basic skills test that assesses proficiency in reading, writing, and math. This test is a common requirement in many states for teacher certification. It's sort of like passing the bar to be certified to teach. Now, new teachers have the option to demonstrate their competency in basic skills by submitting SAT, ACT, or GRE scores as long as they are in the the top third percentile for the year they were taken.

The New Jersey Education Association (NJEA) believes that eliminating the basic skills test will remove unnecessary barriers to the teaching profession and promote equity. In a statement, the NJEA expressed its intention to eliminate the basic skills test, referring to it as another barrier that needs to be abolished following the removal of the edTPA last year.

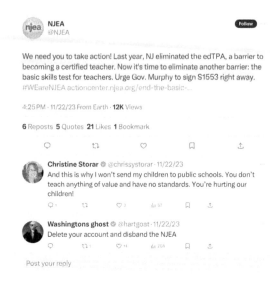

NJEA
@NJEA

Follow

We need you to take action! Last year, NJ eliminated the edTPA, a barrier to becoming a certified teacher. Now it's time to eliminate another barrier: the basic skills test for teachers. Urge Gov. Murphy to sign S1553 right away. #WEareNJEA actioncenter.njea.org/end-the-basic-...

4:25 PM · 11/22/23 From Earth · **12K** Views

6 Reposts **5** Quotes **21** Likes **1** Bookmark

Christine Storar ✓ @chrissystorar · 11/22/23
And this is why I won't send my children to public schools. You don't teach anything of value and have no standards. You're hurting our children!

Washingtons ghost ✓ @hartgoat · 11/22/23
Delete your account and disband the NJEA

Post your reply

edTPA is a performance-based, subject-specific assessment and support system used by teacher preparation programs throughout the United States to emphasize, measure, and support the skills and knowledge that all teachers need from Day 1 in the classroom.

However, this proposed change has raised concerns among parents and community members. The idea of having their children taught by teachers who may not have proven their proficiency in reading, writing, and math is unsettling. While the union suggests using SAT, ACT, or GRE scores as an alternative, it is important to note that being in the top third percentile with these scores does not necessarily guarantee recent knowledge or up-to-date skills. In fact, someone who took these tests years ago could still be eligible to teach.

New Jersey already removed the edTPA assessment requirements to be a certified teacher; now, the union wants them to drop the PRAXIS assessment test. Essentially, they are lowering the bar and making it so anyone can be a teacher. Before long they won't even require you to have a degree. Opponents of this change argue that it would lead to a lowering of the standards for teachers. This shift in standards raises concerns about the level of mastery and knowledge that teachers will be expected to possess.

While the intention behind this proposed change is to promote equity within the teaching profession, there are doubts about whether it will truly achieve that goal. Critics argue that lowering grading and testing standards may not necessarily result in a more equitable education system. Instead, it may perpetuate a system where everyone is required to do less to prove their mastery of educational concepts.

The question at hand is whether lowering standards is necessary in order to achieve equity. Is it implying that minorities are unable to meet the same assessment criteria or obtain certification unless the process is made easier for them? A notion that should be offensive to all minorities.

The union is asserting that it will promote "equity" in the teaching field. However, there is a concern that their approach involves reducing the standards for teachers. This is further compounded by the fact that grading and testing standards for students have already been lowered. The overall fear is that these actions will result in a situation where everyone involved in education, both teachers and graduates, will be required to demonstrate less mastery in their respective areas. It is important to consider the potential impact of these changes on the quality of education being provided[23].

Is there any wonder why grades and test scores continue to fall?

Teachers are Making Union Executives Wealthy

Let's delve into an analysis of the salaries of union leaders in New Jersey, specifically focusing on the NJEA (New Jersey Education Association). According to a report by Michael Lilley of the Sunlight Policy Center of New Jersey, union bosses in New Jersey have been paying themselves exorbitant salaries. This is particularly concerning considering that teachers' unions generate their income from the hard-earned money of teachers, who are often required to pay monthly dues automatically deducted from their paychecks.

Lilley's report compared the compensation of NJEA leadership from 2018 to 2022, based on IRS filings, with the National Education Association (NEA) and the three largest state unions in the country: New York State United Teachers (NYSUT), the California Teachers Association (CTA), and the Pennsylvania State Education Association (PSEA). Despite the fact that the NEA and these three state organizations have larger memberships and higher revenues than the NJEA, there is no justification for the excessive compensation received by NJEA executives.

For instance, NJEA pays one executive an astounding $2,052,199 per year, which is more than double CTA's highest-paid executive and significantly higher than other unions. This raises the question of how NJEA can afford to pay such exorbitant salaries and still remain financially viable. One factor may be the fact that NJEA members pay the highest annual dues in the country.

To put the NJEA's salaries into perspective, let's analyze the numbers provided by Lilley. The average pay of the NJEA's top ten highest-paid executives was $752,726 per year, which is 59percent higher than the NEA, 65percent higher than the CTA, 128percent higher than the NYSUT, and 160percent higher than the PSEA.

In 2018-2020, eight of the top ten highest-paid executives among all unions belonged to the NJEA, with four of them earning over $1 million. Notably, former executive director Ed Richardson appeared on the list three times. Richardson, often referred to as the NJEA's $9.3 million political pro, accumulated a staggering $9,311,371 in compensation over his thirteen-year career as a NJEA executive. On average, this amounts to $716,259 per year, which would place Richardson among the top ten highest earners across all unions.

It is clear that NJEA leadership is enriching themselves at the expense of teachers in New Jersey. If teachers were aware of these facts, they would undoubtedly be outraged.

An interesting comparison can be made between the NJEA and the NEA. Despite having significantly fewer members (200,200 compared to NEA's nearly three million) and lower revenues ($150 million compared to NEA's $400 million in 2020), the NJEA pays its executives much more than the national union does.

The highest salaries within the NJEA are not allocated to the president, vice president, or secretary but rather to headquarters staff. In 2018, the average compensation for the top nine headquarters staff members was over a million dollars. These individuals are primarily political operatives and organizers who are involved in promoting desired legislation and legislators, as well as advancing the agenda of the national union.

Ultimately, NJEA members contribute to this rigged system through their annual dues, which are 30percent higher than CTA dues, 74percent higher than PSEA dues, and 164percent higher than NYSUT dues. Unfortunately, teachers rarely witness the fruits of their contributions as the money goes towards lavishly compensating NJEA executives.

Hundreds of millions of dollars, with salaries ranging from 700k to several million for individuals, is quite impressive for a non-profit. It does raise the question of how these funds are being utilized, particularly in relation to teacher contributions. Are these contributions primarily being used for salaries rather than furthering the mission of the organization? This is a concern for all teachers, not just those in New Jersey. They deserve to know what they are getting in return for their contributions.

When researching this topic, I came across numerous articles on the internet from state and national teachers' unions, claiming that teachers receive great benefits from being part of the union. However, when I interviewed teachers in union-controlled states and asked them what they actually receive from their union, they struggled to provide a clear answer. The most common response was that the

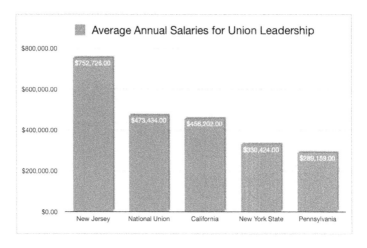

union has their back, but it seems that the tangible benefits are less apparent.

While it may be true that the collective strength of unions allows them to negotiate better contracts for teachers, there doesn't seem to be a significant improvement in educational outcomes as a result. This raises a valid question about the value of these high salaries. It is natural to wonder what the teachers and taxpayers are truly getting in return beyond enriching a select few individuals.

This issue highlights a broader problem with non-profits in general. Although there are no specific salary restrictions outlined in the legal code or by the IRS, there is an expectation that salaries should be "reasonable." However, what constitutes reasonable is subjective and can vary depending on who is receiving the high salary. Those earning 700k a year will likely find numerous justifications to support

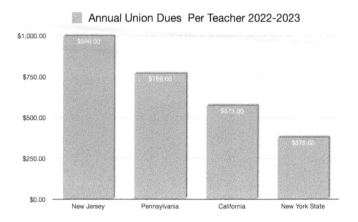

their pay, even within the non-profit sector. Unfortunately, many non-profits seem to allocate a significant portion of their contributions towards top-level salaries. In my experience, it seems that non-profit status is often manipulated to avoid taxes and generate additional funds under the guise of virtuous goals.

Putting all this aside, it is crucial for teachers in this country to reassess the value of their contributions and what they are receiving in return. From my perspective and based on conversations with several teachers, it appears that unionized teachers are not receiving substantially more benefits compared to their non-union counterparts in other states[24].

Maybe the Tide is Turning Against the Unions

In a recent poll conducted by Echelon Insights on behalf of the Illinois Policy Institute in late 2023, it was revealed that there has been a significant decline in support for the CTU among registered Chicago voters. The findings showed that only 37 percent of voters have a favorable view of the CTU, while 46 percent hold an unfavorable view.The recent findings indicate a considerable decrease in public support for the CTU compared to earlier this year. According to the poll conducted in February, 44 percent of respondents held a favorable view of the CTU, while 42 percent expressed an unfavorable view. In essence, the CTU's net favorability among Chicago voters has dropped from a positive two to a negative nine in just eight months, marking an 11-point decline. This shift in sentiment serves as a cautionary tale for unions that may be overplaying their hand, and it also serves as a warning to legislators who continue to defer to their short-term power. If the CTU can lose its grip on public opinion, it underscores that no union stranglehold can last indef-initely[25].

The dissatisfaction with the CTU extends across party lines, with Republicans and independents reporting net favorability levels of -52 and -20, respectively. Furthermore, voters from all political backgrounds believe that the CTU has "too much influence over the City of Chicago." Even among Chicago Democrats, 40 percent agree that the CTU has "too much influence," while 28 percent believe they have "about the right amount of influence," and only 14 percent feel that they have "too little influence."

In addition to its actions against the Invest in Kids Tax Credit Scholarship program, CTU has also faced criticism for its stance on reopening public schools during the COVID-19 pandemic. Their decision to keep schools closed was met with backlash, especially when it was revealed that one of their board members was vacationing in Puerto Rico while claiming it was unsafe for teachers to return to in-person teaching[26].

Furthermore, the union faced controversy when they posted and later deleted a tweet suggesting that the push to reopen schools was rooted in sexism, racism, and misogyny. Once again, they are showcasing their strategy of labeling any decision they disagree with as sexist, racist, or misogynistic. This statement received significant backlash from the public.

Unfortunately, the strike initiated by CTU in 2022, citing concerns related to COVID-19, further impacted low-income students who were already disadvantaged. This strike disrupted their education and limited their opportunities to attend alternative schools.

It is worth noting that the decision to oppose the Invest in Kids Tax Credit Scholarship program and the actions taken by CTU during the COVID-19 era have been met with criticism and were not supported by a majority of Chicago voters. A recent poll showed that 65 percent of voters in Chicago, including Republicans, Democrats, and independents, were in favor of the program. This demonstrates a disconnect between the union's actions and the preferences of the local community[27].

If that wasn't already enough negative information regarding the CTU, it was revealed in January 2024 that the union had not released any audits detailing their utilization of teacher dues for the past four years. According to the Chicago Teachers Union's own internal rules, they are required to provide an annual audit of their financial activities. However, they have failed to meet this obligation for the past four consecutive years.

Despite this lack of transparency, the union has proceeded to increase members' dues by 13percent, amounting to over $1,400 for the 2024 fiscal year. Those who have questioned the CTU's financial practices have faced targeted insults from its president, Stacy Davis Gates. As a result, some members have chosen to discontinue their membership with the union altogether.

---

1. https://daily.jstor.org/the-rise-of-teachers-unions/
   http://hechingered.org/content/the-rise-of-teacher-unions-a-look-at-union-impact-over-the-years_5601/
2. https://www.opensecrets.org/industries//totals?cycle=2018&ind=l1300
3. https://www.brookings.edu/books/special-interest/
4. https://nypost.com/2021/07/08/teachers-union-president-randi-weingarten-defends-critical-race-theory/
   https://www.washingtonpost.com/local/education/teachers-union-critical-race-theory-weingarten/2021/07/06/ef327c20-de61-11eb-9f54-7eee10b5fcd2_story.html
   https://www.wsj.com/articles/randi-weingartens-racism-rant-1500845156
5. https://cynicaltheories.com/
6. https://nypost.com/2021/07/04/teachers-union-vows-to-fight-back-against-critical-race-theory-critics/
   https://pjmedia.com/stacey-lennox/2021/07/05/teachers-union-commits-to-shoving-critical-theories-down-the-throats-of-students-and-parents-nationwide-n1459480
7. https://faculty.utah.edu/u6007892-Eunice_Sookyung_Han,_Ph.D./hm/index.hml
8. https://www.epi.org/people/jeffrey-h-keefe/
9. https://www.edweek.org/policy-politics/what-a-teachers-union-leader-saw-in-ukraine/2022/10
   https://www.washingtonexaminer.com/policy/education/randi-weingarten-ripped-for-visiting-ukraine
   https://www.influencewatch.org/person/randi-weingarten/
10. https://www.foxnews.com/media/teacher-union-boss-randi-weingarten-claims-school-choice-undermines-democracy
11. https://edreform.com/2017/08/randi-weingartens-hypocrisy/
12. https://chicago.suntimes.com/education/2023/9/7/23863532/ctu-president-defends-sending-her-son-private-school-result-unfair-choices-south-side-families
13. https://www.illinoispolicy.org/teachers-unions-hand-nearly-1-5-million-to-lawmakers-ahead-of-invest-in-kids-vote/
   https://www.wbez.org/stories/illinois-controversial-private-school-scholarship-program-is-ending/849c1d35-b525-4dde-adbf-9147aa38a224

14. https://www.foxnews.com/media/ny-teachers-union-accused-hypocrisy-approving-expansion-randi-weingartens-charter-school
    https://nypost.com/2023/04/23/uft-opposes-charter-schools-except-for-boss-randi-weingartens/

15. https://www.foxnews.com/media/success-academy-ceo-speaks-out-against-uft-for-being-silent-about-randi-weingartens-charter-school-expansion

16. https://www.philipkhoward.com/not-accountable

17. https://www.edweek.org/teaching-learning/how-teachers-unions-are-influencing-decisions-on-school-reopenings/2020/12
    https://www.usatoday.com/premium-registration/?return=httpspercent3Apercent2Fpercent2Fwww.usatoday.compercent2Fstorypercent2Fnewspercent2Feducationpercent2F2021percent2F01percent2F25percent2Fbi wants-schools-open-but-teachers-unions-have-other-ideaspercent2F4165684001percent2F
    https://edsource.org/2020/california-teachers-unions-affirm-opposi tion-to-opening-schools-without-more-safety-precautions/645460
    https://nypost.com/2023/05/09/randi-weingarten-fact-checked-by-twitter-after-claiming-she-advocated-to-reopen-schools-during-covid/
    https://bongino.com/teachers-union-leader-demands-schools-stay-closed-while-vacationing-from-puerto-rico/

18. https://www.dailymail.co.uk/news/article-9105697/Teachers-union-leader-blasted-pushing-schools-closed-vacations-Puerto-Rico.html

19. https://www.foxnews.com/media/chicago-teachers-union-panned-for-video-demanding-safe-return-to-schools-through-interpretive-dance

20. https://justthenews.com/politics-policy/education/colorado-teachers-union-passes-resolution-stating-capitalism-inherently

21. https://parentalrights.org/parental-rights-are-not-anti-education/

22. https://foxbaltimore.com/news/project-baltimore/maryland-teachers-union-revenues-and-assets-hit-record-highs-as-student-test-scores-plummet-maryland-state-education-association-cheryl-bost-anirban-basu-baltimore-city-school-board
    https://www.detroitnews.com/story/opinion/2023/02/15/allen-balti more-shows-why-students-need-options/69908775007/
    https://readlion.com/parents-left-unaware-of-stunning-illiteracy-in-a-baltimore-public-high-school/

23. https://www.northjersey.com/story/news/education/2023/11/16/njea-teacher-basic-skill-test-end/71608947007/

24.

25. https://www.msn.com/en-us/news/us/new-poll-reveals-what-voters-really-think-of-americas-most-powerful-teachers-union/ar-AA1lnNsA

26. https://bongino.com/teachers-union-leader-demands-schools-stay-closed-while-vacationing-from-puerto-rico/

27. https://wirepoints.org/new-poll-reveals-what-voters-really-think-of-the-chicago-teachers-union-fox-news/

12

TO HOMEWORK OR NOT TO HOMEWORK...THAT IS THE QUESTION

"I have always felt there should be a balance between home-work and family time."
   Annie Lopez
   Teacher

In recent years, there has been a surge in headlines and complaints from parents about homework. Some parent groups have even started petitions to ban homework altogether. These complaints generally fall into two categories: the homework being too difficult, or there being an excessive amount of homework, or sometimes both. Fueling these complaints are the numerous studies that have been circulating online, claiming that homework has no benefit for students. These studies have been widely shared on platforms like Facebook, garnering millions of views.

However, it's important to note that I personally have become skeptical of studies in general. With the abundance of information available on the internet, it has become increasingly difficult to discern between credible and unreliable sources. It's all too easy to find a study that contradicts another study, and people often share studies that align with their existing beliefs without critically evaluating the source, the participants, or the methodology. In today's digital age, many people have become accustomed to reading headlines without delving deeper into the nuances of an article, which often provides exceptions to the key points highlighted by the headline. Unfortunately, this has led to the spread and acceptance of misinformation, even in the face of contradictory evidence from other sources. The COVID-19 pandemic serves as a prime example of this phenomenon.

Let me illustrate this point with an anecdote from the summer of 2016. An article appeared on a relatively unknown website, claiming that a child's mathematical intellect solely came from their mother. This headline was widely republished and shared on social media, mentioned in news broadcasts, and became a topic of discussion on Facebook. If you were the mother of exceptionally intelligent children, you may have felt proud. Conversely, if your children were not deemed brilliant, you might have experienced a sense of disappointment. However, reputable scientists and researchers quickly debunked this study, but their findings were hardly shared at all. Consequently, many people continue to blame their mothers for their perceived lack of mathematical prowess. In reality, the study and the article were nothing more than a fraud. It is crucial to emphasize that there are studies that present arguments both in favor of and against homework. Therefore, from this point forward, I will rely on common sense and insights from teachers who work with children on a daily basis.

In recent years, there has been a noticeable decrease in complaints regarding excessive homework. This positive shift can be attributed to the fact that schools have taken feedback into consideration and made adjustments to address the issue. It is likely that the implementation of the Common Core curriculum prompted schools to reevaluate the amount of homework being assigned, leading to a more balanced workload for students.

First and foremost, it is important to note that very few teachers argue against homework entirely or argue that it is unnecessary for effective education. The debate among educators primarily centers around the amount of homework. It should also be noted that teachers do not receive any additional compensation for assigning homework. In fact, creating and grading homework assignments adds to their workload. So why do teachers assign homework? The answer lies in the fact that it is logical for a child who learns something new on Tuesday at 9 am to review that information before being tested on it at a later date. The saying "repetition is the mother of learning and the father of action, which makes it the architect of accomplishment" resonates with many people. However, it is worth mentioning that the daily review of previous lessons has become less prevalent in our current education system due to the increasing rigor of the curriculum. As one teacher explained, "Because I have an extensive amount of content to teach each week, I don't have the luxury of spending extra time ensuring that everyone fully understands yesterday's lesson. We have to keep moving forward; otherwise, we risk falling behind." In this context, homework serves as a valuable tool for teachers to gauge each student's understanding of the material and identify areas that require additional assistance. It also enables teachers to assess the overall comprehension of the class as a whole, thereby informing their future teaching strategies. Many students are able to solve problems or grasp concepts more confidently in a classroom setting, where a teacher is readily available to provide guidance. Completing homework assignments at home fosters independence and problem solving skills. Additionally, homework instills lessons in time management, responsibility, and the importance of completing tasks, even when they are undesirable. These are all essential qualities that contribute to a strong work ethic. Homework also helps students develop effective study habits.:

Below is a list of ten benefits that educators cite in support of homework:

- •Homework teaches students about time management.
- •Homework teaches students how to set priorities.
- •Homework helps teachers determine how well students understand the lessons and materials.
- •Homework teaches students problem-solving skills.
- •Homework provides students with an additional opportunity to review class material.
- •Homework allows parents to gain insight into their child's learning progress.
- •Homework teaches students the importance of fulfilling obligations, even when they lack motivation.
- •Homework encourages students to take responsibility for their own education.
- •Homework fosters independent work habits.
- •Homework emphasizes the significance of planning, organization, and taking action.

Despite these benefits, there are several factors that have

contributed to the negative perception of homework and those who assign it. Today, parents lead busier lives compared to previous generations. Between their children's extracurricular activities and demanding work schedules, parents often seek ways to alleviate the time pressure at home. Sports and after-school activities are voluntary, and I wish more parents would dedicate as much time and motivation to their children's school work as they do in sports. I've heard from many teachers that parents will write a note asking for their child to be granted forgiveness or extra time because their nine-year-old child was out playing sports till 10 pm. Sadly, some people will read that last line and not see a problem. As someone who coached baseball and played for many years and also coached softball for my daughter, I understand the value of sports in teaching valuable life lessons. However, considering the slim chances of a child pursuing a professional sports career, it is crucial to ensure that they are adequately prepared for higher education or technical fields that require intellectual aptitude.

Another common complaint revolves around the perceived difficulty of homework, especially in subjects such as mathematics. Once upon a time, textbooks were brought home by the student, and the parents could use the textbook to walk through the problem or lesson together. I empathize with parents who feel frustrated by the lack of resources or support accompanying homework assignments. This is an area where many schools and districts seem to be blind. In my experience, they simply do not see this as a problem. However, sending homework without the proper resources to review it is a problem that needs to be fixed. Their mentality is that there's plenty of resources on the internet. However, parents are often unsure about the reliability and accuracy of the resources they come across, as well as the suitability of the content for their children's assignments.

It is worth noting, however, that there is such a thing as too much homework. Determining the optimal amount of homework is a significantly more contentious topic. After all, practice makes perfect, which is why you take your kids to practice sports or dance, etc. So it should be understandable that a teacher would like your kids to practice as well.

Maybe There are Some Exceptions to Consider

I recently had a conversation with a retired principal who had a wealth of experience in both upper-middle-class schools and schools that primarily served disadvantaged neighborhoods. One particular piece of advice that he shared with all his teachers in the school serving the disadvantaged community struck a chord with me. It was an aspect I hadn't previously considered, but it made complete sense. He emphasized the importance of assigning homework to students, while taking into account their unique circumstances.

Within the school, there were students who faced responsibilities beyond their academic pursuits. Some of these students would go home and take on the role of caretaker, cooking for younger siblings and even working late into the night until 11 pm or midnight. They would then squeeze in their homework either on the bus or before school started. These students were driven by a desire to support their families or because the adults in their households were unable to fully care for them. It became evident that their lives were the opposite of those students whose parents preferred they not work during their school years.

It is clear that his teachers highly regarded this principle, as he never imposed new teaching methods or curricula on them. Instead, he trusted their professional judgment and allowed them to determine what would be most effective. However, he was equally aware of the challenges his students faced and was committed to their success. Recognizing that overwhelming them with excessive work would only lead to discouragement or hinder their progress, he prioritized their well-being and academic achievement.

Time is an Issue

Let me bring attention to a crucial point that often goes unnoticed by most parents: time. The average teacher, particularly in elementary and middle school, faces a significant time constraint when it comes to covering all the required subject matter. If you were to ask educators with over a decade of experience, you would discover that the time allocated to each subject has consistently decreased as school districts continue to add more responsibilities to their already extensive teaching to-do lists. This includes not only instructional time but also review sessions and ensuring that every student is adequately prepared to progress. Unfortunately, teachers nowadays have very limited extra time and are compelled to adhere to the curriculum map that must be completed by the end of the academic year. Consequently, there is little room for additional review or reinforcement. It is important to note that high school teachers who specialize in a single subject face fewer challenges in this regard. However, elementary teachers must find a way to incorporate all subjects into their daily schedule. I have spoken to several elementary and middle school teachers who have revealed that they only have approximately 15 minutes of class time dedicated to science, 15 minutes to social studies, and 15 minutes to other subjects. This paints a clear picture of the time constraints they face. In order to assess student under-standing and identify those who may be falling behind, teachers often rely on homework assignments. Falling behind can occur due to incomplete homework or a lack of comprehension of the lesson. Therefore, assigning home-work serves as a valuable tool for teachers to gauge student comprehension and prepare them for future assessments. This underscores the importance of parents ensuring that their children complete their homework assignments.

But let's not forget again...practice makes perfect. And that is the goal.

13

SCHOOL CHOICE & VOUCHERS

"I may disagree with your choice, but I respect your right to choose it."

When it comes to education, parents have a range of options to consider for their children. While most parents opt for their neighborhood public school, there are several alternative choices available. These include public charter schools, magnet schools, private schools, parochial schools, online schools, and even homeschooling.

School choice is a term for education options that allow students and families to select alternatives to public schools. According to Amy Smith, the interim dean of the School of Education at the University of St. Thomas in Minnesota, school choice is fundamentally about empowering parents and guardians to make decisions about their children's education, regardless of the funding sources involved.

At present, a total of 32 states, along with Washington, D.C., have implemented some form of school choice program, as reported by EdChoice, a nonprofit organization that advocates for school choice. Robert Enlow, the president and CEO of EdChoice, highlights that the past two years have witnessed an increasing number of states adopting educational choice programs, demonstrating a growing trend towards providing families with more options in education[1].

As mentioned earlier in the book, it is interesting to note that there are 42 states where public schools actually spend more per student than it costs to send that same student to a private school. This particular observation raises an important consideration: the potential benefits of implementing a voucher program. By allowing parents to choose private schools for their children and utilizing vouchers, it is possible to argue that such a program could lead to cost savings for taxpayers. This is because the state would only have to pay the lesser amount required to send kids to private schools.

Proponents of school choice policies strongly believe that these programs have a significant impact on educational outcomes and provide greater opportunities and access for historically disadvantaged students. By offering alternative options beyond traditional public schools, school choice policies empower parents to make decisions about their child's education based on their individual needs.

Furthermore, advocates argue that the introduction of competition through school choice programs not only benefits the students who participate but also has a positive effect on traditional public schools. The presence of alternatives encourages these schools to innovate, improve their programs, and provide a higher quality education to attract and retain students.

However, critics of school choice policies raise concerns

about the potential negative consequences. They argue that diverting funds from traditional public schools to support school choice programs can result in or exacerbate the existing inequalities among students. This diversion of resources may limit the capacity of public schools to provide the necessary support and education to all students, especially those in economically disadvantaged areas[2].

In addition, opponents of school voucher programs and Education Savings Accounts (ESAs) express concerns about the allocation of tax dollars to religious organizations that operate many private schools. This raises questions about the separation of church and state and the potential implications for the diversity and inclusivity of educational options[3].

Democrat politicians have frequently expressed opposition to choice programs, while state unions have resorted to lawsuits in an attempt to halt school choice and voucher programs, although with limited success. However, the notion that reduced funds to local public schools, resulting from students opting for other school choices, is not substantiated by the outcomes observed in states where choice and vouchers have been available for several years. Even if it were true, it would not justify allowing others to remain in a failing system just to avoid defunding it. If districts were aware that they would be competing with other school choices for funds, they would be compelled to make significant efforts to improve their district schools. This would necessitate identifying effective strategies and retaining their best teachers.

In 2023, Tennessee Governor Bill Lee introduced the Education Freedom Scholarship Act, which aims to extend school choice to every family in both rural and urban Tennessee communities. Under this plan, 20,000 scholar-

ships would be made available to Tennessee students, with
10,000 scholarships earmarked for students at or below 300
percent of the federal poverty level, students with disabilities, and those eligible for the existing pilot program. An
additional 10,000 scholarships would be open to a universal
pool of students entitled to attend public schools. However,
State Senator Heidi Campbell raised concerns, accusing
Governor Lee of scamming Tennessee residents. Senator
Campbell argues that in states where similar programs have
been implemented, state scores have declined, and public
schools have suffered from reduced funding for economically disadvantaged students.

I am uncertain about the source of Senator Campbell's
data, but information available on the internet from other
states actually contradicts her claims. It seems that her main
concern stems from the fact that funding intended for
public education is now being allocated to non-public
schools. This seems to be an attempt to manipulate the data
in order to support the narrative that everyone should
support the public school system, regardless of the quality
of their local schools. Somehow, it is perceived as wrong to
abandon government schools in favor of better alternatives[4].

Vouchers

Voucher programs are primarily targeted toward families
with low income, enabling parents to utilize public education funding to partially or fully cover the tuition fees at
private schools that would otherwise be financially out of
reach. These programs encompass both religious and non-
religious educational institutions. According to EdChoice,

sixteen states, along with Washington, D.C., currently implement voucher programs. The eligibility criteria based on income also differ across states and specific programs, with certain states offering multiple voucher programs[5].

Education Savings Accounts

In these programs, eligible parents who choose to remove their child from public school receive a deposit of state funds into an educational savings account, commonly referred to as an ESA. These funds can be utilized for various educational expenses, providing parents with greater flexibility compared to other school choice initiatives. Notably, ESAs can be used for private school tuition and fees, as well as other approved expenses such as online learning programs and tutoring. Some states, such as Arizona, even allow remaining funds to be allocated towards higher education pursuits. According to Martin West, an academic dean and education professor at Harvard University's Graduate School of Education, education savings accounts differ from vouchers in that parents receive funds that can be utilized for any approved educational purpose rather than solely for private school tuition. In certain states, ESAs can also be utilized to support homeschooling, including the coverage of necessary supplies. Currently, eleven states have implemented ESA policies, as indicated by EdChoice. Among these states, four (Arkansas, Florida, Iowa, and Utah) have recently introduced new programs with universal eligibility, set to take effect in 2023. It is worth noting that some states' programs have specific criteria, such as income thresholds

---

or special needs requirements, in order to determine eligibility for participation[6].

Tax-Credit Scholarships

Sometimes referred to as Tax Credit Scholarships. These programs provide individuals or corporations with the opportunity to receive full or partial tax credits when they donate to nonprofit scholarship funds. It is worth mentioning that these scholarships are specifically aimed at helping eligible families, typically those with low or middle incomes, who are seeking financial assistance to cover private school tuition expenses. To apply for these scholarships, families can submit their applications through the scholarship-granting organization operating in their respective states.

Cons as Listed by Opponents

Opponents of school choice present weak and illogical arguments. Let's examine their main points, as outlined on the unions' website:

1. Detractors of school choice often raise concerns about its impact on educational inequality. They contend that only privileged parents are able to take advantage of school choice, while lower-income families are left with limited options. They

argue that this creates a system where wealthier parents can move to areas with high-performing schools or afford private education, while less affluent families are left with potentially underperforming schools in their neighborhoods. From their perspective, school choice exacerbates existing inequities and raises questions about fairness and social justice. By focusing on the potential disparities in access and quality of education, critics of school choice emphasize the importance of ensuring all students have equal opportunities for success. They argue that every child should have access to a high-quality education regardless of their socioeconomic background. From their viewpoint, the ability of some families to choose better schools can perpetuate systemic inequalities and hinder efforts to provide a level playing field for all students.

2. Critics argue that implementing school choice will not have a positive impact on public education. Their main concern is that if a large number of parents choose to transfer their children to other schools, it could potentially result in the closure of some public schools.

3. Another important consideration is that not all parents are equipped with the necessary information to make well-informed decisions when presented with a wide range of options. Although implementing a lottery system simplifies the application process, families still face the responsibility of visiting different schools, comparing the various offerings, and

ultimately making educated choices for their children's education.

4. Opponents of this viewpoint argue that not all individuals prioritize the needs of their own children. They assert that the assumption that rational self-interest benefits everyone is flawed. Some parents and students may feel a sense of loyalty towards struggling schools and prioritize the well-being of others over their own children.

Critics argue that public funds should be directed toward schools that provide equal access and support to all students. Jessica Levin, the deputy litigation director at the Education Law Center and director of Public Funds Public Schools, highlights the concern that private education vouchers enable private schools to cherry-pick students based on their own criteria. In contrast, public schools are legally required to accept all students living within their district boundaries. It is important to note, however, that many school choice programs in most states allow parents to choose charter schools or other public schools as alternatives, not just private schools. This provides parents with additional options and flexibility in finding the best educational fit for their children.

First and foremost, let's address the argument that highlights the issue of fairness in the context of school choice. While it is true that some parents have the means to choose a different school for their children, while others may not have that luxury or may opt not to exercise it, it is essential to approach this matter from a more mature perspective. Fairness, or the lack thereof, is a fundamental aspect of life that we must acknowledge. However, it is counterproductive to impede certain families from pursuing educational opportunities simply because others may not have access to them.

In a free and democratic society, it is crucial to empower parents to make decisions based on what they believe is best for their children. While the extent of our societal freedom may be subject to debate, we must still embrace the idea of allowing parents to act in their children's best interests when it comes to education. It is worth noting that wealthier parents already exercise their choice by relocating to areas with superior schools or opting for private education. Therefore, the concept of school choice primarily aims to assist lower-income families whose parents may not have the financial means to move to a more desirable school district.

Secondly, it is important to note that the intention behind school choice is not to guarantee a universal improvement in public education. Rather, it aims to provide children with the opportunity to attend schools that are considered "better" in terms of quality. By allowing parents and students to choose the most suitable educational environment, school choice ultimately promotes a higher standard of education. It emphasizes the concept that schools should be accountable for the education they provide, and those that fail to effectively serve their students cannot truly claim to offer a quality education.

While it can be unfortunate if a school is forced to close due to an exodus of students to other schools, this outcome reflects the failure of that particular institution to fulfill its responsibilities effectively. In the realm of business, consumers have the power to choose where to spend their money, and a similar principle should apply to education. Schools that consistently fall short of expectations should either work to address their shortcomings or, if necessary, consider the possibility of ceasing operations. The purpose is to ensure that students are receiving a satisfactory education, and retaining students without achieving satisfactory results serves no purpose in that regard.

The third argument against school choice is illogical. If parents are willing to invest time and effort into researching, visiting schools, and making informed decisions, they should be allowed to do so. After all, they are motivated by concerns that their current neighborhood school is not adequately meeting their child's educational needs or is unsafe. By having the freedom to choose a school, parents can explore alternative options that may provide a better learning environment for their children. They can consider factors such as academic programs, extracurricular activities, teacher-student ratios, and safety measures to ensure their child's well-being and educational growth.

Finally, argument number four appears to be redundant as it echoes the sentiment expressed in the first point. It states that not all parents will take the initiative or make the effort to transfer their child to a better school. While it is indeed true that some parents may not prioritize education in their children's lives, as discussed in earlier chapters of this book, it is unfortunate but a reality. However, the laziness of these parents should not be a reason to hold all other students and parents hostage in failing school districts. On the contrary, this situation may inadvertently benefit the students who remain in lower-performing schools. The reduced class sizes can facilitate better management for teachers and provide more one-on-one instruction opportunities.

In my perspective, the only valid argument against implementing school choice would arise if all schools provided an equivalent level of education, with minimal deviation between them. However, since this is not the reality we face, it is essential to grant parents the freedom to make choices that they believe would be most beneficial for their children.

To those who oppose the idea of school choice, I present a thought-provoking question. Imagine yourself residing in an area where schools consistently demonstrate underperformance each year, leaving no doubt that your children are not receiving a quality education. Would you persist in keeping your children in that school solely to uphold your ideological standpoint against school choice?

One unintended consequence of implementing school choice is that highly successful schools may reach their capacity and become unable to admit additional students in a given year. In states where there is a high demand for charter schools but limited availability, a lottery system is utilized. This means that parents who are interested in enrolling their children in these schools have to rely on luck in order to secure a spot. Ultimately, the market will step in and create new Charters and private schools to fill the additional need for more schools.

As we explored in previous sections, failing schools often mirror the circumstances of the surrounding community. While some individuals may find this statement uncomfortable, it is crucial to address such matters without being constrained by political correctness. Parents within these communities are well aware of the situation, which is precisely why they actively seek alternative educational opportunities for their children.

Pros

In my view, the primary justification for advocating school choice lies in the autonomy it affords parents to select the optimal educational path for their children. However, it is worth delving into the seven most compelling rationales that parents frequently put forth, backed by extensive research and data.

I. Parents who choose to exercise school choice often prioritize the safety of their children as one of the main reasons for doing so. This concern for school safety is especially prominent in communities where violence is prevalent. By providing alternative education options, school choice allows students to escape environments plagued by issues like bullying, gang-related violence, and other forms of school violence. An example that highlights the positive impact of school choice can be seen in Milwaukee, where research has shown that participants in school choice programs were half as likely to commit felonies and misdemeanors compared to those who attended their local public schools. This demonstrates the potential of school choice in not only improving safety but also reducing criminal activity among students. Furthermore, various empirical studies have consistently found that students who participate in private school choice programs experience enhanced safety and receive a better quality of education. This evidence supports the notion that school choice can have a positive impact on the overall well-being and academic outcomes of students. This notion is further reinforced by two additional studies conducted in different contexts. In the largest-ever survey conducted on a private school choice program in Florida, school safety ranked among the top three priorities for parents when selecting a school, with 36 percent of nearly 15,000 respondents listing it as a crucial factor. Similar motivations related to school safety have also been reported by parents exercising education choice in settings such as Washington, D.C.

2. School choice has been proven to have a significant influence on parental satisfaction and active involvement in their child's education. Numerous studies have consistently shown that parents who have the freedom to choose their child's school are overwhelmingly content with the decisions they make. For example, in Arizona, where the education savings account option is available, a remarkable 70 percent of respondents with children enrolled in this program reported being "very satisfied." This statistic serves as a powerful testament to the positive impact that school choice can have on parents. Another notable example is the D.C. Opportunity Scholarship Program, which has yielded similar outcomes. Parents whose children participate in this program have expressed higher levels of satisfaction and increased engagement in their children's learning journey. This compelling evidence suggests that when parents are empowered with

the opportunity to select their children's schools, they become more personally invested and actively involved in shaping their educational experience.

3. School choice offers a valuable opportunity for low-income families who seek more educational options. By implementing school choice, we can break the arbitrary link between a child's housing situation and the school they can attend, providing a fair chance for all students to access a high-quality education. They no longer have to settle for a school solely based on their zip code or financial status. While some middle-income and upper-income families already have the means to send their children to private schools and support the public education system through taxes, this privilege is not extended to lower-income families. For these families, school choice becomes an essential element in ensuring that their children receive the education they deserve. The introduction of school choice creates a system where a family's ability to purchase an expensive home or pay twice does not determine their access to a quality education. This step is crucial in leveling the playing field and providing equal opportunities for all students, regardless of their socioeconomic background.

4. School choice has been consistently proven to have a profound positive impact on graduation rates. Studies have shown that when students are given the opportunity to participate in school choice programs, they are more likely to

successfully complete their high school education. This is exemplified by the remarkable success of the D.C. Opportunity Scholarship Program, which is specifically designed to support low-income students by offering them the chance to attend private schools of their choice. The data collected from the D.C. Opportunity Scholarship Program presents compelling evidence of the effectiveness of school choice. It reveals an impressive 21 percentage point increase in graduation rates among participating students. This evidence demonstrates the clear benefits of empowering students with the option to select the educational environment that best suits their individual needs. By granting students the freedom to choose their educational path, we are providing them with opportunities to thrive academically and increase their chances of successfully completing high school.

5. School choice initiatives have a positive impact on the quality of local schools through the introduction of competitive pressures. The mere existence of alternative education options fosters improvement. Research indicates that the threat of competition alone generates positive outcomes, as exemplified by empirical studies conducted in Florida and Milwaukee. These studies have shown that the implementation of new school choice opportunities resulted in noticeable enhancements in the academic performance of students in public schools. In Florida, the introduction of school choice

initiatives led to increased competition among schools, forcing them to strive for excellence in order to attract students. As a result, public schools implemented various improvements, such as innovative teaching methods and specialized programs, to distinguish themselves from other educational options. This not only benefited the students attending these schools but also raised the overall educational standards in the community. A similar trend was observed in Milwaukee, where the introduction of school choice options created a healthy competition between public schools and alternative education providers. Public schools in the area recognized the need to improve their offerings to remain competitive and retain students. This led to the implementation of rigorous academic programs, enrichment activities, and additional resources to enhance the learning experience for students.

6. School choice has the potential to greatly enhance accountability within the education system. By giving parents the freedom to choose the schools their children attend, a direct line of accountability is established between schools and parents. This is because parents who are not satisfied with their children's education have the option to transfer them to alternative schools and redirect education funding accordingly. Unlike the centralized, top-down approach employed by district schools, a market-based education system empowers parents as immediate stakeholders in their children's education. This dynamic fosters a

feedback loop that encourages innovative and collaborative solutions to cater to the diverse needs of students. It is essential for policymakers to demonstrate trust in the ability of parents and education providers to work together and drive educational improvements. By implementing school choice, we create an environment where schools are incentivized to provide high-quality education and meet the needs of their students. Competition among schools encourages them to constantly improve and innovate in order to attract and retain students. This not only benefits parents and students by giving them more options, but it also raises the overall quality of education in the system.

7. School choice offers a superior solution for meeting the varied needs of students. Each child possesses a distinct set of learning styles, abilities, and interests. With school choice, parents have the freedom to select educational institutions that are specifically designed to meet their child's unique requirements, resulting in a more individualized and custom-tailored learning experience. By opting for school choice, parents gain the ability to explore a wide range of schools and educational programs that may align more closely with their child's learning preferences. Whether it's a school that focuses on arts and creativity or one that emphasizes STEM education, school choice provides the means to find the perfect fit for each student. This personalized approach to education ensures that students receive the attention and resources they

need to excel academically and maximize their potential for success. Whether a child thrives in smaller class sizes, benefits from specialized support services, or requires a curriculum that aligns with their specific interests, school choice allows parents to make informed decisions that will optimize their child's educational journey.

Moving in the Right Direction

It's important to clarify that school choice encompasses various educational options, such as charter schools, magnet schools, and public schools. However, the statistics provided in this section specifically focus on Education Savings Accounts (ESA), school vouchers, and education tax credit scholarships.

When it comes to providing families with taxpayer funding for private education or homeschooling, several states have implemented policies to support school choice. Notably, Wisconsin emerged as a trailblazer in 1989 by becoming the first state to pass a law creating a school choice program. The Milwaukee Parental Choice Program was introduced to offer eligible students in Milwaukee funding to attend private schools within the city.

Fast forward to 2023, and the momentum for school choice continues to grow. Five states enacted new Education Savings Account (ESA) programs, with four of those programs covering all or most K-12 students. Furthermore, in 2022, two states expanded their existing programs to include all or most students.

Currently, thirteen states have enacted ESA programs. Among these states, Florida, Iowa, Utah, West Virginia,

Arizona, Arkansas, and North Carolina stand out as they have programs that cover all or most students.

In addition, twenty states have implemented voucher programs, offering families more flexibility in choosing the educational environment that best suits their needs.

Twenty-five states have enacted tax-credit programs, providing individuals and businesses with the opportunity to receive tax credits for contributions made to scholarship programs. These scholarship programs allow students to utilize the funds for educational expenses outside of the public school system.

Last but not least, twenty-three states have enacted tax-credit scholarship programs, which allow individuals or businesses to write off their contributions to scholarship programs. These scholarships can then be used to cover various educational expenses beyond the public school system.

Finally, it's worth mentioning that eleven states have implemented policies allowing individuals to write off or deduct their educational expenses from their personal taxes, further supporting the concept of school choice[7].

1. https://www.usnews.com/education/k12/articles/what-school-choice-is-and-how-it-works
2. https://schoolchoicewi.org/wp-content/uploads/2017/07/How-does-school-choice-affect-public-schools.pdf
3. https://www.nea.org/about-nea/media-center/press-releases/supreme-court-decision-funnels-taxpayer-dollars-private-religious-schools
4. https://www.wkrn.com/news/tennessee-politics/gov-lee-announcement-nov-28-2023/
    https://www.foxnews.com/media/tennessee-democrat-calls-gop-governors-school-choice-expansion-plan-real-scam
5. https://www.edchoice.org/school-choice/types-of-school-choice/what-are-school-vouchers-2/
6. https://www.edchoice.org/wp-content/uploads/2022/01/2022-ABCs-FINAL-WEB-002.pdf

https://www.edchoice.org/wp-content/uploads/2023/11/ABCs-2024-Online.pdf

7. https://www.educationnext.org/origins-milwaukee-parental-choice-program-no-struggle-no-progress-fuller/

https://www.edchoice.org/school-choice/types-of-school-choice/education-savings-account/

https://www.edchoice.org/school-choice/programs/wisconsin-milwaukee-parental-choice-program/

14

PRIVATE & CHARTER SCHOOLS

"If you are a Black family living in a Black community, high-quality neighborhood schools have been the dream, not the reality."

Stacy Davis Gates

President of the Chicago Teachers Union and Executive Vice President of the Illinois Federation of Teachers

Charter schools and private schools are at the top of the list of school choices. These two types of schools have distinct approaches to school funding and curriculum decisions. Additionally, they both have commendable track records in terms of educational outcomes. In most cases, both charter and private schools are small, often single-location establishments. However, it's worth noting that Catholic private schools and some charter school organizations have multiple locations.

When it comes to cost, private schools exhibit significant variability depending on their location and exclusivity. On the other hand, charter schools do not have the same level of variation in cost as they are free to attend. Private schools rely solely on enrollment fees for funding. In contrast, charter school funding is a more complex matter that varies slightly from state to state and district to district. On average, charter schools receive approximately 61 percent less funding compared to their public school counterparts.

While teacher's unions argue that public schools are just as good as charter and private schools, it is important to examine the hard data on outcomes and results. It is worth noting that I have made a conscious effort to rely on unbiased data and studies, avoiding those sponsored by unions or any entity with a vested interest in the debate. Gathering this data was a challenge, as the unions and affiliated organizations have flooded the internet and various publications with information contradicting studies that demonstrate better outcomes for alternative school choices.

Let's now take a closer look at each of these school options, analyzing their characteristics and benefits in more detail.

Charter Schools

Charter schools, as are public schools, are funded based on their enrollment, which is also referred to as average daily attendance (ADA). They receive funding from both the district and the state, depending on the number of students attending. However, the funding mechanisms for charter schools vary significantly from their district counterparts, both at the state level and within individual communities.

On a national scale, charter schools receive an average of 61 percent of the funding that conventional district public schools receive. This translates to an average of $6,585 per pupil for charter schools, compared to $10,771 per pupil for district public schools[1].

This disparity in funding highlights the financial challenges that charter schools face. With limited resources, charter schools must find innovative ways to provide a high-quality education to their students.

Despite the funding differences, charter schools do their best to fulfill their mission of providing educational opportunities to students, often with a unique curriculum or educational approach. Some Charter schools are more engineering-centered or STEM-focused. When searching for Charter schools, the focus of their curriculum is typically a part of their mission statement or their charter.

By operating as public schools, charter schools contribute to the overall landscape of public education, providing families with alternative options and fostering healthy competition among schools. This diversity within the public education system ultimately benefits students and promotes a more robust educational environment.

The first charter school, which is an independently operated public school, was established in Minnesota in 1992. Since then, the popularity and enrollment of charter schools have significantly increased. According to the National Center for Education Statistics, around 3.7 million students attended approximately 7,800 charter schools in the fall of 2021. This represents a substantial growth in comparison to previous years. In fact, the enrollment in charter schools more than doubled between 2010 and 2021. Additionally, the number of charter schools themselves grew by almost 50 percent during the same period. Charter schools have also made significant strides in terms of diversity. Over the past decade, these schools have become more racially diverse, contributing to a more inclusive educational landscape[2].

In the fall of 2021, around 8 percent of public schools were charter schools, representing a notable increase from 5 percent a decade earlier. This growth and diversification of charter schools demonstrate their increasing relevance and appeal in the education sector. As the demand for alternative educational options continues to rise, charter schools are playing an important role in providing students with more choices and opportunities for academic success[3].

In a previous chapter on System Error, we discussed several positive statistics related to Charter Schools. However, it is important to note that numerous studies have been conducted comparing traditional public schools and charter schools across different states. These studies consistently show that Charter Schools outperform their public counterparts in terms of results and outcomes. While it is not an absolute statement that all Charter Schools are excellent, the percentage of A-rated Charter Schools in comparison to A-rated public schools is significantly higher. This data indicates that Charter Schools have a higher likelihood of achieving higher ratings and delivering quality education.

It is worth mentioning that this information is based on extensive research and analysis conducted in various states. These findings provide substantial evidence that Charter Schools have a competitive advantage over traditional public schools when it comes to academic performance and overall success.

According to a comprehensive study conducted in 2018, it was found that charter schools in Indiana outperformed traditional public schools in terms of academic ratings. The research revealed that an impressive 20.3 percent of charter schools obtained an A rating in 2017, compared to only 11.4

percent of traditional public schools. These findings were highlighted by Ron Sandlin, a distinguished researcher and the Senior Director of School Performance and Transformation at the Indiana State Board of Education.

Furthermore, the study also examined the academic growth of students attending brick-and-mortar charter schools as compared to their counterparts in traditional public schools. The results indicated that students enrolled in charter schools exhibited slightly more substantial growth in grades 4 through 8, while demonstrating significantly higher levels of academic achievement in high school. These compelling findings not only emphasize the effectiveness of charter schools in Indiana but also provide valuable insights into the benefits of enrolling students in these alternative educational institutions. The report also noted that students with special needs fared better in charters than in traditional public settings[4].

In 2023, EdWeek Magazine conducted a study that examined the performance of students in 6,200 charter schools across the United States. The study revealed that from 2014 to 2019, charter school students showed significant academic growth compared to their peers in traditional public schools. On average, charter school students gained the equivalent of 16 days of learning in reading and six days in math. Moreover, 83 percent of charter school students performed the same as or better than their peers in reading, while 75 percent performed the same as or better in math.

The study also highlighted specific states and cities that witnessed remarkable improvements in school outcomes. For instance, charter school students in New York gained 75 days of reading and 73 days of math compared to traditional public school students. Similarly, Rhode Island and Tennessee experienced significant gains, with students in

Rhode Island gaining 90 days of reading and 88 days of math and Tennessee students gaining 33.5 days of reading and 39 days of math.

Interestingly, this study suggests that the overall performance of charter schools in reading and math has consistently surpassed the national trend since the 2000-01 academic year. While national student performance plateaued during this time period, charter schools continued to excel, as evidenced by data from the National Assessment of Educational Progress (NAEP).

To conduct the study, researchers utilized standardized testing data from state education agencies and schools. They compared the performance of 1,853,000 charter school students with their peers in traditional public schools that they would have otherwise attended.

Margaret "Macke" Raymond, the founder and director of CREDO (Center for Research on Education Outcomes), which operates out of Stanford University, expressed her perspective on the study. She emphasized that the findings do not serve as a comprehensive endorsement of Charter schools but rather highlight the flexibility that charters provide, both to the schools themselves and to their staff. This flexibility enables educators to explore different approaches and experiment with new ideas, ultimately leading to improved outcomes for students.

Rather than advocating for a complete overhaul of the education system, Raymond emphasizes the importance of incremental improvements and adaptation within existing schools. By empowering school teams with the capacity to adapt and experiment, lasting improvements in student performance can be achieved over time[5].

This study underscores the value of charter schools in allowing educators the freedom to pursue effective teaching methods and innovate. By encouraging a culture of continuous improvement, charter schools create an environment where educators can try new strategies without being constrained by rigid standards[6].

One of the most extensive and rigorous studies put together, researchers from the Harvard Graduate School of Education and MIT have recently conducted a groundbreaking study that sheds light on the performance of Charter school students in Boston compared to their peers in other public schools. The results of the study, published in a report by The Boston Foundation titled "Informing the Debate: Comparing Boston's Charter, Pilot and Traditional Schools," are based on an innovative research design using school lotteries to directly compare charter and pilot school students with their peers.

The research team, led by Thomas Kane, faculty director of the Project for Policy Innovation in Education and Professor of Education and Economics at the Harvard Graduate School of Education, and Joshua Angrist, Ford Professor of Economics at MIT, utilized data provided by the Massachusetts Department of Elementary and Secondary Education. They found that charter school students in Boston demonstrate higher levels of achievement than their counterparts in traditional public schools.

The study revealed the positive effects of Charter schools on student achievement at both the middle school and high school levels across various subjects. Notably, there was a significant impact on middle school math, with the effect equivalent to moving a student from the 50th to the 69th percentile in student performance in just one year. This effect was even half of the black-white achievement gap. At the high school level, charter students showed stronger performance in English Language Arts, math, writing topic development, and writing competitions[7].

"This report emphasizes the potential impact of education reform," stated Paul Grogan, president and CEO of the Boston Foundation. He highlighted the need to apply the successful practices of charter and pilot schools to serve all families who desire to benefit from this culture of success, as it can help close the achievement gap that has affected Boston's schools, renowned as one of the best large urban systems in the country[8].

In order to address the common criticism that charter school applicants are "different" from their counterparts in traditional public schools, the research team tracked the outcomes of students who had participated in school admission lotteries. By comparing those who were offered a slot with those who were denied, they were able to show that the students being compared were very similar in terms of family background, motivation, and other relevant factors, except for the likelihood of attending a charter or pilot school.

"At the time of admission, the only difference between applicants who were offered admission and those who were not was a coin flip," explained Kane. "The fact that there are substantial differences in subsequent performance suggests that charter schools are indeed making a significant impact. The next step is to identify the elements that are working in charter schools and incorporate them into traditional public schools to enhance student achievement.[9]"

If you want to read a much deeper dive into Charter Schools, then I highly recommend Dr. Thomas Sowell's book Charter Schools and Their Enemies[10].

Private Schools

The history of private schools in the world extends back hundreds of years. In most countries throughout history, public education was not available to all citizens. Instead, education was reserved for the upper class, mainly males in those societies. In the early days of America, there were no public schools, and children in small townships would take breaks from farm work to attend classes in small one-room classrooms. These classrooms accommodated students of all ages, and the curriculum primarily focused on reading, writing, and arithmetic. If you've ever watched "Little House on the Prairie," you've witnessed a fairly accurate depiction of schools during that time. However, there were variations as not all factors, such as town population and resources, were equal.

Fast forward to the 21st century, and while there are still expensive elite private schools catered to the upper class, there are now more localized private schools available that are somewhat more affordable. Many of these schools are affiliated with churches or have religious leanings, although some are not. And many that are affiliated with churches are not teaching religion in the private school. Interestingly, many teachers I have worked with or interviewed have expressed that if they could afford it, they would send their own children to private schools. While this may not be a glowing endorsement for public schools, it aligns with the historical context we've discussed so far.

According to data from the National Assessment of Educational Progress (NAEP), in the most recent academic year, private school students consistently outperformed their public school counterparts in almost all subjects. Additionally, the National Association of Independent

Schools (NAIS) reports that private school students tend to score higher on college entrance exams such as the SAT[11].

One key advantage of private schools is that they often set enrollment limits to ensure smaller class sizes. This allows teachers to develop closer relationships with their students. On average, the student-to-teacher ratio in private schools is 12:1, which is considerably lower than the ratio of 25:1 or higher in public schools, as stated by the Princeton Review. With smaller class sizes, teachers in private schools can provide individualized attention to each student.

Unlike public schools that are bound by state-mandated testing, private schools, being mainly funded through tuition and donations, are not obligated to follow the same requirements. Therefore, private school teachers can prioritize their students' overall learning experience rather than solely focusing on preparing them to pass standardized tests. This flexibility allows private school teachers to create lesson plans that are more creative and dynamic.

Another advantage of private schools is their autonomy. Unlike schools that are part of larger administrative groups like school districts, private schools operate as independent entities. This means that there are fewer layers of bureaucracy, and issues can be addressed more directly. The organizational structure of private schools typically consists of staff, department heads, the head of the school, and the board. While larger schools may have additional layers, even these institutions maintain relatively thin management structures. According to the most recent data, which is from fall 2019, there were approximately 4.7 million students enrolled in private schools from kindergarten through grade 12, representing about 9percent of the student population[12].

Choosing to send a child to a private school is an investment, with parents spending anywhere from $2,000 to

$32,000 annually, as reported by the National Center for Education Statistics (NCES). Given the significant financial commitment, parents are often more involved in their children's education at private schools compared to public schools. However, this increased involvement also comes with challenges. Private schools consider parents to be clients, taking their goals and aspirations into account when making decisions. As a result, each family's expectations may vary, adding a level of complexity to the school's decision-making process[13].

While teaching in a private school has many advantages, one potential drawback is lower pay. According to the Bureau of Labor Statistics (BLS), the median annual salary for kindergarten teachers in private schools is $46,520, while high school teachers earn a median annual salary of $56,510. In contrast, elementary school teachers in public schools have a median annual salary of $61,760, as reported by PayScale. The reason for this pay discrepancy is that private schools generally do not face teacher shortages and, therefore, do not need to increase their pay scale to attract new teachers[14].

Despite the salary difference, statistics show that private school teachers are not significantly more likely to move to public schools. This can be attributed to the lower stress levels and greater freedom that private school teachers enjoy.

During my research, I had the privilege of engaging in conversations with four experienced teachers who made the transition from public education to private schools. Their unanimous feedback shed light on the immense level of satisfaction and contentment they experienced in their new roles. They emphasized a plethora of advantages that accompanied the switch, including reduced working hours, diminished stress levels, increased flexibility, decreased involvement in politics and bureaucracy, and enhanced behavior management solutions.

Undoubtedly, these teachers did express a desire for higher pay in their new positions. However, they concluded that the benefits of lower stress and greater class autonomy far outweighed the smaller paycheck. It is worth noting that I also had the chance to meet teachers who made the opposite transition, moving from private to public schools in pursuit of a pay increase. Interestingly, they shared their perspectives on the challenges they encountered in their new roles, highlighting the increased difficulty and stress. In fact, one teacher openly expressed doubts about whether the higher salary was worth sacrificing personal happiness.

Academic Performance

If you were to believe the claims made by the teachers union, you would think that private schools fall short of meeting the standards set by public education. However, let's delve into the data provided by the ACT test to gain a more accurate understanding.

In 2018, over 1.9 million students, accounting for approximately 55 percent of high school graduates, took the ACT. Among these test-takers, a total of 198,464 students hailed from private schools. On October 17th, the ACT released its annual report titled "The Condition of College & Career Readiness 2018," which evaluates the preparedness of high school graduates for college.

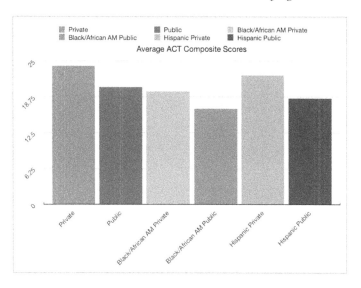

The data reveals that the advantage enjoyed by private schools remained consistent across all subject areas. In English, private school students achieved a mean score of 24.7, while their public school counterparts scored 19.7. Similarly, in reading, private school students achieved a mean score of 24.8 compared to 20.9 for public school students. In math, private school students obtained a mean score of 23.1, surpassing the 20.2 achieved by public school students. Lastly, in science, private school students earned a mean score of 23.4, outperforming the 20.4 achieved by public school students. It's important to note that the ACT scoring scale ranges from 1 to 36, with higher scores indicating greater proficiency[15].

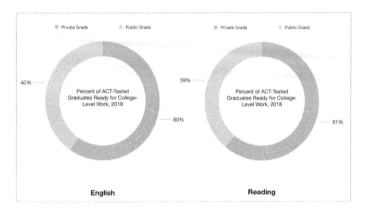

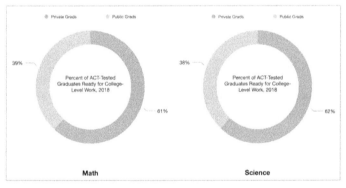

Finally

If you're in the process of choosing a private school or a charter school for your child, I highly recommend scheduling an appointment to visit the school, take a tour of the facilities, and get a comprehensive understanding of what they have to offer. By doing so, you'll have the opportunity to evaluate whether the school aligns with your family's values, educational philosophy, and budget. It's important to remember that each private school operates differently, and not all of them may be well-suited to your child's needs. By exploring multiple options and comparing their offerings, you can make a more informed decision about the best fit for your family. Visiting the school allows you to see firsthand the teaching methods, extracurricular activities, and resources available to students. It also gives you the opportunity to interact with the faculty and staff, who play a crucial role in shaping your child's educational experience. In addition to the practical considerations, it's vital to assess the overall atmosphere and culture of the school. Ultimately, by taking the time to explore different private or charter schools and gathering as much information as possible, you can make an informed decision that will set your child up for success both academically and personally.

---

1. https://edreform.com/2011/09/how-are-charter-schools-fund ed/#:~:text=Nationwidepercent2Cpercent20onpercent20averageper-cent2Cpercent20charterpercent20schools,costpercent20ofpercent20securingperc

2. https://www.edweek.org/policy-politics/charter-schools-now-outper form-traditional-public-schools-sweeping-study-finds/ 2023/06#:~:text=Thepercent20firstpercent20charterper-cent20schoolpercent20opened,50percent20percentpercent20inper-cent20thatpercent20time.

3. https://www.edweek.org/policy-politics/charter-schools-now-outper form-traditional-public-schools-sweeping-study-finds/ 2023/06#:~:text=Studypercent20showspercent20apercent20longper-cent2Dtermpercent20trend&text=Theirpercent20enrollmentper-cent20morepercent20thanpercent20doubled,5percent20percentpercent20aperce

4. https://www.wfyi.org/news/articles/indianapolis-city-charter-innova tion-schools-credo-test-study
      https://files.eric.ed.gov/fulltext/ED594809.pdf

5. https://www.edweek.org/policy-politics/charter-schools-are-outper forming-traditional-public-schools-6-takeaways-from-a-new-study/ 2023/06

6. https://credo.stanford.edu/wp-content/uploads/2021/08/ncss_2013_fi nal_draft.pdf

7. https://cepr.harvard.edu/files/cepr/files/cepr-ma-charter-schools.pdf

8. https://promiseofplace.org/research-evaluation/research-and-evalua
   tion/informing-the-debate-comparing-bostons-pilot-charter
9. https://promiseofplace.org/research-evaluation/research-and-evalua
   tion/informing-the-debate-comparing-bostons-pilot-charter
10. https://www.cato.org/regulation/fall-2020/charter-schools-their-
    enemies
11. https://nces.ed.gov/nationsreportcard/pubs/studies/2006461.aspx
12. https://nces.ed.gov/programs/coe/indicator/cgc/private-school-enroll
    ment
13. https://soeonline.american.edu/blog/pros-and-cons-of-teaching-at-a-
    private-school/
14. https://www.indeed.com/career-advice/pay-salary/private-teacher-
    salary#:~:text=Averagepercent20salarypercent20forpercent20aper-
    cent20privatepercent20schoolpercent20teacher&text=Theper-
    cent20BLSpercent20alsopercent20statespercent20that,schoolspercent20ispercent2
15. https://www.lcs.education/private-school-students-perform-better-on-
    act/

facility.

nt20earlier.

15

HOMESCHOOL

"It is a thousand times better to have common sense without education than to have education without common sense." – *Mark Twain*

Homeschooling is an educational option that allows parents to teach their children at home instead of sending them to school. In today's society, homeschooling has gained acceptance and popularity due to the vast array of resources and opportunities available to homeschooling families. This educational alternative originated in the 1970s and 1980s, driven by both progressive educational reformers aiming to foster children's creativity and conservative evangelical leaders concerned about public school environments. As of 2022, approximately 4.3 million children are being homeschooled, resulting in an increasingly diverse homeschooling community in terms of race, class, and parental motivations[1].

Parents opt for homeschooling for various reasons. Some are concerned about the social environment or academic quality of local public schools. Others want to ensure that their children receive an education aligned with their religious beliefs. Some believe that child-directed learning outside of a traditional classroom setting is more conducive to their children's learning style. Additionally, some parents make the decision to homeschool due to factors such as their children being bullied in school, health issues, or demanding extracurricular schedules. The flexibility of homeschooling provides families with the freedom to tailor their children's education to fit their unique needs. Some children discover that homeschooling aligns well with their natural learning styles and personalities[2].

Let's delve into the opportunities available to parents who have the flexibility to restructure their daily routines to incorporate homeschooling into their lives. This option provides them with the freedom to tailor their children's education to their unique needs and interests while also allowing for a more personalized and individualized learning experience.

While homeschooling is legal across the United States, the extent of oversight and regulations for homeschools vary from state to state. Most states require parents to notify state or local education officials of their intent to home-school, with approximately half of the states having some form of assessment requirement. Additionally, most states have guidelines for the number of instructional days or subject requirements, while a few states impose parent qualification and bookkeeping obligations. However, there are still a handful of states with no specific requirements for homeschooling. The patchwork nature and inconsistent oversight of homeschooling present challenges in ensuring the well-being and educational interests of homeschooled children[3].

Research demonstrates that homeschooled children

can excel academically, particularly when they receive support and resources from their parents. Many home-schooling parents are actively involved and highly motivated in their children's education. They take on the role of facilitators or coordinators, seeking additional resources, tutors, or classes for subjects they may not be proficient in teaching themselves. However, academic success in homeschooled children is not guaranteed. In cases where parents lack motivation or do not prioritize their children's academic progress, homeschooled children may face academic struggles or even fail to receive a proper education.

Homeschooling is not a one-size-fits-all approach, and many parents are unable to dedicate the time and resources necessary for teaching their children at home. However, it's important to note that homeschooling has made significant advancements over the past two decades.

In the past, homeschooled children were often perceived as isolated and lacking socialization opportunities. However, as time progressed, people recognized the potential drawbacks of keeping children at home without social outlets. Today, homeschooled children are actively engaged in a wide range of social activities outside of their homes. They participate in homeschool cooperatives, where they collaborate with other homeschooling families to provide a comprehensive education experience. These cooperatives offer opportunities for interaction and collaboration among students of different ages and backgrounds.

In addition to homeschool cooperatives, homeschooled children also participate in extracurricular activities such as dance and music lessons, church and Sunday school activities, field trip groups, and various classes, clubs, and organizations. These activities allow homeschooled children to interact with peers, develop friendships, and cultivate important social skills.

The advent of the internet has further expanded the socialization opportunities for homeschooled children. Online communities and forums provide platforms for collaboration, discussion, and networking with other homeschooling families. Homeschooled children can engage in virtual classrooms, participate in online group projects, and connect with students from around the world.

It's worth noting that the increasing acceptance of homeschooling by society has also played a significant role in expanding socialization opportunities. As the stigma surrounding homeschooling diminishes, more families are actively seeking social outlets for their children.

An increasing number of states now allow homeschooled children to enroll in public school part-time, enabling them to take individual classes or participate in extracurricular activities such as athletics. Some studies indicate that up to 20 percent of homeschooled students choose to enroll in public school part-time. Certain states even offer programs such as public school at home or public/charter correspondence programs that allow children to be educated at home while still benefiting from enrollment in a public school system. Additionally, "cyber-charters" and innovative charter schools have emerged as popular options among homeschoolers, providing children with the opportunity to attend physical school for classes once or twice a week while receiving the majority of their education at home. The increasing diversity in educational options offers homeschooling families a plethora of flexible and creative alternatives.

The education resource that I was a part of creating was incredibly popular among homeschooled families. This comes as no surprise, as homeschool families are often responsible for finding and purchasing their own educational materials. We were fortunate to have several homeschool cooperatives that actively utilized our resources and regularly engaged with our website. In fact, the homeschool community quickly became the fastest-growing segment of our business[4].

Snapshot of Homeschoolers

Public education faces numerous challenges, such as social education issues and controversial subject matter, as outlined in various reports and studies. These issues have significantly contributed to a surge in the number of families choosing to homeschool their children. This shift represents one of the most significant increases in home education in recent history.

Research conducted by the National Home Education Research Institute (NHERI) indicates that during the 2020/2021 academic year, there were approximately 3.7 million homeschooled students in the United States alone. Additionally, from late March to early May 2022, 5.22 percent of all school-aged children received their education at home, reflecting a Compound Annual Growth Rate (CAGR) of 10.1 percent for homeschooling between the years 2016 and 2021.

Homeschool 2022	Homeschool 2021	Homeschool 2020	Homeschool 2019
4.3 Million	3.721 Million	2.65 Million	2.5 Million

The Census Experimental Household Pulse survey has shown that the COVID-19 pandemic had a significant bearing on the rising trend of homeschooling. According to the survey data, the number of households opting for home-schooling in the U.S. doubled during the pandemic period between March 2020 and March 2021. The migration to homeschooling during and after the pandemic was driven by several factors that became apparent during the lock-downs. Firstly, parents who were at home with their children while they attended online classes became aware of the curriculum and ideologies being taught. This revelation alarmed many parents who were previously unaware of the social issues being addressed in schools. Secondly, the resis-tance to reopening schools in various states left parents with no choice but to homeschool their children. Additionally, as many parents continued to work from home, they saw homeschooling as a viable option to ensure their children's education continued uninterrupted.

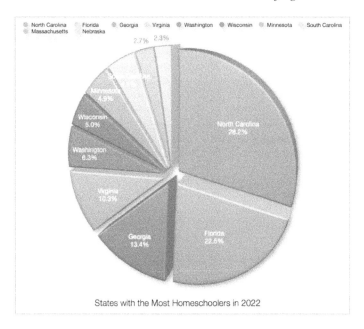

States with the Most Homeschoolers in 2022

NHERI's data also reveals that North Carolina, Florida, and Georgia are the states with the highest numbers of homeschooled students, respectively. In 2021, North Carolina led the way with 179,900 homeschooled students, with Florida closely trailing at around 143,431 and Georgia with 85,510 students.

Homeschool demographic consists of 52 percent female students and 48 percent male students. The breakdown across grade levels shows that 23 percent of homeschooled students are in Kindergarten through 2nd grade, 22 percent are in 3rd through 5th grade, 24 percent are in 6th through 8th grade, and 31 percent include those in 9th through 12th grade. This according to a study by the National Center for Education Statistics.

Reasons for Homeschooling	Percentage
Safe environment concerns	25%
Bad academic quality	14.5%
Provide religious instruction	13%
Provide moral instruction	6.6%
Health problems	3.6%
Special needs	7.3%
Provide non-traditional education	7.7%
Emphasis on family	8.3%
Other	14%

Interestingly, homeschooling has shown a gradual increase among minority communities, primarily due to concerns about safety within traditional schooling environments. With safety as a major concern, high school-level students make up the majority of homeschooled individuals, with parents viewing the home as a considerably safer environment for their teenagers, protecting them from potentially harmful encounters such as physical violence, drug exposure, or inappropriate sexual incidents.

Geographically, 34 percent of homeschooling families surveyed reside in urban areas, 31 percent in rural regions, 28 percent in cities, and a smaller portion, about 7 percent, live in towns.

According to the Home School Legal Defense Association, strict laws regulating homeschooling exist in 10 percent of U.S. states, including New York, Vermont, Rhode Island, Massachusetts, and Pennsylvania. A further 18 states have moderate regulations, with low regulations evident in 16 states.

White	Black	Hispanic	Asian	Other
70%	6%	17%	2%	6%

Category	Price Range
Curriculum	$350-$750
Supplies & Materials	$150-$300
Field Trips	$100-$250
Extracurriculars	$100-$500
Total	$700-$1,800

Interestingly, 11 states provide parents complete freedom when it comes to homeschooling. For instance, in New Jersey, parents are not obligated to inform any authority about their decision to homeschool their children, and likewise, there is no need to provide proof that their children have indeed been homeschooled.

In stark contrast, Florida maintains strict regulations on homeschooling, wherein parents actively seek suitable adult instructors for their children's education. Unlike other states, there are no mandatory homeschooling hours stipulated for students in Florida, allowing flexibility with regard to learning both inside and outside their homes[5].

Is Homeschooling Effective

There are numerous advantages to homeschooling compared to traditional institutional schooling. One of the key benefits is that homeschooling enables children to tailor their education to suit their unique nature and schedule. When homeschooling is well-planned and organized, it not only provides opportunities for socialization but also yields highly effective outcomes. By allowing students to focus on their specific career interests and incorporating extension courses, homeschooling provides a well-rounded education that effectively prepares students for college.

Furthermore, homeschooling offers additional benefits when homeschooled students have the opportunity to participate in extracurricular activities, community sports, and community service groups. These experiences contribute to a holistic education and further enhance the development of homeschooled students.

A study conducted by Michael Cogan at the University of St. Thomas revealed that homeschooled students have a higher graduation rate compared to students from public schools. In fact, homeschooled students graduated college at a rate of 66.7 percent, which is 10 percent higher than their counterparts.

In addition to higher graduation rates, homeschooled students also demonstrate superior performance on standardized academic achievement exams. According to The National Home Education Research Institute, in 2015, homeschoolers scored 15 percent-30 percent higher than students in public schools. This remarkable achievement holds true regardless of the educational level or financial status of the parents, highlighting the effectiveness of homeschooling as an educational approach.

Clearly, not all homeschooling experiences are identical, and it is evident that the educational level may vary considerably. It is possible that a parent who did not excel academically during their school years may need to refresh their knowledge in certain subjects to teach their children effectively. As a result, many parents opt to send their high school-aged children to external educational institutions. The complexity of certain lessons may surpass the parent's educational background or comprehension. However, it is worth noting that homeschooling parents who devote their time and effort to educating their children have a greater determination and focus on their children's academic progress. They have the flexibility to slow down or speed up the pace of learning to suit their children's individual needs and understanding. This adaptability may contribute to the success of homeschooled students in standardized tests such as the SAT or ACT. Additionally, the availability of high-quality educational resources online serves as a valuable aid in the homeschooling process and has made it easier to acquire quality teaching tools and materials[6].

1. https://fordhaminstitute.org/national/commentary/hard-lessons-veteran-homeschooler#:~:text=Accordingpercent20topercent20thepercent20Censuspercent20Experimental,steadypercent20andpercent20expectedpercent20topercent20continue.
2. https://nces.ed.gov/programs/coe/indicator/tgk/homeschooled-children
3. https://hslda.org/legal
4. https://www.homeschoolfacts.com/hybrid-homeschooling-as-an-alternative-education-model/
   https://nces.ed.gov/blogs/nces/post/higher-rates-of-homeschooled-students-than-enrolled-students-participated-in-family-learning-activities-in-2016
   https://www.thehomeschoolmom.com/what-is-homeschool-co-op/
5. https://www.nheri.org/how-many-homeschool-students-are-there-in-the-united-states-during-the-2021-2022-school-year/
   https://hslda.org/legal
6. https://orisonorchards.com/homeschooling-statistics/#:~:text=Michaelpercent20Coganpercent20ofpercent20thepercent20University,studentspercent20frompercent20publicpercent20highpercent20schools.
   https://www.nheri.org/research-facts-on-homeschooling/

16

CURRICULUM

*No! Thats not the way we learned it in class! You'll never pass
the test doing it the most efficient way.*

Curriculum is a term used to describe the collection of
courses and subjects offered in a school, college, university,
or any educational institution. Dictionary.com defines it as
the "aggregate of courses of study given in a school, college,
university, etc." It can also refer to the regular or specific
course of study within an educational institution.

For individuals who are not familiar with the term "curriculum," it encompasses all the subjects and courses that
are taught in a school, as well as the schedule and grade
level at which they are introduced. It is essentially a blue-
print that outlines what students will learn and when they
will learn it.

Currently, every school system across the country is
actively developing its own curriculum map, either by
purchasing pre-made curricula or creating its own. The
intention behind this is to ensure that all the schools in the
district are aligned in teaching the same curriculum.

However, as we will explore later, the implementation of a unified curriculum, such as the Common Core, faced significant challenges and did not yield the desired results.

The specifics of what is covered in a curriculum and when it is taught can vary from district to district. For example, the introduction of graphing trigonometric functions could occur in 6th grade, 8th grade, or any other grade level, depending on the curriculum framework being implemented.

Curriculum plays a crucial role in shaping the educational experience for students, as it determines what knowledge and skills they acquire during their academic journey.

In 2012, there was a rallying cry in many states to get rid of the Common Core Curriculum. Before the 1990's changes to a state's curriculum took place, on average, about once every ten years. Since the 1990's, and ever since politicians began campaigning with education reform as an issue, many states have changed their curriculum, on average, every 3 to 4 years. While the changes have been made in the name of improving education, some very clear negative consequences follow frequent curriculum changes.

When I was in school, and I didn't understand my math homework, my dad would tell me to get out the textbook, and we'd follow along with the chapter that my homework was based on, and with plenty of fussing, we'd work through it till my homework was finished. No more than a decade ago, textbooks served this purpose. Most people I talk to assume the reason textbooks have disappeared from their children's book bags is that they are now digital or online. However, the same parents who believe they are digital have never seen them online and couldn't show you where their child's school is hiding them. Most textbook publishers do make digital, online versions of their textbooks, but very few school systems have purchased the rights to distribute them to their students. In reality, the death of textbooks has not come at the hands of the internet but rather the unintended consequences of state and federal politics. But don't expect the politicians to recognize the role they are playing in the extinction of textbooks. So now that I've pointed the finger, let me explain how the political promises and good intentions of those trying to get re-elected have led directly to the extinction of textbooks.

Let me go back to 2011; it was national news at the time that Common Core would become the curriculum used in most states. In Georgia, this replaced the curriculum that Georgia had only adopted four years earlier. As I began to talk with teachers and discuss my company's decision to use Common Core as our curriculum map, a trend in their responses became noticeable. In a nutshell, they warned us not to get too hung up on any one type of curriculum because it will change again very soon. The consensus was that Common Core wouldn't last more than three or four years. At the time, none of the teachers had seen or taught Common Core yet. Their prognostication was based on history. Common Core was instituted in Georgia and most states in 2012. By 2015 Georgia changed the curriculum again, making the teacher's predictions accurate. Most states changed or renamed their curriculum in 2015 or 2016, moving away from Common Core.

Why am I telling you this story? Every time a state changes its curriculum, the county must find new books to follow along with the new curriculum. An average-sized county will pay millions for math textbooks alone. In the past, a purchase that large wasn't as much of a burden since the books would often wear out before the curriculum would wear out. In most states around the country, curriculum changes have become commonplace. In the 1970s and 80s, almost no states made significant curriculum changes. Starting in the '90s, politicians began seizing on education to stump on during election seasons. In most cases, the mantra was a cry to increase test scores and increase rigor, which state, local, or federal politicians do not know how to do, so they changed the one thing that would be noticeable: the curriculum. The average state now changes curriculum every 3 to 4 years. The average county can not spend millions of dollars every 3 to 4 years, and so they have settled on going forward without textbooks. I can point to several counties in Florida and Georgia that purchased new math textbooks in 2009, only to have all the textbooks sitting in warehouses three years later when the curriculum was changed to Common Core.

I'm not going to give a thumbs up or down on anyone's curriculum; we'll get into that later, but every time we elect people who promise to change education, we should understand that those changes are often very costly and, in my view, a huge waste of school funds. Counties must adapt tests and paperwork, and everyone from teachers to administrators must re-learn and re-organize what they are teaching. Any books purchased based on the former curriculum must be sidelined, and new materials must be bought. States do not provide a change of curriculum fund for the counties, which means that expenses come out of the county's general education funds. They use the same funds to upgrade schools and hire employees.

If this is all new to you, that's because most changes are kept quiet, and some curriculum changes are more subtle. For instance, the backlash and anger about Common Core caused most states to declare they were moving on from Common Core. But did they really? NO. They simply renamed, relabeled, and re-organized common core to reduce the backlash. Many did, however, tinker with the curriculum map. Moving subjects and topics around in response to parents complaints.

To provide further clarification, it is important to note that the implementation of curriculum changes has evolved over time. While the Common Core initiative stood out as it was driven by the federal government, nowadays, most curriculum alterations occur at the district or local level, often without much public attention. Previously, the presence of textbooks and workbooks limited the flexibility of making such changes. However, with the shift away from traditional instructional materials, counties now have the freedom to procure and implement different curricula regularly.

These shifts can be motivated by various factors. For instance, grants provided alongside a particular curriculum may incentivize counties to adopt it. Additionally, some curricula are marketed as solutions to address declining academic performance. Interestingly, the rationale behind these decisions is not always openly discussed, even among teachers who are at the forefront of classroom instruction. In fact, many educators may find themselves adjusting to new changes just as they become accustomed to the previous ones.

The Downside of Changing Curriculum

While the changes have been made in the name of improving education, some very clear negative consequences follow frequent curriculum changes.

First, curriculum changes are often sold to the public as a means of making grades better when, in fact, the opposite result often occurs, especially in the short term. Since curriculum changes happen about every 3 to 4 years, there is rarely long-term term data to show whether the curriculum changes produced positive results. In fact, it's increasingly rare these days for a student to graduate under the same curriculum they started in. To understand why grades would be adversely affected by a change in curriculum, you must understand the primary differences between curricula. Math curriculums vary, mostly by what grades you introduce and teach the core math domains that are commonly taught from kindergarten through the twelfth grade. For example, one math curriculum may teach solving for decimals in fifth grade, while another may not teach it until sixth grade. If you can understand that example, then it will be easy to understand how changing the math curriculum too often can introduce gaps in a student's math knowledge.

To explain this, let me use another example. In the state of Georgia, students who graduated in 2016 and 2017 endured three curriculum changes from kindergarten to graduation. A student who was in middle school when the change to Common Core took effect had math lessons that they were supposed to learn in the grade above suddenly move back to the grade they were leaving. Since math education builds upon itself to get progressively harder, this left many students with gaps in their understanding of math. They were now trying to learn math when they had missed the previous building block to understanding it. Those same students had the same thing happen to their math curriculum again in their freshman or sophomore year in high school when the change away from Common Core began. Introducing more gaps in their math education.

Some states have tried to stagger the introduction of the new curriculum by introducing changes at the elementary and middle school levels first and slowing the transition at the higher grade levels. But teachers often complain that the transition is usually two years or less, hardly enough time to make a difference. At this point, it is impossible to know what curriculum works best because we never see a curriculum in place long enough for students to finish using the same curriculum they started.

Second, if you've read this far into the book, you undoubtedly have seen how frequent changes to the curriculum cause stress and frustration for many teachers. Often, curriculum changes come with a lack of resources to mirror the changes. The end-of-the-year assessments are often a year or two behind the new curriculum, so the teachers who are being forced to teach the new curriculum will find that their students are now being assessed in the old way. Furthermore, many state curriculum changes come with new methods that must be learned and mastered with very little time to prepare.

I'll let the readers make up their minds as to the value, good or bad, of future changes to the curriculum in their states. The curriculum should be finely tuned and adjusted rather than uprooted and made over. From my point of view, there are much more effective changes needed to education that would cost less and make a much bigger difference in the education of our children. If politicians understood the inner workings of education, they would have already made proposals that dealt with the real needs of schools and not the proposals that sit well on a billboard.

The Rise and Fall Common Core

A report by Elaine McArdle from Harvard provides a comprehensive overview of the Common Core standards. I will give you the bullet points. Common Core standards were developed in 2009 by a group of educators and assessment experts in response to a request from the National Governors Association and the Council of Chief State School Officers. The standards gained rapid acceptance, with 40 states and the District of Columbia adopting them in 2010. Over the next two years, five additional states also embraced the standards.

While the Common Core standards received support from a wide range of stakeholders, including U.S. Secretary of Education Arne Duncan, former Florida Governor Jeb Bush, and the business community, there were also concerns raised by some parents. Particularly, some parents found the math component of the standards to be challenging, as highlighted by comedian Louis C.K., who thanked educators for making his kids hate math. Furthermore, critics argued that the adoption of these standards lacked sufficient democratic processes and empirical evidence to support their value. There were also suspicions regarding the potential influence of corporate interests and the significant funding provided by the Bill & Melinda Gates Foundation.

Starting in 2014, several states began to withdraw their support for the Common Core standards. Indiana was the first state to back out, followed by South Carolina and Oklahoma. Other states were also considering slowing down the implementation of the standards. A notable shift in support came from Louisiana Governor Bobby Jindal, who had initially been a strong proponent of the Common Core but later opposed it. Wisconsin Governor Scott Walker also called for the removal of the standards.

Proponents of the Common Core standards, who were once enthusiastic about their adoption, found themselves facing opposition and attempted to address concerns. They emphasized the importance of giving the standards a chance and highlighted their focus on critical thinking and reasoning, which they believed would better prepare students for higher education and the workforce. Moreover, they expressed concerns that abruptly abandoning or stalling the Common Core standards after four years of preparation could disrupt teachers and students without providing a suitable alternative.

Amity Conkright, one of the contributors to the English and Language Arts portion of the Common Core, pointed out that the standards demanded increased rigor, with greater emphasis on text complexity and higher reading levels. She also highlighted that the standards aimed to develop practical skills needed in real-life situations, such as technical and writing skills.

Professor Paul Reville, former Secretary of Education for Massachusetts, explained that the central concept of the Common Core was to provide a high-quality education to all K–12 students across the nation, regardless of their geographic location. This notion resonated with governors who were concerned about the significant variations in curricula among the nation's 14,000 school districts, which disadvantaged some students purely due to where they lived.

However, Professor Reville's statement took on a different perspective a few years later. The increased complexity of the Common Core standards, particularly in math, led some districts to manipulate grading and scores to artificially boost the performance of low-performing students and schools. This undermined the idea of uniform standards across the board and highlighted the need to address the educational challenges faced by inner-city schools and failing districts.

Another concern raised by Professor Eleanor Duckworth was the limited involvement of K-12 teachers in the development of the standards. She expressed skepticism about the standards devised without significant input from educators and questioned the top-down approach of imposing standards nationwide.

The math component of the Common Core standards attracted the most criticism. The focus on "conceptual" math, aimed at developing problem-solving skills applicable to various aspects of life, required students to understand the rationale behind correct answers. This shift posed difficulties for many parents in helping their children with homework. It also required significant adjustments from teachers.

Considering the implementation challenges and criticisms, opponents of the Common Core standards argued that they seemed like a federal mandate despite the fact that states were not obliged to adopt them but were incentivized with federal funding.

In addition, the expansion of testing and assessments was a contentious issue. Parents were dissatisfied with the difficulty of the math assessments, especially as they struggled to comprehend the new math methods. Teachers also expressed frustration as their evaluations became tied to their students' performance on the assessments.

Ultimately, the long-term impact of the Common Core standards will remain unknown, as they were gradually phased out from most state curriculums. The concerns raised by teachers about curriculum changes and the lack of firsthand experience of K-12 schools among academics involved in developing new ideas are worth considering in reflecting on this situation[1].

For Rigor Sake

For the past several years, when I was in meetings with educators, the word rigor has come up. It's always under the response of "increasing the rigor" or "we must increase the rigor." States and local administrations around the country have had the rallying cry to increase the rigor of their curriculum branded on their core message. In most states, the curriculum for math is so much harder than it was 25 years ago that kids today are learning math in 5th grade that people in their 30s didn't learn until 8th or 9th grade. What's funny about this mantra to increase rigor is it coincides with the same concerns that every state and local school system has about falling test scores. I've yet to hear anyone make the connection that the increased rigor may have been increased too much. Please understand that I'm all for increasing the goals and intellect of our kids, but sometimes, in the process, we must stop and make sure that common sense has prevailed. If the rigor is so tough that more and more of your students aren't getting the lesson, does it make sense? Maybe there's a correlation between the increase in rigor and the increased number of students being put into special ed programs? I've even had a teacher tell me that half of the students in special ed or RTI programs wouldn't be considered "low" if they had to perform at the education levels of the 1990s. That's sad when you think about why some kids give up or why they feel like they've fallen so far behind that school is a hopeless cause. Then, we as a society blame the teachers because they failed to teach the students. Is it possible that the students weren't ready for the curriculum? When I talk with college academics who study learning, they often talk about how students, especially those below ten years old, develop at very different rates. A group of 10 students who are starting out in elementary school will progress at different speeds but, given the right attention, can all be on the same academic level by 7th or 8th grade. That is why kindergarten students who had more pre-K and early learning time before entering kindergarten are academically higher entering kindergarten than the average student their age but often are not smarter on average by the end of 5th grade. Some would argue that this is the idea behind special education, and maybe that's true, but a special education teacher continues to try to teach the current curriculum through more direct attention. As one teacher put it, "They are trying to shove too much knowledge into their heads at too young of an age."

One new feature of the math curriculum, to increase the rigor of math, is teaching multiple methods or strategies for solving the same math problem.

Most parents have heard their child say, "That's not how I'm supposed to do it." For instance, to add two numbers, you might use the standard algorithm, the way most of us learned it, by stacking one number on top of another and adding down through each place value column (see illustration to the right). Now they must use adding in chunks, counting on, use compensation, use place value, using friendly numbers, using a number line, or using the counting method. In fact, teachers in some districts are not allowed to teach the standard algorithm until after 5th grade. It seems logical that a student who understands every strategy would be better at math. And indeed, that is true. However, the consensus that I hear from teachers is that the students who are already good in math are the students who understand all the strategies. The students who struggle in math are now more confused by all the

$$\begin{array}{r} 16 \\ +17 \\ \hline 33 \end{array}$$

Standard Algorithm

methods, which shows up even larger when you require them to use one method over another[2].

I understand that academics who love math think that the world would be great if all students could see using mental math, speak math, and love math. That's not reality. Most parents and many teachers, who will not say it publicly, believe that the right answer is the right answer, and if one child needs to use the standard algorithm and one prefers another method, even using their fingers, the correct answer should be the goal. There's nowhere else in life where you are told you must be able to perform your task successfully using every possible method. Our bosses just want the correct numbers on a report. We want our quarterback to put points on the board; whether he gets it done by passing, running, or handing it off is less important to us. Some kids are visual learners, while others may be more analytical. Let them solve the problems using whatever process or strategy makes sense to them.

It is true that increasing the complexity or difficulty of something will challenge and strengthen those who practice it. But just as there is a ceiling to how much each person will deadlift no matter how much they practice, there's a ceiling to what the average student will do efficiently when the complexity rises above their ability.

When I was in high school, we used to ask our trig teacher when we'd ever use this outside of the classroom. Now, 7th graders are being asked to solve Polynomial Functions using Synthetic Division. Something that they are too young to have a need for at their age and have no understanding of. For me, one of my children was good in math, and one was average. There are plenty of good careers where you do not need math. To be clear, I'm not pointing any fingers, and I think everyone is doing what they feel is best and with the best of intentions. But I know from experience that sometimes when we set a goal that we must "reach at all costs," we lose sight of the "cost."

The funniest part about these arguments is that many teachers have told me they can get their students to learn higher math if allowed to teach the way they know how. But they get handcuffed to use additional strategies by the districts they teach. Often something that was only recently introduced. Once the teacher's autonomy is taken away, you are now asking the teachers and the students to learn something new, often at the same time.

---

1. https://www.gse.harvard.edu/ideas/ed-magazine/14/09/what-happened-common-core
2. https://www.sciencedirect.com/science/article/abs/pii/S0732312397900079

17

SOCIAL & EMOTIONAL LEARNING

"If someone is going down the wrong road, he doesn't need motivation to speed them up. What they need is someone to educate them to turn them around. "
    Jim Rohn

Social & Emotional Learning (SEL) is a multifaceted concept that encompasses various aspects of personal growth and development. It includes self-awareness, self-management, social awareness, relationship skills, and responsible decision-making. Originally, SEL was designed to support children who faced challenges in managing their social and emotional well-being, which could hinder their academic progress or their emotional maturity.

Over time, the scope of SEL has expanded beyond its initial focus on children's understanding of their own circumstances. It has evolved to address broader societal issues, such as power dynamics and the impact of oppression and dominance on children's experiences and learning. This reimagined perspective is often associated with the Diversity, Equity, and Inclusion (DEI) movement, which emphasizes the importance of creating equitable learning environments.

However, there has been some criticism and concerns raised regarding the direction in which SEL is heading. Some argue that the notion of ensuring equality of outcome is unrealistic and can potentially undermine the importance of individual effort. They believe that guaranteeing equal opportunities, rather than equal outcomes, should be the focus.

Another criticism pertains to the expanded scope of SEL and its potential impact on young children. Critics argue that introducing complex concepts such as victim/oppressor dynamics, gender ideology, and explicit sexual content at a developmentally inappropriate age can undermine children's innocence. They contend that educational materials and programs should prioritize age-appropriate content and ensure that children are not exposed to topics that may be beyond their comprehension or emotional maturity[1].

Concerns have been raised specifically about books that contain inappropriate sexual content being included in school libraries. While these books may be written and illustrated in a way that appears appealing to young children, the explicit content within them raises red flags. Parents who have protested against the inclusion of such materials argue that their presence goes against the principles of age-appropriate education and can potentially have a negative impact on children's well-being. And that the content appears to have no educational value except to groom young kids for early sexual activity.

Furthermore, there are books like "The Long Dark Shadow" by Allyn Walker, which attempt to de-stigmatize the desires of "Minor Attracted Persons" or what is commonly referred to as pedophiles. This normalization of such desires raises alarm among parents and creates a genuine cause for concern[2].

The convergence of these ideologies, SEL, and MAPs, is concerning to parents, especially considering the rise in the crime of sex trafficking of minors. It is crucial to address these legitimate concerns and ensure that educational materials prioritize the well-being and appropriate development of children.

Transformative SEL

SEL, or Social and Emotional Learning, has evolved to a new level known as Transformative SEL, which places a strong emphasis on building robust relationships between young people and adults to encourage co-learning. This approach goes beyond individual growth and delves into critically examining the root causes of inequity while also collaboratively developing solutions that promote well-being at personal, community, and societal levels. In Transformative SEL, responsible decision-making expands beyond individual choices and encompasses the collective. It embraces ethical responsibility, distributive justice, and collective well-being. The aim of distributive justice is to allocate resources equally to achieve equitable outcomes, highlighting a sense of collectivism, or socialism, in the learning process. This aligns with the ideology found in Karl Marx's writings on equity and collectivism.

An influential organization driving the implementation of Transformative SEL within the DEI (Diversity, Equity, and Inclusion) field is CASEL. Their mission is to address and dismantle inequity while promoting intentional outcomes through SEL. Their ultimate goal is to achieve equity. CASEL relies on various forms of data collected from our children to shape strategies and policies that cultivate anti-racist mindsets and achieve equitable outcomes. This data includes diversity surveys, mental health questionnaires, and bias testing.

CASEL obtains the necessary data from schools, which may then share or sell data-mining contracts to organizations like the for-profit Panorama Education, DEI consultants such as The Glasgow Group, and research collaboratives like SPARC (School Participatory Action Research Collaborative). SPARC, a consortium of private schools, collaborates with the University of Pennsylvania's Graduate School of Education to improve school culture, policy, and practice. While the intentions may appear vague, it is clear that these organizations utilize the data to introduce concepts such as Critical Race Theory, gender theories, and sexuality to our children.

Professors from The University of Pennsylvania involved with SPARC focus on empowering students to become social justice activists. This has been reported by Forbes and openly acknowledged on the organization's website. Unfortunately, accessing this information has become increasingly challenging as organizations remove web pages from their websites. For example, NAIS recently took down the webpage listing its Officers and Executive Board to remove the faces and names of the people involved.

In the field of education, the National Association of Independent Schools (NAIS) plays a significant role in implementing the CASEL framework for its Annual Conference on Social and Emotional Learning (SEL) presentations. They also have influence over independent schools seeking accreditation by advocating for the application of transformative SEL practices in various aspects of education, including classes, sports, service learning, and field trips. NAIS emphasizes that for SEL to be truly authentic and equity-focused, it should actively address systemic racism and oppression. Without the implementation of Transformative SEL, new private schools may not receive accreditation from CASEL. It is important to note that to date, most private schools are not involved with CASEL, only a select group, but that list is growing.

Some individuals argue that this approach aligns closely with Critical Race Theory (CRT), which examines how race and racism are embedded in institutions. NAIS also conducts its own data collection through AIM (Assessment of Inclusivity and Multiculturalism) surveys to provide schools with strategic equity goals.

Another significant entity in this landscape is Big Tech, referring to large technology companies. These organizations engage in data mining, research, and strategy development and receive funding from progressive education entities such as Emerson Collective, XQ Institute, and the Chan-Zuckerberg Initiative. Tech titans like Laurene Powell Jobs and Mark Zuckerberg support these entities. However, critics argue that these groups are using our children as involuntary test subjects in their efforts to promote cultural Marxism. Additionally, they leverage their power to label dissenting parents as domestic terrorists, as evidenced by the recent actions of United States Attorney General Merrick Garland.

The amount of time dedicated to SEL by teachers who may be ill-equipped or inadequately prepared to understand the complex theoretical and psychological aspects of this approach has a negative impact on the teaching of core academic skills. Valuable instructional time is redirected towards group projects and "grading for equity." It is important to note that, according to critics, the ultimate goal of SEL is to foster a mindset of activism and collectivism (Marxism)[3].

Where Common Sense Ends

It is important to acknowledge that life does not always unfold in a fair and equal manner for everyone, no matter how much we tinker with the details and options. While it is tempting to believe that everyone should start off on the same footing, the reality is quite different. Celebrating the achievements of individuals who have overcome significant challenges in their lives and achieved success is commendable. However, it is crucial to strike a balance between recognizing personal responsibility and acknowledging the external factors that may contribute to one's circumstances. This is why equal outcomes will never work and never be a reality.

This was the stated goal of all socialist and communist dictators, but to date, no one can show me a socialist or communist country where equity was a reality. Someone told me in a conversation that China's citizens were all equal thanks to the government. Thats true! Equally poor, unless you are a member of the elite class in China. The citizens of China have little or no autonomy and have no opportunities to strive for greater circumstances in their lives.

Equity cannot be achieved without equity of effort, a concept that highlights the inherent differences in work ethic amongst individuals. The notion of changing human nature to eliminate these disparities is a futile pursuit.

Throughout history, human nature has demonstrated that some individuals will consistently work harder while others may prefer to rely on the efforts of their peers. This divergence in effort can have profound consequences, as exemplified by the early colonies in America.

When the first colonies initially distributed farmland as shared property, unforeseen challenges emerged. Unfortunately, some people chose not to exert the same level of effort in cultivating crops and maintaining the land as others did. Consequently, they consumed more than their fair share, leading to famine and what economists refer to as the "tragedy of the commons." The absence of equal effort distribution resulted in a strained dynamic, with resentment growing amongst those who contributed more.

However, the situation took a transformative turn when the colony's governor, William Bradford, advocated for a different approach. He proposed that each family be assigned a parcel of land to treat as their own. This shift from communal ownership to private property had a profound impact. It instilled a sense of personal responsibility and incentivized individuals to invest more in cultivating their land. As a result, a significant increase in corn planting occurred, marking a departure from the previous scarcity. Private property became the catalyst for ensuring an abundant food supply, as those who invested greater effort reaped the rewards, while others were compelled to step up their work efforts to survive.

How does this relate to social and emotional learning (SEL)? Well, it is evident that in this scenario, those who exerted the most effort experienced greater success and accumulated more wealth. They were able to generate income by selling the surplus food they cultivated. On the other hand, individuals who lamented their lack of wealth argued that it was unfair for others to have more. However, it is worth noting that in this straightforward illustration, those who possessed more wealth worked diligently and intelligently to attain their additional prosperity[4].

Neither DEI or SEL promote the idea that effort is the key to success. Rather, it teaches the opposite. It teaches children to be resentful of those who have more or who have chosen to exert more effort than others. This can create a mindset that diminishes the value of hard work and perseverance. Instead of encouraging individuals to strive for excellence, these approaches may inadvertently foster a sense of entitlement and discourage personal growth. It is important to recognize that while factors like privilege and opportunities can shape outcomes, it is ultimately individual effort and determination that lead to success. This is why most wealthy families are only wealthy for 1 or 2 generations, because the children and grandchildren, who did not earn the wealth, do not understand or put forth the effort to create the same success that lead to their families wealth.

Teaching children to blame others or the world around them for their problems is not productive. In fact, I view critical theory as kindergarten thinking. As a parent, I understand that children often express their discontent when they perceive others as having more than they do or when they expect everyone to share, even if they themselves haven't put in the effort to earn more. The practice of critical theory teaches kids to continue to think this way. If you tell kids to always find the problems in every situation, they will always find the problems even when the problems are not real or are not affecting their situation. It's also raising kids to grow up and be unhappy. If you are programmed to identify how you are oppressed, you live life weary of how your situation might be better if not for someone else. This type of mindset doesn't teach kids to look at themselves as the reason they have problems in their life. It also fails to teach that everyone has talents and nature gifts that sometimes lead to a person earning more because their talents just happen to pay better. The athlete who can hit a 99 mile an hour fast ball 400 feet. That person, based on our societies love of sports, will earn millions because there aren't very many people with that gift. Just as very few people can write a hit song. That doesn't mean your life if less valuable and it definitely doesn't mean that systemic racism has kept you from playing baseball or being a famous rapper or rockstar.

The world is diverse, and it will never conform to a one-size-fits-all model. Some individuals may need to exert more effort and work harder than others to accomplish their goals. As someone who has lived through my fair share of experiences, I have witnessed individuals who were born into privilege but failed to thrive because they did not appreciate the value of hard work and the rewards it brings. Easy to understand if you grow up with everything being given to you with little effort.

My own upbringing was in a middle-class family until my parents divorced during middle school. During that time, my mother worked tirelessly, attending school at night and working a job at Walmart during the day. To support her and contribute to the household, I worked and willingly shared a portion of my paycheck to help with bills and necessities. Although I may have resented it at the time, looking back, I can see how the struggles and the additional effort put into finding solutions ultimately led to a better future. It also taught me that a working towards a goal is the best way to better your situation, no matter how hard it is or how long it takes. I could have spent useless time complaining about the situation and how others had it much easier. But identifying how many were born with better circumstances would have solved nothing and certainly wouldn't have made my life better.

Critical theory, or whatever it's called this year, teaches that every situation is plagued with bigotry. It teaches that anyone with power over you is the problem. But life is built on hierarchy. Unless you own the business where you work, you will be under a manager or boss. Your parents are in charge until you are old enough to move on and become in charge of your life or, eventually, your kids. Now, you are in power over them. Your teachers are going to be in charge of you while you are in school. I could go on with lots of examples, but you get the point. Identifying who is at the top of the power dynamic in your life is not helpful, and it certainly doesn't lead to self-sufficiency.

However, it is important to recognize that power dynamics exist in various aspects of life. Understanding these dynamics can provide valuable insights and help navigate relationships and systems more effectively. While critical theory may emphasize the negative impact of power imbalances, it is also crucial to acknowledge that hierarchies are often necessary for organizational structures and societal functioning. The military is an organization that operates within a well-defined hierarchical structure. This structure is essential for the efficient functioning and coordination of military operations.

For instance, in the workplace, having a manager or boss ensures that tasks are delegated, goals are set, and performance is monitored. This hierarchical structure enables efficient decision-making and coordination within the organization. Similarly, within the family unit, parents play a crucial role in providing guidance and support and ensuring the well-being of their children.

By recognizing the power dynamics in our lives, we can develop a better understanding of how to navigate these relationships and work towards achieving self-sufficiency. Rather than viewing those in positions of authority as inherently problematic, it is more productive to focus on building skills, gaining knowledge, and developing autonomy. This will empower individuals to take control of their own lives and work towards their goals, regardless of the power dynamics they may encounter. Teach your children to do well in school or in a trade so they can climb to the top of the hierarchy and have fewer people over them.

Instead of fostering a mindset where children believe that identifying their oppressors and complaining about their circumstances is the solution, it is more beneficial to teach them about individuals who have displayed determination and resilience in the face of obstacles. These are the stories that inspire mental toughness and resilience in young adults. Take, for example, the inspiring journey of Francis Ngannou. At the tender age of 10, he was working in sand mines in his native Cameroon. Driven by his dream of becoming a boxer, he attempted numerous times to reach France, enduring countless beatings, robberies, injuries, and even arrests. On his seventh attempt, he successfully made it to Spain and eventually to France, overcoming incredible odds. I encourage you to explore his remarkable story, along with the narratives of Ayaan Hirsi Ali and Yeonmi Park. These stories can serve as powerful examples for our children[5].

The world does not often hand us roses; instead, it teaches us that we must venture out and find them ourselves. This mindset of perseverance and self-reliance is a valuable lesson to impart to the next generation. And that doesn't mean teaching them that their problems are caused by someone else who has achieved or been handed more opportunities than them.

Examples of Images found in Elementary, Middle, and High Schools

The images below are from books that parents with common sense want removed from schools. After seeing them, you can make your own decision.

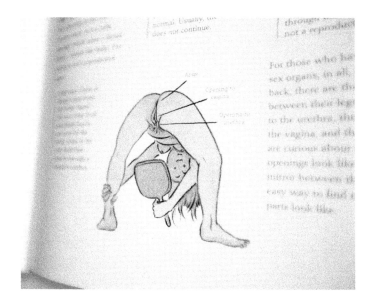

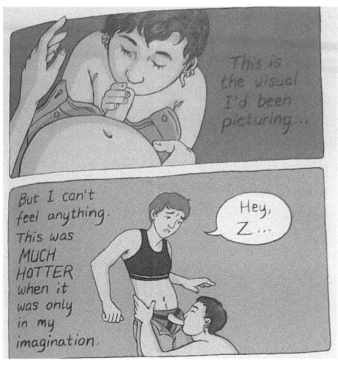

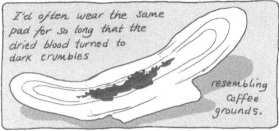

HIDING MY PERIOD BECAME EXTREMELY IMPORTANT TO ME. FOR TWO ENTIRE SCHOOL YEARS I SUCCESSFULLY AVOIDED EVER USING A SCHOOL BATHROOM.

I'd often wear the same pad for so long that the dried blood turned to dark crumbles

resembling coffee grounds.

TO THIS DAY A HUGE NUMBER OF MY NIGHTMARES INVOLVE MENSTRUAL BLOOD.

I'll feel the familiar sensation of hot blood gushing from my body—

!!! ...

When I make it to the bathroom I'll find my legs smeared with blood from waist to knees.

36

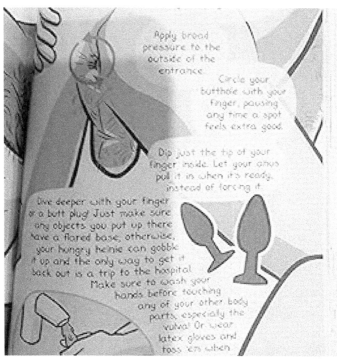

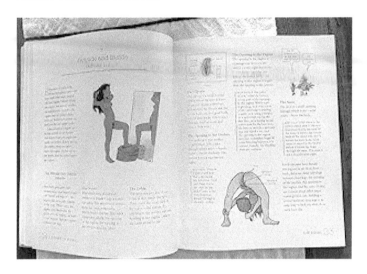

1. https://casel.org/fundamentals-of-sel/
    https://www.dpi.nc.gov/districts-schools/districts-schools-support/nc-social-emotional-learning/defining-social-and-emotional-learning-sel
2. https://www.allynwalkerphd.com/longdarkshadow
3. https://casel.org/fundamentals-of-sel/how-does-sel-support-educational-equity-and-excellence/transformative-sel/
    https://www.city-journal.org/article/equity-in-disguise
    https://civicsalliance.org/equity-in-disguise/
    https://newdiscourses.com/2022/03/critical-education-transformative-social-emotional-learning-sel/
    https://rumble.com/v224el9-the-occult-and-new-age-origins-of-sel.html
    https://www.nais.org/analyze/assessment-of-inclusivity-and-multiculturalism/
    https://www.emersoncollective.com/
    https://chanzuckerberg.com/
    https://sparcopen.org/our-work/innovator/penn-data-refuge-project/
4. https://www.onlineathens.com/story/opinion/2013/12/01/stossel-early-colonial-history-and-tragedy-commons/15549074007/
5. https://www.espn.com/espn/feature/story/_/id/33100543/francis-ngannou-miraculous-journey-ufc-stardom
    https://abcnews.go.com/WNT/story?id=2854474&page=1
    https://www.nbcnews.com/news/north-korea/yeonmi-park-s-long-journey-north-korea-chicago-n849516

18

NO ONE WAY TO LEARN

*If you think education is expensive, try estimating the cost of
ignorance.*

Dr. Howard Gardner

If you have made it this far, you have already delved into the
ever-changing landscape of school districts and their
constant adjustments to curriculum, methods, and styles. In
today's education system, there is a persistent quest to
discover the one-size-fits-all approach to teaching that will
cater to the diverse population of K -12 students. However,
numerous studies have revealed that individuals do not all
learn in the same way or through the same methods, highlighting the need for adaptable teaching practices.

During my interviews with teachers, many of them
expressed frustration over the fact that the principles they
were taught in college regarding teaching and the cognitive
processes of children and young adults are often disre-
garded by decision-makers. It is disheartening to witness the
abandonment of evidence-based research and scientific
findings on the most effective ways to impart knowledge.

Interestingly, I have encountered individuals within the education field who vehemently argue against this notion, asserting that there exists a definitive best practices method that, if discovered or honed in on, will yield exceptional results. However, this perspective fails to acknowledge the inherent diversity among individuals and their unique personalities, which influence the way they learn.

This chapter is intentionally concise, as its purpose is to emphasize the need for adjustments in public education that allow teachers the freedom to employ a variety of methods in their classrooms, catering to the individual needs of their students. It is crucial that students are given the opportunity to progress at their own pace, accelerating their learning when they are ready while also providing support and flexibility for those who require additional time to grasp concepts. Montessori schools, to some extent, have embraced this approach, recognizing the importance of individualized instruction and self-directed learning.

Gardner's Theory of Multiple Intelligences[1]

The concept of multiple intelligences, as proposed by Harvard psychologist Howard Gardner, challenges the traditional notion that intelligence is solely determined by a single measure, such as IQ testing. In his influential 1983 book "Frames of Mind: The Theory of Multiple Intelligences," [2]Gardner put forth the idea that individuals possess a diverse range of intelligences. Rather than viewing intelligence as a fixed trait, Gardner suggests that it is composed of various dimensions or "intelligences." According to Gardner, there are currently eight recognized intelligences, with the potential addition of a ninth. These intelligences include musical, interpersonal, spatial-visual, and linguistic intelligences, among others. Each intelligence represents a specific talent or ability that individuals may possess to varying degrees. For instance, someone could be exceptionally skilled in musical intelligence while also exhibiting strengths in verbal and naturalistic intelligence. It is crucial to acknowledge and foster these different intelligences in order to support individuals in realizing their full potential.

By embracing the concept of multiple intelligences, we can create a more inclusive and diverse education system that values and celebrates the unique talents and abilities of each individual. This means providing opportunities for individuals to develop their intelligence through specialized education, training, and enrichment programs. For example, a person with strong linguistic intelligence may excel in writing, public speaking, or language-based professions. On the other hand, someone with high spatial-visual intelligence may have a natural inclination towards art, design, or architecture. By recognizing and nurturing these diverse intelligences, we can create a society that thrives on the talents and contributions of individuals from all walks of life.

The theory of multiple intelligences challenges the traditional view of intelligence by emphasizing the presence of various intelligences within individuals. By acknowledging and embracing these intelligences, we can unlock the full potential of individuals and foster a society that values and celebrates the richness of human diversity.

Visual-Spatial Intelligence

People who possess strong visual-spatial intelligence have a remarkable ability to visualize concepts and ideas. Their proficiency in this area extends to various aspects, including their aptitude for understanding and interpreting visual information such as maps, charts, videos, and pictures. This unique cognitive strength enables them to excel in tasks that require visual and spatial judgment. Here are some examples that highlight their strengths in this domain:

Reading and Writing for Enjoyment: Individuals with strong visual-spatial intelligence often find pleasure in reading and writing. They have a knack for immersing themselves in vivid descriptions and mentally visualizing the scenes and characters portrayed in books. Whether it's a thrilling adventure or a heartfelt romance, they are able to create a vivid mental movie as they read.

Puzzle Solving: These individuals excel at putting puzzles together. Their ability to mentally manipulate and visualize the pieces allows them to quickly identify patterns and find solutions. With an eagle eye for detail, they can spot even the smallest clues and utilize their visual-spatial skills to solve puzzles with ease.

Interpretation of Visual Data: Visual-spatially intelligent individuals possess a keen eye for interpreting pictures, graphs, and charts. They can effortlessly extract meaningful insights from visual representations, making them adept at analyzing and understanding complex information. Whether it's deciphering a complex infographic or interpreting a complex diagram, they can make sense of visual data in a way that others may struggle to do.

Artistic Expression: People with strong visual-spatial intelligence often have a deep appreciation for the visual arts. They not only enjoy admiring artistic creations but also actively engage in artistic expression themselves. Whether it's drawing, painting, or engaging in other forms of artistic expression, they can bring their ideas to life on paper or canvas with their exceptional visualization skills. Their creations are visually captivating, as they have a unique ability to translate their thoughts and emotions into art.

Pattern Recognition: Recognizing patterns comes naturally to individuals with strong visual-spatial intelligence. They have an innate ability to identify recurring motifs, sequences, and relationships. This allows them to make connections and draw conclusions more easily. Whether it's spotting patterns in data, identifying trends in the stock market, or understanding the structure of a mathematical sequence, their visual-spatial skills give them an advantage.

In summary, individuals with strong visual-spatial intelligence possess a range of strengths that revolve around their exceptional visualization skills. Their ability to mentally manipulate and interpret visual information, coupled with their affinity for artistic expression and pattern recognition, sets them apart in various domains.

Linguistic-Verbal Intelligence

Individuals with strong linguistic-verbal intelligence possess an exceptional ability to effectively use language, both in written and spoken form. These individuals excel in various language-related activities, showcasing their talent for crafting compelling narratives, retaining information through reading and memorization, and engaging in articulate conversations. Here are some key traits of people with linguistic-verbal intelligence:

1. Firstly, they demonstrate an impressive capacity to retain and recall written and spoken information. Their sharp memory allows them to

absorb and remember a vast amount of information, enabling them to participate actively in discussions and debates.

2. Secondly, they derive great pleasure from the act of reading and writing. For them, the exploration of written works is not only a hobby but also a source of joy and fulfillment. They find solace and inspiration through books and take delight in expressing their thoughts through writing.

3. Moreover, individuals with linguistic-verbal intelligence have a knack for engaging in debates and delivering persuasive speeches. With their linguistic prowess, they are able to effectively convey their arguments and influence others through their well-articulated points.

4. Furthermore, they possess the ability to explain complex concepts in a clear and concise manner. This skill makes them effective communicators and teachers as they can break down intricate ideas into easily understandable explanations. Their clarity of thought and expression helps others grasp difficult concepts more easily.

5. Lastly, individuals with linguistic-verbal intelligence employ humor as a powerful tool when sharing stories. They utilize their wit and cleverness to captivate their audience and leave a lasting impression. By infusing their narratives with humor, they engage their listeners and make the storytelling experience more enjoyable.

In conclusion, individuals with linguistic-verbal intelligence have an exceptional command of language. Their ability to retain information, their passion for reading and writing, their persuasive speaking skills, their aptitude for explaining complex concepts, and their use of humor make them highly effective communicators and storytellers.

Logical-Mathematical Intelligence

Logical-mathematical intelligence is a cognitive ability that encompasses a range of skills, including strong reasoning abilities, pattern recognition, and logical problem-solving skills. Individuals who possess this intelligence are adept at conceptual thinking related to numbers, relationships, and patterns. Here are some key characteristics of people with logical-mathematical intelligence:

1. Excellent problem-solving skills: Individuals with logical-mathematical intelligence possess a natural talent for solving complex problems. They have the ability to break down problems into smaller components and analyze them systematically to arrive at effective solutions. Their logical and analytical thinking allows them to approach problems from different angles and consider various possible solutions.

2. Enthusiasm for abstract ideas: People with logical-mathematical intelligence have a strong interest in exploring abstract concepts and theories. They are fascinated by the underlying principles and theories that govern various phenomena. They enjoy delving into complex ideas and understanding the fundamental aspects that drive them.

3. Passion for scientific experimentation: Individuals with logical-mathematical intelligence find joy in conducting scientific experiments. They are naturally curious about cause-and-effect relationships and strive to uncover new knowledge through empirical investigation. Their love for experimentation enables them to test hypotheses and gather evidence to support their theories.

4. Proficiency in complex computations: People with logical-mathematical intelligence possess the ability to handle intricate calculations with ease. They can navigate through complex mathematical operations and arrive at accurate results. Their computational skills enable them to solve complex mathematical problems, make precise calculations, and analyze data effectively.

By leveraging their logical-mathematical intelligence, individuals can excel in various fields such as mathematics, computer science, engineering, finance, and research. Their analytical thinking and problem-solving skills make them valuable assets in these professional settings, where they can contribute to the development of innovative solutions and advancements in their respective fields.

Bodily-Kinesthetic Intelligence

Individuals who possess a high level of bodily-kinesthetic intelligence are known for their exceptional proficiency in body movement, executing actions, and maintaining physical control. This specific type of intelligence is character-ized by their remarkable hand-eye coordination and dexterity. People with bodily-kinesthetic intelligence exhibit a range of traits that showcase their unique abilities.

1. Proficiency in dancing and sports: Individuals with bodily-kinesthetic intelligence excel in physical activities such as dancing and sports, where they can demonstrate their skill and talent. Their ability to master complex movements and techniques sets them apart.

2. A strong inclination towards hands-on creation: Those with bodily-kinesthetic intelligence experience joy and satisfaction in the process of crafting and building things using their hands. They possess a natural talent for bringing their creative ideas to life through manual work.

3. Remarkable physical coordination: Individuals with this intelligence type have an innate ability to perform tasks that require precise movements and control. Their coordination skills allow them to excel in activities that demand fine motor skills and agility.

4. Active engagement in learning: People with bodily-kinesthetic intelligence tend to remember information through active engagement and physical involvement. They rely on doing and experiencing things firsthand, rather than solely relying on auditory or visual stimuli, to enhance their understanding and retention of knowledge.

Collectively, these traits make individuals with bodily-kinesthetic intelligence unique and valuable in various domains that prioritize physical skills and mastery. Their exceptional control over their bodies enables them to excel in activities that involve movement and coordination, making them a valuable asset in fields such as sports, dance, crafts, and other physical pursuits.

Musical Intelligence

People with strong musical intelligence have a unique ability to think in patterns, rhythms, and sounds. This intelligence allows them to excel in musical composition and performance, showcasing their deep appreciation for music. Here are some key characteristics that individuals with musical intelligence often exhibit:

Enjoyment of singing and playing musical instruments: Those with musical intelligence find immense pleasure in engaging in activities such as singing or playing musical instruments. The act of expressing themselves through music brings them solace and fulfillment.

Proficiency in recognizing musical patterns and tones: Individuals with musical intelligence possess a keen sense of perception when it comes to identifying musical patterns and tones. They have the ability to discern the intricacies and nuances present in different musical compositions.

Exceptional memory for songs and melodies: People with musical intelligence have an exceptional ability to remember songs and melodies. They effortlessly recall and reproduce musical pieces, showcasing their remarkable auditory memory.

In-depth understanding of musical structure, rhythm, and notes: Those with musical intelligence possess a profound understanding of the fundamental elements of music. They have a rich knowledge of musical structure, rhythm, and notes, which enables them to analyze and appreciate music on a deeper level.

Overall, individuals with musical intelligence possess a unique set of skills and talents that allow them to excel in the realm of music. Their ability to think in patterns, rhythms, and sounds, coupled with their appreciation for music, sets them apart and enables them to create and perform music with great proficiency.

Interpersonal Intelligence

Individuals with strong interpersonal intelligence possess a remarkable ability to comprehend and engage with others. They excel in perceiving and interpreting the emotions, motivations, desires, and intentions of those they interact with. This unique aptitude enables them to:

1. Communicate effectively through verbal means, articulating their thoughts and ideas with clarity and precision. They are skilled in expressing themselves using appropriate language, tone, and delivery to ensure their message is understood by the listener.

2. Demonstrate exceptional proficiency in nonverbal communication, utilizing body language, facial expressions, and gestures to convey messages and establish rapport. They have a keen awareness of how their nonverbal cues can impact the overall communication

process and use this knowledge to enhance their interactions.

3. Exhibit a remarkable capacity to view situations from various perspectives, allowing them to understand different viewpoints and appreciate diverse opinions. They are able to put themselves in others' shoes, which helps them to navigate complex social dynamics and build bridges between people with different ideas or values.

4. Foster positive relationships with others by establishing genuine connections, demonstrating empathy, and actively listening to their needs and concerns. They have a natural ability to connect with others on an emotional level and create a welcoming and supportive environment where individuals feel understood and valued.

5. Skillfully navigate and resolve conflicts within group settings, employing their interpersonal skills to mediate and find mutually beneficial solutions. They have a knack for diffusing tense situations, facilitating open dialogue, and finding common ground among conflicting parties.

Overall, individuals with strong interpersonal intelligence possess a valuable set of skills that enable them to thrive in social interactions, build meaningful connections, and contribute to harmonious relationships. These skills not only benefit personal relationships but also prove to be advantageous in various professional settings, such as team collaborations, leadership roles, customer service, and sales.

Intrapersonal Intelligence

Individuals with strong intrapersonal intelligence have a remarkable capacity for recognizing and comprehending their own emotional states, feelings, and motivations. They possess an innate proclivity for self-reflection and analysis, engaging in activities such as daydreaming, exploring their relationships with others, and evaluating their personal strengths. People with intrapersonal intelligence exhibit a range of characteristics that set them apart:

1. First and foremost, they demonstrate a keen ability to thoroughly analyze their strengths and weaknesses. By doing so, they gain valuable insights into their own abilities and areas for improvement. This self-awareness allows them to make informed decisions and take appropriate actions to enhance their personal growth.

2. Moreover, individuals with intrapersonal intelligence find immense joy and fulfillment in delving into theories and ideas. They derive a sense of satisfaction from unraveling and dissecting complex concepts, constantly seeking intellectual stimulation, and expanding their knowledge.

3. Notably, these individuals possess exceptional self-awareness. They have a deep understanding of their own thoughts, emotions, and behaviors. This heightened self-awareness enables them to navigate their internal landscape with clarity and insight, making conscious choices that align with their values and aspirations.

4. Furthermore, people with intrapersonal intelligence possess a profound comprehension of the underlying factors that drive their own motivations and feelings. This heightened self-knowledge empowers them to effectively manage their emotions and make decisions in a way that aligns with their personal growth and development.

Overall, individuals with intrapersonal intelligence have a unique ability to introspect and gain a deep understanding of themselves. Their self-knowledge serves as a foundation for personal growth and development, empowering them to make choices that align with their values and aspirations.

―――――

Naturalistic Intelligence

According to Gardner's theory of multiple intelligences, individuals with a high level of naturalistic intelligence have a deep appreciation for the natural world and possess a strong desire to explore and learn about it. They have a remarkable ability to recognize and understand even the most subtle changes that occur in their environment. People with naturalistic intelligence often:

1. Show a strong interest in subjects such as botany, biology, and zoology. These fields provide them with an opportunity to delve deeper into their passion for the natural world. They enjoy

studying and understanding the intricate
workings of various species and ecosystems.

2. Have a natural talent for organizing and
categorizing information effortlessly. They
possess an innate ability to collect and make
sense of the vast amount of knowledge they
acquire about the natural world. This talent
enables them to create connections and
relationships between different aspects of nature.

3. Take immense pleasure in engaging in outdoor
activities like camping, gardening, hiking, and
exploring the wonders of the natural world. They
find solace and inspiration in immersing
themselves in the beauty of nature and seek
opportunities to connect with the environment
around them.

4. Have a preference for learning topics that are
directly connected to nature. They find it more
challenging to engage with subjects that lack this
connection, as their naturalistic intelligence
thrives when it can be applied and observed in
real-life contexts.

Individuals with naturalistic intelligence possess a
unique perspective and a deep understanding of the natural
world. Their passion and curiosity drive them to explore
and appreciate the wonders of the environment, making
significant contributions to areas such as ecology, conserva-
tion, and environmental studies.

Existential Intelligence

Existential intelligence, as proposed by Gardner, is considered the ninth type of intelligence that complements his original theory. This form of intelligence entails an individual's ability to contemplate and delve into the profound questions that surround life and existence. By possessing existential intelligence, individuals not only ponder over the meaning of life but also explore how their actions can contribute to larger goals.

One of the notable strengths associated with individuals who possess existential intelligence is their holistic perspective. This perspective allows them to recognize and understand the interconnectedness of various aspects of life, enabling them to see the bigger picture.

When it comes to characteristics, people with existential intelligence exhibit several distinct qualities:

Long-term Outlook: Individuals with existential intelligence adopt a forward-thinking mindset, considering how their current decisions and actions can shape future outcomes. This long-term outlook empowers them to make choices that align with their overarching goals and aspirations.

Interest in Questions about the Meaning of Life and Death: Those with existential intelligence possess a deep curiosity regarding the fundamental aspects of human existence. They find themselves engrossed in profound questions about the purpose and significance of life, as well as the nature of mortality.

Strong Interest and Concern for Others: Empathy and compassion towards others are intrinsic to individuals with existential intelligence. They genuinely care and seek to understand the well-being of those around them, motivating them to support and uplift others.

The Ability to See Situations from an Outside Perspective: People with existential intelligence have the remarkable ability to step back and view situations from an objective standpoint. This unique vantage point allows them to gain a broader understanding of complex issues, enabling them to make well-informed decisions.

Overall, individuals with existential intelligence possess a distinct set of qualities that empower them to explore the deeper facets of life and make meaningful contributions to the world.

***

Criticism of Multiple Intelligences

Gardner's theory of multiple intelligences has faced criticism from both psychologists and educators. These critics argue that Gardner's definition of intelligence is too broad and that his nine different "intelligence" simply represent talents, personality traits, and abilities. They believe that this intelligence does not accurately capture the complexity of human cognition and that intelligence should be measured using more standardized and objective assessments. Additionally, Gardner's theory lacks sufficient empirical research to support its claims, which further weakens its credibility in the eyes of skeptics.

However, despite these criticisms, the theory of multiple intelligences remains popular among educators and has found significant traction, especially in private schools. Many teachers incorporate Gardner's theory into their teaching philosophies and strive to integrate it into their classrooms. While there is a lack of concrete evidence to demonstrate that learning according to one's "intelligence" leads to better educational outcomes, exploring the concept of multiple intelligences can still provide insights into how different students engage with or process information.

Understanding that individuals have different skills and strengths can help educators tailor their teaching methods to better meet the needs of diverse learners. For example, a teacher who recognizes that a student excels in spatial intelligence can incorporate more visual and hands-on learning activities into their lesson plans. By doing so, they create a more engaging and effective learning environment for that particular student. By acknowledging and valuing the various intelligences that students possess, educators can foster a more inclusive and empowering educational experience.

Personally, I have observed the diversity of abilities and behaviors in individuals. For instance, while I struggled with math and received average grades in the subject, many of the math teachers I hired excelled in understanding mathematical concepts effortlessly and did so at a young age. Similarly, I have friends who effortlessly picked up the guitar and became skilled players without formal lessons. In my previous career as a video/commercial director/editor, I excelled at visualizing the final product based on the script and direction provided by producers. I was able to piece together scenes shot out of order and create a cohesive narrative. I also wrote and produced concepts, which required me to explain my ideas and vision to agencies for approval.

Even if the nine different intelligences are indeed traits and abilities, they still play a role in driving one's interests and how their brain processes information. That's why a person who is mathematically inclined may grasp complex equations more easily, while someone with a strong musical intelligence may find it challenging. It is important to note that these intelligences are not mutually exclusive, and individuals can possess multiple intelligences simultaneously. For example, a musician may also have strong mathematical skills.

It is not uncommon to encounter individuals who possess exceptional skills in specific areas despite their performance in traditional academic settings. In fact, I personally know several successful people who were average or below-average students during their K-12 education. However, once they discovered a career path that aligned with their strengths or had the opportunity to study subjects they were genuinely interested in, they excelled in college and beyond. This raises the thought-provoking question of whether incorporating the concept of multiple intelligences into high school education could be beneficial in helping students better understand themselves and find their areas of passion and strength.

---

1. https://www.verywellmind.com/gardners-theory-of-multiple-intelli gences-2795161
2. https://www.goodreads.com/book/show/294035.Frames_Of_Mind

19

RACISM

The word racism is like ketchup. It can be put on anything - and demanding evidence makes you a racist.
   Dr. Thomas Sowell

As someone who grew up in the South, I have witnessed firsthand the presence of racism in the community. While most instances were subtle, there was a period during my elementary school years when the Ku Klux Klan would march through the center of our small town on a monthly basis. Though I was too young to fully comprehend the significance of what I saw, my parents, who were devout Catholics, made sure to educate me about the importance of loving everyone without prejudice. They emphasized that the Klan's message went against our Christian faith.

Over the years, I have seen race relations steadily improve, especially since I have spent the majority of my life in the South. By the time I reached college, it was becoming increasingly common to see students of all races socializing, attending parties, and even dating each other. I knew white students with black roommates, which was a testament to the progress being made. Of course, there were still some traditional Southerners who frowned upon interracial relationships, and I personally knew people who kept their relationships hidden from their parents or grandparents - both from white and black families.

During the 90s and early 2000s, I co-owned one of the largest wedding video production companies in Georgia. My ex/partner grew up in California and Oregon. Together, we worked at countless weddings and had conversations about the misconceptions regarding race relations in the South, particularly among people from the West Coast. Weddings served as eye-opening events. We frequently observed predominantly white weddings with black groomsmen or best men, and vice versa. The same held true for bridesmaids. These experiences confirmed to us just how far race relations had come, although we were not naive to the fact that racism still existed, albeit as isolated incidents or among those who lacked exposure and understanding.

Unfortunately, in recent times, there seems to be a push to regress and disregard the progress that has been made. Some individuals want us to believe that nothing has changed and that racism remains as prevalent as it was in the past. Singer John Mellencamp, for instance, made a statement on Bill Moher's YouTube show claiming that only 1 to 2 percent of black people in the country live better lives now than during the days of slavery. Such a statement reflects a sheltered perspective, and I would love to show him around where I live. I know black professors, doctors, and lawyers who would be more than eager to debate him on this issue. Mellencamp's statement is an example of the hyperbolic rhetoric that frequently permeates discussions on race, often exacerbating tensions and creating an atmosphere of heightened drama[1].

What troubles me is how this backslide affects younger generations. Many have embraced the idea that all injustices and disparities should be attributed to racism. Consequently, students in schools are growing up believing that their skin color determines their potential for success. Some think their dark skin denies them opportunities, while others feel burdened by guilt because they have light skin. This is a harmful outcome that hampers their sense of self-worth and obstructs their paths to success.

Unfortunately, there are individuals who resort to playing the race card when it suits their purposes. This often happens when they find themselves in a difficult situation or when their circumstances are not favorable.

This tactic involves manipulating race-related issues to divert attention from their own shortcomings or to gain sympathy and support. It is important to recognize that this behavior is not only unfair but also perpetuates stereotypes and undermines genuine efforts toward racial equality and understanding.

In considering this debate, it is important to recognize that much of the negative discourse comes from higher-level leaders. It raises questions about their motives. However, when it comes to everyday parents, this is not their primary concern. If you doubt my assertion, I encourage you to search on YouTube for videos of parents who are fighting against the teaching of critical race theory in public schools. You will find that a significant percentage of these parents are black and they reject the idea that racism is a barrier to their children's progress. These minority parents represent the 1 to 2 percent that Mellencamp should listen to - they believe in the potential for success in their lives and do not want outdated labels or divisive rhetoric to stand in the way of their children's future achievements in both their careers and family lives[2].

In fact, telling a young minority student that they cannot achieve something because of systemic racism is more harmful than the racism itself. By conveying this message, we are essentially telling them that success is unattainable regardless of their efforts because the system is inherently rigged against them. This discourages them, effectively urging them to give up before even trying. At the same time, we inadvertently place blame on young white individuals, insinuating that their mere existence is the cause of someone else's inability to achieve their dreams. This divisive narrative serves no purpose other than to perpetuate feelings of resentment and inequality.

Interestingly enough, the same individuals who ardently support such sexually explicit content in schools are quick to advocate for the banning of books like To Kill a Mockingbird and other renowned classics that deviate from their own vision of an ideal society. In Washington State, four teachers embarked on a mission to have Harper Lee's novel removed from the school curriculum, and while they were partially successful, their attempt to ban it entirely was thankfully unsuccessful.

In their formal challenge against the inclusion of To Kill a Mockingbird, the teachers argued that the book excessively focuses on whiteness, thus hindering an authentic understanding and appreciation of the Black perspective during the Civil Rights era. They insisted that this literary work should be eradicated from the curriculum[3].

In Chicago, there was a teacher who expressed offense at the idea of a white man being portrayed as the savior for black defendants in a historical story. However, it is important to recognize the context of the time period in which the story takes place. During that time, black people had no power or influence in the legal process and were systematically oppressed. In such a climate, it required great courage for someone, regardless of their race, to stand up against the injustices being committed. This individual risked their reputation and faced threats to their own safety and the safety of their family in order to challenge the prevailing narrative and advocate for what was right[4].

The moral of this story serves as a valuable teaching moment for all individuals, regardless of their race. It emphasizes the importance of speaking out against oppression, even in the face of serious consequences. The white man in the story demonstrated integrity by recognizing the inherent wrongness of the situation and taking action to rectify it. It is worth noting that only a small number of individuals who champion social justice causes would be willing to go to the same lengths if their own livelihood or security were at stake.

Sports writer Claire Smith, a notable black woman who was honored in 2017 for her outstanding achievements in sports journalism, eloquently highlighted the pivotal role played by individuals like Yogi Berra, Pee Wee Reese, and Ted Williams in paving the way for the integration of black players into Major League Baseball. Their acceptance and belief in equality were essential in the journey of players like Jackie Robinson, who broke the color barrier in baseball. Ted Williams, a highly respected figure in the sport, even used his Hall of Fame speech to advocate for the inclusion of exceptional players from the Negro Leagues in the Baseball Hall of Fame[5]. A defining moment is all of sports, not just baseball.

In times of oppression, it requires individuals who hold positions of power and influence to demonstrate bravery and take a stand for what is right. It's important to acknowledge that these acts of support and advocacy from white men towards black players were not a display of superiority, but rather a testament to their honor and integrity. Their actions exemplify the belief that equality should prevail regardless of race.

Similarly, in Harper Lee's renowned novel "To Kill a Mockingbird," the historical significance cannot be overlooked. Published in 1960, a time when racial tensions were high, and segregation was still deeply rooted in the South, the book courageously tackled the prevalent racial issues of the era. Its progressive portrayal of injustice serves as a powerful reminder of the importance of bravery and standing up against discrimination. The enduring influence and relevance of this work make it an essential part of educational curricula, allowing students to appreciate and learn from its timeless message. I find it somewhat ironic that there are individuals who argue that banning critical race theory is a means of avoiding the teaching of slavery and racism's history. Yet, these same individuals also desire to eliminate a story that presents a fictional character who courageously confronts that very racism. It seems contradictory that they would champion the suppression of a narrative that promotes resilience against racial discrimination while simultaneously advocating for the inclusion of comprehensive historical education.

Blaming everything negative on racism is not an effective way to address the issue of racism that still exists. While it is important to acknowledge and confront racism, it is equally vital to recognize the progress that has been made since the race riots of the 1960s. By perpetuating the idea that racism has not improved, we fail to acknowledge the efforts and achievements made in combating it. Instead of focusing solely on the negative aspects of racism, it is important to promote a constructive dialogue that encourages understanding and empathy. When individuals use race as a tool for bullying or to avoid addressing underlying issues, it creates a divisive society where one side becomes hesitant to engage in discussions for fear of being labeled as racist. On the other hand, those who interpret this hesitation as racism further perpetuate the cycle of misunderstanding and polarization.

Where Social Justice Gets it Wrong

For the record, in my opinion, I believe that discussions around social justice sometimes overlook important details. It is evident that people often rush to judgments without conducting thorough research, possibly influenced by social media or their university education. This tendency leads to unnecessary emotional outrage without fully understanding the context or having a comprehensive understanding of the subject matter.

The issue of racism, especially systemic racism in education, has garnered significant attention. There is a prevailing belief that systemic racism is deeply rooted in the education system and impossible to eliminate. However, upon closer examination of the facts, a different perspective emerges. When asked to provide evidence supporting the claim that systemic racism is the root cause of underperformance among minority students, proponents of this view often struggle to present a compelling argument. Usually, they are only able to point out that there are more minorities failing in schools, so that must equal systemic racism in the school system. Their statements seem to rely more on hearsay and repetition rather than concrete evidence. It is important to delve deeper into the causes instead of solely relying on data on racial disparities, as the data doesn't point to the true causes.

Dr. Thomas Sowell aptly states, "*Some things are believed because they are demonstrably true. But many other things are believed simply because they have been asserted repeatedly—and repetition has been accepted as a substitute for evidence.*"

He goes on to say in his book Social Justice Fallacies, "*In New York City, for example, in school year 2017–2018 there were dozens of places in low-income minority neighborhoods where public charter schools and traditional public schools, serving the same local community, were housed in the same buildings. When black and Hispanic students in both kinds of schools took the same statewide test in mathematics, the charter school students achieved the official "proficient" level in mathematics more than 6 times as often as children of the same ethnicities in traditional public schools housed in the very same buildings. These are huge disparities within the same groups, so that neither race nor racism can account for these huge differences. Nor can culturally biased tests[6].*"

This observation sheds light on the prevailing narrative surrounding systemic racism. While there are self-proclaimed experts and academics who advocate for the existence of systemic racism, it is crucial to question their motivations. It is possible that personal gain from lectures and book sales may influence their stance more than a genuine commitment to uncovering the true factors behind unequal outcomes. Furthermore, in many cases, the available data does not support their narratives.

In order to challenge these notions, we can look at the Nigerian population as an example. Nigerian Americans have achieved remarkable success, with average incomes that exceed those of the overall U.S. population. Approximately 76 percent of adult Nigerian Americans are part of the labor force, compared to about 65 percent of the U.S. population. More than half of Nigerian Americans hold professional or managerial jobs, in contrast to roughly 36 percent of the U.S. population. Moreover, over 60 percent of Nigerian Americans over the age of 25 have at least a bachelor's degree, while less than 30 percent of the U.S. population can make the same claim[7].

All of these achievements are made despite skin color. This begs the question: If the United States is indeed plagued by systemic racism, how is it possible for Nigerian Americans to thrive? As mentioned earlier, Nigerian families place a great emphasis on education and strive to further their knowledge. They understand that completing K-12 education and pursuing higher education will contribute to their financial stability. One Nigerian student I spoke to shared that his family did not attend his high school graduation despite his position as the top student in his class, as it was simply expected of him. Education was viewed as a stepping stone to higher accomplishments. While this perspective may seem cold or uncaring, it has proven to be effective for the Nigerian population.

I am not advocating for parents to diminish their pride in their children's achievements. However, it is worth considering that the success of Nigerian Americans is not restrained by their skin color, but rather propelled by their commitment to education and fields that yield prosperity.

Is it fair to suggest that our education system discriminates against minorities, considering that Nigerian children, who are of a different racial background, attend the same schools and live in the same communities as everyone else?

The same can be said for many Asian and Indian families who have an unwavering dedication to their children's education. Are they inherently smarter than black and white Americans? Probably not. From my observations and experiences, it appears that Asian, Indian, and Nigerian parents do not allow distractions to hinder their child's educational success. They limit the use of technology, including cell phones, and are willing to take them away if their child is not putting enough effort into their studies. Excuses are not tolerated, and these parents go to greater lengths than most American families to ensure their children remain focused on the ultimate goal of succeeding in their educational endeavors.

Some individuals may attempt to explain away the success of these three minority groups using convoluted arguments and data. However, most of these arguments fall outside the realm of logical clarity, making it difficult to understand their validity. One counterargument suggests that the immigrants who are willing to pack up everything and migrate to the United States are among the most driven individuals within their population, thus skewing the data to represent exceptional people. However, this argument fails to address how these exceptional individuals can succeed in a country that supposedly oppresses minorities through racism and discriminatory structures. It also fails to explain why people who are already residing in America cannot follow suit and work hard to achieve their goals.

In the end, it is important to recognize that everyone faces obstacles in life. We often celebrate individuals who have succeeded despite facing seemingly insurmountable odds. We also celebrate those who have been told they cannot succeed but defied those odds. Teaching our children to adopt a similar mindset and persevere will serve them well, regardless of the obstacles they encounter. After all, obstacles are an inherent part of life.

I Saw the Signs

While traveling around the southern states to introduce our education company to school districts and principals, I encountered several disheartening incidents of racism. One particular experience stands out in my memory. I had driven two hours to meet with a small district in south Georgia to present our product. Upon entering the meeting room, where I was supposed to set up my laptop and begin my presentation, I noticed a list on the whiteboard. To my surprise and disappointment, the second item on the list read, "Hire fewer white people." This revelation left me with a sinking feeling that my long journey had been in vain. Nonetheless, I proceeded with my presentation, but unsurprisingly, I never heard from the district again.

Another incident occurred during a prominent annual meeting in Dekalb County, Georgia, attended by principals and vice-principals. This conference served as a platform for discussions about upcoming changes in the county's education system, featuring guest speakers addressing various educational topics. As vendors, we were given the opportunity to set up booths and showcase our products and services to district leaders and individual principals. During our first year participating in this conference, a district leader approached our media booth and bluntly informed me that our product would never sell in their community because it was "too lily white." I was taken aback by this statement and explained that 45 percent of the video lessons were taught by black teachers. However, the district leader dismissed this information, stating that they would not purchase anything that did not reflect the racial makeup of DeKalb County. Despite this discouraging encounter, we were able to form partnerships with four elementary schools in DeKalb County, indicating that not all of the district's leadership held the same biases. I remember sharing this story with one of the principals who had consistently renewed their contract with us for three years, and she sadly acknowledged the existence of individuals who opposed racial diversity in their community.

On another occasion, I traveled to Mississippi to showcase our product. Mississippi consistently ranks in the bottom third of education nationwide, so I was hopeful that our educational resources would be well-received. I presented our demo to the curriculum specialist, who expressed her enthusiasm and mentioned that she would have other members of the leadership team join us to evaluate the product. However, she made a perplexing request, asking if I could only show the black teachers in the demo. I explained that creating a separate edit to remove the white teachers would be necessary to fulfill her request. Realizing the impracticality of this suggestion to edit the video on the spot, she proposed rescheduling the meeting after I made the edit. Frustrated by the long drive I had already taken, I voiced my concerns about the feasibility of returning to show a new demo. She then suggested that I email her a link to a demo featuring only black teachers. Ultimately, I decided against making the edit and sending the modified demo as it felt ethically wrong to exclude one race from our presentation. Especially since our video library would contain both white and black teachers if they purchased the rights to use our product. Just imagine a scenario where we made such a concession for someone requesting the removal of black teachers from our demo. The double standard is disheartening, to say the least.

As a result of these distressing encounters, our other salesperson and I discussed the idea of hiring a black sales representative who could navigate these situations more effectively. Though we never implemented this suggestion, these incidents opened our eyes to the realities of racial bias at the local level in certain districts.

If we were to play out these scenarios hypothetically, consider an inner-city school in Chicago where only 12 percent of elementary students tested at or above proficiency level for math[8]. It is inconceivable that such a school would reject valuable resources solely based on the skin color of the teachers featured in those resources. However, the unfortunate truth is that in some districts and individual schools in this country, this is precisely what is happening.

Additionally, we conducted a thorough statistical analysis to determine the popularity and viewership of our videos. Interestingly, we found no significant disparity in the number of views between videos featuring white teachers and those featuring black teachers. In fact, the distribution of content views was quite evenly spread across both white and black teachers.

Moreover, when deciding how to cater to different ethnic groups, we closely monitored schools that were predominantly black and predominantly white. To ensure comprehensive coverage, we created multiple videos for each lesson, as different teachers had varying teaching styles. Surprisingly, we observed that the distribution of video plays was not biased towards the videos of black teachers in predominantly black schools, nor were white teacher views disproportionately higher in predominantly white schools. The video views were consistently and evenly distributed across both groups. This trend was also evident in higher-income districts.

From this data, it becomes evident that parents, overall, do not prioritize the skin color of the person teaching. When searching for video lessons, their main concern is finding someone who can effectively explain the content in a way that students can understand. With multiple teachers to choose from, parents had the freedom to select the most suitable instructor for their child's needs. It is worth noting that Mr. Allen, a black teacher who taught algebra and geometry at the high school level, was one of our most viewed instructors. His videos tended to be longer and more deliberate, which many parents seemed to appreciate.

Critical Race Theory

Critical Race Theory is a deeply rooted belief that asserts systemic racism as the underlying structure of society, with white people benefiting from it. This theory suggests that racism is not just an individual act but rather ingrained in various societal institutions such as law, education, and other foundational structures that uphold and shape our communities.

Advocates of Critical Race Theory argue that it is crucial to educate children about these systemic issues through the educational system. By doing so, they believe that young minds will develop a critical understanding of racism and become equipped to identify and challenge it. The ultimate goal is to initiate a comprehensive social and cultural revolution aimed at rejecting racism at its core.

It is important to note that Critical Race Theorists see themselves as the torchbearers of this revolution, as they possess the specialized knowledge necessary to navigate and unravel the complexities of systemic racism.

Some aspects of the intentions behind the teachings mentioned above may seem commendable. However, it is unfortunate that they go beyond the scope of teaching theory and instead categorize individuals based on their skin color as either oppressors or oppressed. In educational settings where teachers have undergone Critical Race Theory (CRT) training and are imparting the same to their students, white students are being labeled as inherently evil and bad, with no consideration for their individual character or actions. Conversely, students with black skin are being taught that the system is intrinsically biased against them and that white students should face reverse racism as atonement for the sins of their ancestors.

It seems to be based on the baseless notion that different outcomes among students of color are related to systemic racism or racism baked into the situation.

If the aforementioned scenario is perceived as a positive direction for our children, then it appears we have differing views on common sense. This situation starkly contrasts with the renowned words of Martin Luther King Jr., who famously proclaimed, "I have a dream that my four little children will one day live in a nation where they will not be judged by the color of their skin, but by the content of their character."

Ironically, it seems that the current narrative suggests that one's skin color inherently defines their character. Individuals who claim superiority in intelligence insist that by employing reverse racism, we will diminish racism or create a form of racism that somehow heals the sins of the past, even for those whose ancestors did not reside in this country because they have somehow benefited from a system, which their skin color made life easier for them.

Now, let's switch perspectives and consider a reverse statement involving CRT: If I were to assert that black skin is intrinsically bad or evil, it would rightfully provoke outrage. It is worth noting that CRT has not garnered unanimous acceptance within the black community, and many individuals have vocally expressed their opposition to this regressive concept.

When individuals critique or protest the inclusion of CRT in school curricula, they are often unjustly labeled as racist, or if they are black, labeled an Uncle Tom, or accused of attempting to erase the history of racism. However, this could not be further from the truth. The history of racism has been extensively taught throughout the country. As someone who grew up in the South, I can attest to the ample time dedicated to studying this history.

Furthermore, school districts have resorted to renaming their CRT initiatives in an attempt to quell parental objections or to make a claim, with a straight face, that CRT is not included in their curriculum. However, this is merely a matter of relabeling, as administrators and district managers have been caught on secret recordings discussing how to obfuscate the involvement of critical theory in their curriculum.

Essentially, Critical Race Theory (CRT) represents a resurgence of traditional racism, albeit under new leadership. It seems that the advocates of CRT are attempting to convince us that the racism they advocate for is somehow virtuous. For instance, Derek Bell, a key figure in the development of CRT, held the belief that the Supreme Court ruling in Brown vs. Board of Education was incorrect.

Believing that separate but equal was the right idea. He actually supported the idea of maintaining segregated schools and advocated for a return to such a system. This perspective is not viewed as progress by many, including myself[9].

It is counterintuitive to believe that by teaching and endorsing racism, we will somehow eradicate it or reduce its prevalence. As I began this chapter with my perspective on the progress made in race relations, I stand by those observations. There are others who share the same sentiment. When we refer to individuals as racist, we often attribute their behavior to ignorance. So, what do we say about those advocating for a new form of racism[10]?

Unpacking the Idea that Math is Racist

Earlier in this book, we discussed the concerning trend of certain educational authorities attempting to label math as systematically racist. The argument put forth is that in the pursuit of equity, we should be open to the idea that 2 + 2 can equal a number other than 4. While many people find this notion absurd, it is crucial to understand that this idea is gaining some traction and needs to be addressed.

In George Orwell's dystopian novel "1984," there is a well-known math problem: what is two plus two? The protagonist, Winston Smith, is subjected to repeated indoctrination in the story. He is forced to believe that two and two make five. His release from captivity is contingent upon his acceptance of this false reality. The objective of this manipulation is not to establish the correct answer to the math problem but rather to suppress individual dissent and ensure unwavering loyalty to the ruling powers. In this context, the correct answer to the math problem is whatever "Big Brother" dictates.

While the comparison to Orwell's novel may seem extreme, it is essential to examine the current situation in some schools in Oregon and California and other progressive states and counties where the traditional concept of 2+2 equaling four is being challenged. This movement, primarily found in progressive states, is gaining traction. A quick search on Google for "2+2 always equals 4" reveals that 90 percent of the first three pages of results argue against the idea that 2+2 must equal 4. This clearly indicates that the conventional understanding of mathematics is being called into question.

Dr. James Lindsay, a professor and mathematician, has been warning about this for many years. However, most people, including myself, thought that the idea that math was racist was so absurd that it was given very little concern. Lindsay said recently, "America is already near the bottom in math scores from the rest of the world, and now we're going to teach our students that 2 + 2 might equal something other than 4".

The Oregon Department of Education recently sent its guidance on A Pathway to Equitable Math to the states math teachers. This 82-page instructional toolkit is a framework for "deconstructing racism in mathematics" and "dismantling white supremacy in math classrooms." Of course, if there is residual racism in literature, social science, and history, it's easier to understand. But what is "white supremacy" in math?

The guidance reads: "White supremacy culture infiltrates math classrooms in everyday teacher actions. ... We see white supremacy culture in the mathematics classroom can show up when: The focus is on getting the 'right' answer ... [and] students are required to 'show their work." Funny, because I have always held the belief that individuals who identify as white supremacists, Klan members, or skinheads are ignorant and unintelligent. However, it seems that they possess an uncanny level of mathematical proficiency that allows them to arrive at correct answers and demonstrate their problem-solving methods. This revelation prompts me to question the validity of our current approach to mathematics education. Perhaps we should narrow the definition of white supremacy to its original definition.

According to the guidance, teachers are to "choose problems that have complex, competing, or multiple answers" and ask students to "come up with at least two answers that might solve this problem" instead of putting their focus on one "right" answer.

There is something inherently flawed with educators teaching students factually incorrect information. Are we aiming to keep the population uneducated, or do we strive to nurture the brightest minds that will propel our country forward? Math, for instance, is the epitome of objective truth and rationality. The answer is either right or wrong, with no room for interpretation. While people can debate historical events and their impact on the past and future, math remains objective.

The guidance is to train teachers to "challenge standardized test questions by getting the 'right' answer, but justify other answers by unpacking the assumptions that are made in the problem." CNN publicly stated with a headline in 2016, "Math is racist: How data is driving inequality."

However, some schools are now advocating for the teaching of alternative viewpoints, promoting incorrect answers to spare a child's feelings. This misguided approach fails to address the root causes of bigotry and societal issues. It hinders students' intellectual growth and development. By eroding the fundamental principles of mathematics, we undermine the very foundation of our society.

I am very supportive of racial equality. However, having said that no matter what skin color or ethnicity the engineer is building a building or the bridges we drive over, I would like to think that his math is accurate and supportive of the best outcome for the structures they are building. You can make this example in dozens of critical areas of life. It would be hard to run a business when the math you are doing to solve your taxes, expenses, profit margin, etc., has no right or wrong answer. Try telling the IRS you were close enough.

Proponents of equity in math claim that math is Euro-centric and invented by white men. That still doesn't explain why if I hold up two fingers on one hand and two fingers on my other hand, it doesn't equal 4. That's assuming counting is still allowed. We are already dealing with a younger age group that is very entitled, with an increase in narcissism because they've been coddled more than ever. How much worse is the future generation going to act if we are telling them they are "awesome" for choosing 5 for the answer of 2 + 2? In a sense, it's the evolution of everyone getting a trophy. Or maybe it's de-evolution.

This notion of Eurocentric invention is wrong, and unfortunately, for people in education who push this without knowing the history is sad. Algebra was developed through the centuries by many ethnicities. Persian math-ematician al-Khwarizmi is regarded as "the father of algebra ."The word algebra is of Aramaic origin. Much of early math, including algebraic equations, started in the Middle East. The Babylonians may have been the first to create and use mathematical formulas. The Greek, Chinese, and Italian scholars introduced additional equations and methods. Geometry has a similar origin. For example, both the Egyptians and the Babylonians were aware of the Pythagorean theorem about 1500 years before Pythagoras and the Indian Sulba Sutras around 800 BC contained the first statements of the theorem; the Egyptians had a correct formula for the volume of a pyramid. Who wouldn't have guessed that last one?

Those facts do not support the notion that racist white men created math. It appears that those facts are inconvenient to the equity movement, so they are not taught, which means that students are getting an edited knowledge of the history of mathematics. So this means 2 + 2 really does equal 4. I'm sure the people making those claims hope that the high school student making their change at the local grocery store or restaurant will get it right. When approached with these facts, some individuals attempt to divert attention by declaring that focusing on the correct answer is racist. However, it is important to note that this notion is both baseless and absurd. There is no need to further elaborate on this unfounded claim, as it lacks any credible evidence or logical reasoning. But if we aren't holding students of any color to the standards of correct answers, then we have no standards.

Unfortunately, data and statistics often reveal things we hope are not true, but that's the beauty of gathering statistics and doing the math. It allows us to understand better what's going right and wrong and address and correct it without our emotions getting in the way. For instance, how more money doesn't make education better[11]!

───────────────

1. https://nypost.com/2023/08/30/john-mellencamp-ripped-by-bill-maher-over-1-or-2-of-black-people-live-better-than-slaves-claim/
2. https://www.youtube.com/results?search_query=parents+angry+about+critical+race+theory
3. https://nypost.com/2022/01/25/seattle-school-removes-to-kill-a-mockingbird-from-curriculum/
4. https://chicagomonitor.com/2013/06/how-schools-have-killed-the-mockingbird/
5. https://www.nytimes.com/2017/07/29/sports/baseball/claire-smith-becomes-first-female-recipient-of-sports-writing-award.html
6. https://www.goodreads.com/en/book/show/63092727
7. https://www.migrationpolicy.org/sites/default/files/publications/RAD-Nigeria.pdf
8. https://www.usnews.com/education/k12/illinois/districts/city-of-chicago-sd-299-110570
9. https://law.marquette.edu/facultyblog/2011/10/r-i-p-derrick-bell-pioneer-of-critical-race-theory/
10. https://www.heritage.org/critical-race-theory
    https://adflegal.org/article/what-critical-race-theory
11. https://www.newsweek.com/math-racist-crowd-runs-rampant-seattle-portland-opinion-1701491
    https://www.washingtontimes.com/news/2021/jun/6/is-mathematics-racist-california-could-blaze-pathw/
    https://www.seattletimes.com/education-lab/new-course-outlines-prompt-conversations-about-identity-race-in-seattle-classrooms-even-in-math/
    https://apnews.com/article/math-class-tracking-school-gap-e69d6a02e135a2942a975424d1eb4796
    https://www.latimes.com/california/story/2021-05-20/california-controversial-math-overhaul-focuses-on-equity
    https://newdiscourses.com/2020/08/2-plus-2-never-equals-5/
    https://equitablemath.org/#:~:text=Apercent20Pathwaypercent20topercent20Equitablepercent20Math,topercent20gradepercent2Dlevelpercent20prioritypercent20standards.
    https://www.oregon.gov/ode/educator-resources/standards/mathematics/pages/oregon-math-project.aspx
    https://money.cnn.com/2016/09/06/technology/weapons-of-math-destruction/index.html
    https://www.britannica.com/biography/al-Khwarizmi
    https://medcraveonline.com/OAJMTP/evolution-of-mathematics-a-brief-sketch.html
    https://www.superprof.com/blog/learn-maths-history/

20

WHERE'S ALL THIS GOING?

If parents in each generation always or often knew what goes on at their Childs' school, the history of education would be very different.

   C.S. Lewis

If you have read this far into the book, it becomes evident that the future of education is looking bleak. As discussed earlier, those responsible for implementing significant changes in the education system often fail to acknowledge that they themselves are part of the problem. Furthermore, higher administrative positions are often

   resistant to change, as it would directly impact them. Consequently, it is highly unlikely that top administrators will openly admit to their mistakes.

   The current trajectory of the education system is heading towards stagnation and continued decline. While education will continue to exist, its effectiveness is already diminishing due to policies and decisions driven by political motivations, greed, or the desire to appear virtuous. Unfortunately, these factors have no correlation with actual education.

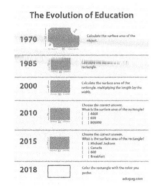

The Evolution of Education

As highlighted in the previous pages, administrators do not possess the answers and often resort to implementing repetitive changes. Despite constant increases in curriculum rigor or alterations in teaching methods, the outcomes and scores continue to deteriorate. This situation can be likened to rearranging the deck chairs on the Titanic - an exercise in futility. They persist in shuffling the same elements and intensifying micromanagement, leading to even greater failure and frustrating the teachers who are at the other end trying to deal with all the minutia.

We are already experiencing a crisis of inadequate teacher numbers, and this shortage of qualified educators is bound to worsen as more individuals abandon careers in education, and others opt not to pursue the field in college. Consequently, class sizes will significantly increase due to population growth and people immigrating into the country. This surge in class sizes will force more teachers to reconsider their career choices. Several districts in Georgia and other states have even been compelled to request permission from the state government to exceed maximum class size limits mandated by state directives. Unfortunately, there are not enough teachers available to alleviate the overcrowded classrooms, leaving the existing teachers burdened with larger student populations. Consider this scenario: You are in need of a surgeon to address an injury, only to discover that a staggering 30 percent of them have been practicing medicine for less than two years. It is concerning to see such a trend in the teaching profession, given its reputation for offering great benefits and the potential to earn a salary above the median income level for most Americans with enough years of experience. However, these incentives alone do not seem to be sufficient to retain educators in the long run. One would assume that the education of our children holds paramount importance for most individuals. Yet, it appears that the necessary steps and concrete actions to address the challenges plaguing the education profession are regrettably lacking.

Additionally, the issue of student behavior must be addressed. As mentioned at the beginning of the book, if eliminating disruptive behavior can enhance the effectiveness of education, then alternative disciplinary measures should be implemented. However, administrators lack the courage to enforce such policies and, therefore, avoid considering this option. I mentioned in an earlier chapter on homework a principal who worked with his teachers on making sure that the students didn't have too much homework and his teachers were not overburdened with curriculum adaptations they weren't fond of. That same principal cleaned up a school that had gang fights and overall poorly behaving students, that was leading to the early retirement of teachers and a lack of safety for the students. He expelled 350 students in one school year to clean up the school. The 350 were sent to alternative schools. That's an administrator with a backbone. What did it do for the school? Behavior issues dropped significantly, and teachers who were trying to transfer out of the school changed their minds. That was over ten years ago. It's unlikely that a district would allow that to happen now. He understood that listening to the students who wanted to be there and the teachers who were having to deal with behavioral problems was the key to fixing the situation. He gained their loyalty by listening and doing what was best for the school as a whole.

In the past, we celebrated teachers who took a hard line against poor behavior and did what was necessary to educate the students, even when the solution was tough love. Movies were made about these exceptional educators, such as Stand and Deliver about Jaime Escalante and Lean on Me about Joe Clark, a maverick ex-teacher who is brought in by a New Jersey school superintendent to clean up the worst school in the state of New Jersey. Both of these stories highlighted individuals who not only maintained high grading standards but also demanded that the students straighten up or get out. They set the bar higher when they arrived in their schools. And it worked.

What's crazy about all the research, anecdotal evidence, and decades of data is that it all points to doing the opposite strategies of what school districts are employing now. We already covered research from economist Seth Gershenson, whose study revealed that students benefited more from teachers who maintained higher grading standards. Gershenson's research highlighted that these more rigorous standards had a positive impact on learning outcomes for students across all major ethnic groups, regardless of their socioeconomic background.

Plus, we have stories of tough love, making the school environments better for the students and the teachers.

We discussed the correlation between raising the rigor and the plummeting of grades.

Teachers have expressed the stresses they have with being micromanaged and told how to teach and having their curriculum thrown out too often for new teaching methods.

You've read about the lack of resources for teachers.

It's clear that teachers are leaving the profession, and fewer are going into the profession.

The list of issues related to the previous bullet points could go on for another page.

If these district or state education leaders have seen the evidence that higher grading standards benefit the students, then why are they lower grading standards?

If these same leaders have seen how being tougher on bad behavior leads to less bad behavior, then why are they dismissing negative consequences from the teachers and school leaders?

If grades and scores drop immediately after increasing the rigor of the lessons, then why keep raising the rigor?

If you are seeing a teacher shortage in your district or state, then why not do what is in the best interest of the teachers who have experience? Instead of lowering the entry requirements for new teachers. Get your teachers the resources they need.

The point here is that despite the evidence and research, which we would assume district and state leaders can also find, they are doing the exact opposite of what good practices would require. It's not rocket science; it's common sense. It's no wonder that some conspiracy theories floating around that point to our education leaders intentionally trying to keep the younger generation dumb.

Furthermore, in states where teaching requirements have been relaxed, it is crucial to recognize that this does not address the underlying pressures that cause both experienced and newly qualified teachers to leave the profession. These policies inadvertently contribute to a situation where a less certified group of individuals may choose to quit in the long run, further impacting the quality of education.

The next thing you will hear is that they're doing a prison release program if you agree to teach.

As someone who loves this country, I want to see our best and brightest become brighter and lead this country into the future. If you watch the news, you've probably noticed that quite a few people have been elected who are the opposite of bright. In the absence of ideas and solutions, the powers that run education around the country have decided that the system is the problem.

Many school districts are already manipulating grading systems and graduation rates to create the illusion of higher student success rates than they actually have. As school districts struggle to cope with increasing student enrollments and the loss of teachers, this trend is likely to become more prevalent.

How Do We Stop the Bleeding?

When addressing the issue of teacher attrition, it is imperative for politicians and administrators to thoroughly analyze the root causes behind teachers leaving the profession. The current practice of implementing yearly policy changes, whether at the federal or statewide level, fails to effectively target the underlying problem. In fact, some of these policies exacerbate the challenges faced by both teachers and their students. While many people believe that teacher pay alone is the issue, it is important to recognize that this is not the sole factor at play here. Therefore, it is essential to shift the focus from advocating for more money to the districts and, instead, consider redistributing the funds to the schools and teachers directly.

In my conversations with retired district leaders, I have discovered a concerning trend. These leaders have expressed their belief that district leaders are paying themselves exorbitant salaries, especially when considering their poor performance as leaders. It seems that there are too many cooks in the kitchen, with highly paid individuals micromanaging the very people who already possess the necessary expertise to fulfill their roles effectively.

Simply lowering the grading standards and passing students who have not fully grasped the curriculum will not lead to the production of more capable graduates. It is disheartening to see a significant number of students struggling to read and write at levels expected of elementary school students. This approach of dumbing down the educational standards does not contribute to the overall strength of our society.

The individuals responsible for overseeing the education system ought to feel a sense of embarrassment, given the disappointing outcomes and the difficulties they encounter in recruiting sufficient personnel. However, it appears that they remain unfazed by these challenges. This lack of concern stems from the fact that, as I have previously mentioned, they are unaware of effective strategies. If, by chance, they do possess this knowledge and intentionally choose not to adopt successful approaches, it may lend credibility to certain conspiracy theories.

In order to bring about change and align our education system with our values, it is crucial for everyone to actively participate in the decision-making process. This requires more than just a one-time protest or expressing concerns during a school board meeting. We need to develop a sustained effort to hold school boards accountable and make informed decisions during elections. Its time to micro-manage the decision makers.

One of the challenges we face is resistance from school boards that may try to silence vocal parents. However, we have seen that when parents come together and inform local news outlets about the challenges faced by our district, it can draw attention to the actions of school board members who often operate in anonymity. By shining a light on their decisions and actions, we can create awareness and push for change. Maybe it's time to bring back good old-fashioned shaming.

Additionally, it is important to hold administrations accountable at the district level. Flood their phone lines with complaints and make it clear that the community is dissatisfied. Furthermore, we should consider the impact of student enrollment or attendance on school funding. If parents start removing their children from underper-forming schools, it will send a powerful message and force schools to take action. Too many parents who are dissatis-fied with education are also too complacent when it comes to taking action.

If the head of the district does not respond or implement positive changes, attending board meetings and demanding their removal becomes necessary. Our determination and persistence will demonstrate that we will not settle for anything less than the improvements our district's schools need.

Many school boards and districts underestimate the resolve of parents and believe they can pacify them long enough for their demands to fade away. It is crucial to prove them wrong by showing up at board meetings with a list of specific changes that the community wants to see and posing challenging questions regarding the lack of progress in education and test scores. By holding everyone accountable, we can ensure that these positions are not merely a source of easy money with little or no responsibility.

It is disheartening to see that very few people actually hold school board members accountable for falling grades and test scores. We need to demand answers and ask what they are doing to address these issues. We cannot allow them to shift blame onto others or claim that the students and parents are the real problems. The majority of parents want their children to receive a good education and do not want the district to fail them.

This is why school choice and vouchers are important additions to the education landscape in all states. Just like we vote with our feet when we receive poor service or products, parents should have the ability to seek a better education for their children. School choice and vouchers provide parents with options and the means to choose a better education for their children.

The education system should be more than just another government agency lacking care, competition, and accountability. It is crucial to advocate for positive change and ensure that the education system caters to the needs of our children, communities, and the future of our country. It is concerning when district administrators introduce curriculum that does not align with the district's population or allow schools to support or promote transitioning without parental consent. Furthermore, it is important to address the issue of inappropriate books in schools and the use of bathrooms by individuals who identify as a different gender than their biological sex. We must express our concerns and opinions loudly, without advocating for violence but utilizing the leverage of the community and parents. If we choose not to permit our daughters to compete against biological males in sports, we run the risk of hindering female representation in school sports. However, by taking a stand, we can encourage schools to acknowledge the importance of supporting girls in sports without compromising their safety. Schools would be compelled to address the issue and make necessary changes to ensure that girls can actively participate in sports while feeling safe and respected.

The absence of female representation in sports would not be the desired outcome, but it would provoke necessary conversations and actions from the schools. These discussions would aim return sports to a state of common sense, allowing our daughters to compete on a level playing field and showcase their talents without fear of injury.

It is therefore necessary to make our voices heard and demand the necessary changes in the education system. And if no is the answer then we should do as the teachers have been doing. Teachers have been voting with their feet; now it's time for the people in the communities to vote with theirs before the entire education system crashes.

If you think my concerns about the education system are exaggerated and a potential crash seems unlikely, consider the following data, which we have already discussed in this book. According to a survey conducted in November 2022, a significant 48 percent of teachers had contemplated changing jobs in the past month, a substantial increase from the previous figure of 32 percent in June 2021. To compound this issue, the Economic Policy Institute estimates that there are currently approximately 118,000 vacant teaching positions throughout the country. This shortfall is projected to rise to 200,000 by 2025. It is worth noting that the school-age population is expected to grow by an additional 1 million children by 2030, largely due to immigration. As a result, the number of students is set to increase significantly. So, the question arises: who will educate these students if we are projected to lose even more teachers? With this forecast, the existing problem will only worsen as we lose teachers while simultaneously accommodating more students. Some optimistic individuals may put their faith in technology to resolve this issue, but implementing such a solution comes with its own set of challenges. Imagine a scenario where technology is responsible for instructing students to be quiet or return to their seats. Clearly, this is not an ideal approach. However, until substantial changes are made to attract qualified individuals to the teaching profession, we may witness a surge in attempts to address this predicament through the use of technology. It remains to be seen whether this approach will prove effective in the long run. Meanwhile, in the immediate term, the pressing need for competent teachers persists.

21

SOLUTIONS

Never stop learning, because life never stop teaching - Proverbs

To write a book that solely identifies problems and points fingers at individuals would leave readers questioning whether the author believes in the possibility of saving our education system. As mentioned at the beginning of the book, it is evident that public education in this country is in dire need of a comprehensive overhaul. However, implementing such changes would be challenging, as many individuals benefit from the current state of affairs and lack the motivation to initiate any reforms. If there were a genuine desire for change, we would have already witnessed progress. Regrettably, those in charge of our public education system seem to repeat the same mistakes and make ill-informed decisions year after year. It is almost as if they are trapped in a cycle of repetition; as the saying goes: "Insanity is doing the same thing over and over again and expecting different results." By the way, a book on education should correct the quote being attributed to Einstein because he never actually made that statement.

Based on my observations and discussions with educators, I have identified some fundamental aspects that could immediately make a significant difference and would be warmly received by teachers. Throughout my research and introspection, while writing this book, I have developed several suggestions. Many of these focus on alleviating the pressure and stress faced by teachers, who are entrusted with the important task of educating our children. I hope that parents, upon reaching this point in the book, begin to realize the extent of the challenges faced by teachers. It is crucial that we have a system where teachers feel valued and are not burdened with tasks that are beyond their scope of responsibility. Making these changes would have a profound impact on improving the overall educational experience.

If we are to stem the attrition of both experienced and new teachers, it is imperative that we reduce their workload and alleviate the stress associated with the profession. It saddens me to read about the teacher shortages and the increasing number of teachers leaving the profession on a daily basis. Yet, it is disheartening that very few districts are willing to acknowledge these issues and actively seek solutions. In fact, most district administrators exploit the high attrition rate as a plea for additional funding despite the fact that this money rarely benefits the educators themselves. Instead, the funds are often used to employ more individuals who further add pressure to an already challenging environment, thereby exacerbating the problem at hand.

It should come as no surprise that while private school teachers may earn less money, they are often more satisfied with their work. This is not to say that I am promoting lower salaries for teachers; rather, I am advocating for a reduction in the workload and stress levels of public school teachers.

One of the main reasons why private school teachers report higher job satisfaction is due to the freedom they have to teach and adapt their methods to the needs of their students. This flexibility is highly valued and contributes to a more positive teaching experience. Interestingly enough, implementing similar changes in public school districts would require minimal effort.

Cutting the Curriculum in Half

Maybe half is a bit excessive, but it is crucial to revise and streamline the curriculum in order to better serve today's students. While district leaders may have good intentions with regard to social education, it is important to recognize that this responsibility primarily lies with parents and families. Requiring thousands of teachers across the country to teach social issues can lead to a wide range of interpretations and perspectives on what is right and wrong, including among the teachers themselves. I have spoken to numerous teachers who express discomfort with certain mandates related to social-emotional learning (SEL). It seems odd to ask math or science teachers to teach lessons on social values when their expertise lies elsewhere. Consider the people you work with or live near and the diverse range of personal values they hold. Designing a curriculum that accommodates such broad interpretations can be challenging. Even within my own extended family, there are individuals who hold social values or beliefs that differ from my wife and I. While we love them as family, we do not wish for them to impose their values on our children. Let math and science teachers focus on teaching math and science, which have concrete right and wrong answers that can be agreed upon.

Another aspect to consider is the information overload that students face. Much of the math and writing curriculum taught in elementary school today was introduced much later in the past. For example, some math lessons that fourth graders now learn were not taught until ninth grade in the 1980s. Elementary students today have several more years before they embark on their careers. It would be beneficial to reduce the rigor of the curriculum so that they can thoroughly grasp foundational math concepts before moving on to more advanced topics such as Slope Intercept Form, which is now taught in some fifth grades. Math, in particular, builds upon itself, and a solid understanding of multiplication and division is essential for proficiency in algebra. Given the prevalence of computers and advanced smartphones, it is unnecessary to require sixth graders to reason abstractly and quantitatively when they lack real-world experiences to fully comprehend its significance or how it will be applicable in their adult lives.

Perhaps one reason for the decline in math scores is that students are grappling with problems that are too complex for their cognitive abilities, leading them to disengage and believe that they have no chance of mastering the curriculum. It is ironic that educators continue to increase the rigor of math instruction at a time when most students will rely on computers to solve problems in

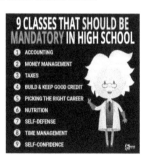

437

their chosen career or trade. Let's not overwhelm young minds with excessive information and limit math requirements to basic geometry and algebra. Similar to college, any math beyond that level should be elective based on the student's interests and intended career path. This approach allows students who excel in math to explore more advanced concepts, while those who have no interest in higher-level math can avoid the frustration of poor grades in a subject they struggle to comprehend. It is disheartening to see millions of students graduate each year having learned math lessons they will likely never encounter again until they are forced to relearn them to assist their own children with math.

If the goal is to cultivate well-rounded students, high schools could offer classes that align with potential career paths. In fact, let them explore classes for different career choices. In many cases, advanced math does not contribute significantly to students' future success. However, for those interested in pursuing careers in engineering or other fields heavily reliant on math or statistics, it is essential to provide the necessary courses to support their ambitions.

Let's make some changes to the curriculum by removing certain classes and adding ones that will truly have a positive impact on our students' lives. When I was in school, we had an economics class that taught us how to balance a checkbook. This was a crucial skill back then because there were no banking apps or software to keep track of our checking accounts. However, times have changed, and there are now many other skills that young adults need to learn in order to thrive in today's world.

If the purpose of education is to prepare students for their future, then it's important to educate them on subjects that are relevant to their lives. For example, classes on staying healthy, time management, credit, and money management would be much more beneficial than trigonometry. Additionally, teaching high school-age students about investing and saving could provide them with valuable knowledge and skills that will have a lasting impact on their financial well-being.

By updating our curriculum to include these practical and essential life skills, we can ensure that our students are better equipped to navigate the challenges and opportunities that lie ahead. It's time to prioritize education that truly prepares our students for success in all aspects of life, not just academically.

Teacher Board of Directors

I have to assume that administrators of school districts would strongly oppose the implementation of including teachers on a board of advisors, as it would potentially diminish their power. However, I firmly believe that incorporating teachers into the decision-making process would yield significant benefits. Drawing inspiration from corporate practices, my proposal is to establish a board of directors composed of experienced teachers who have taught in the district for more than ten years. This representative board would hold the authority to vote on critical matters, such as curriculum decisions, spending measures, and budgetary items that directly impact the district schools.

While some districts already involve educators on their boards, these individuals often hold limited influence, with their votes merely "taken into advisement" or restricted to a narrow range of options. In contrast, my vision is to ensure that every school within the district is represented on the board of directors, guaranteeing that the voices of teachers from all corners of the district are heard and valued

In practical terms, this system would require district administrators to present their cases to the board of directors. By doing so, teachers would have an opportunity to actively participate in decisions that directly affect them. Additionally, teachers in the district would have the privilege to vote for educators from each school to serve as their representatives on the board. This inclusive approach would prevent teachers from feeling uninformed about spending, grant, and hiring decisions and instead empower them to actively shape these choices.

For example, in a scenario where a teacher believes that allocating additional funds towards hiring more special education teachers is crucial, they could exercise their voting power to reject a spending item until such allocation is made. This would enable teachers to genuinely influence decisions and advocate for their specific needs within the district. By modeling our education system after corporate governance, where CEOs or presidents must adhere to the decisions of the board of directors, we can truly empower teachers and ensure their voices are not only heard but also respected in the decision-making process.

Parent Book Approval

Throughout the United States and Canada, there has been a significant number of parents voicing their concerns about inappropriate books and materials in libraries. The controversy revolves around books that many reasonable and well-balanced individuals believe are too sexually explicit for both high school students and elementary-age children. Without passing judgment, I decided to examine some of these debated books for myself. To my disbelief, what I saw and read was completely inappropriate for elementary school students, let alone a high school student.

Let's break down this issue into smaller components. Many of the books that have sparked parental outrage contain extremely graphic sexual content. I personally believe that even the depiction of two people making love is inappropriate for students in kindergarten through eighth grade. If that were the extent of the content, one could argue for its inclusion in higher grade levels. However, these books go well beyond that. They describe and depict explicit acts such as blow jobs, anal sex, sex toys, and multiple sex partners to children who are below the age of 10. These materials are far beyond what would be acceptable in an elementary school setting, and reading and showing such content a few years ago to underage kids would certainly lead to legal consequences.

So, how is it that adults in the education sector are not only allowing this but also promoting and defending it? At school board meetings across the nation, which can be viewed on platforms like YouTube, outraged parents attempt to read excerpts from these books to the board members, only to be shut down and, in some cases, even arrested. I find this aspect of the issue truly perplexing and view it as a disturbing force aimed at robbing our children of their innocence or worse.

There is an abundance of data from numerous studies that highlight the negative effects of children being exposed to sexual content at too early an age. This alone should be enough to prevent any school or school board from allowing such materials through their doors. The consequences that may arise from continuing this trend can be seen in the lives of those who have grown up in sexually abusive environments or have fallen victim to sex trafficking, which has been on the rise over the past decade.

One cannot help but wonder if the goal is to encourage early sexual activity among children. If that is not the case, then what exactly is the goal? Despite passionate arguments from parents who wish to have these types of books banned from school libraries, school board members throughout the country have yet to provide a single scientifically sound study that justifies the inclusion of sexually explicit material in educational settings.

Parents already face challenges in shielding their children from age-inappropriate content on various media platforms, such as television, phones, and videos. Now, they find themselves unable to trust their local schools to do the same. It is disheartening to see how much trust the administrations have lost due to this issue, and the concerns voiced by the people are valid.

In light of the current circumstances, I propose the implementation of a comprehensive book selection system that empowers parents to actively participate in the decision-making process for their children's school libraries and classrooms. This system would consist of a carefully curated book list that parents can review and vote on each school year, ensuring that their preferences and values are taken into account. To facilitate a streamlined and efficient process, a line-by-line voting system would be established, allowing parents to provide their input on each book individually.

While some schools may express concerns about the potentially time-consuming nature of this process, it is important to highlight that with the right strategies in place, any challenges can be overcome. For instance, books that have received approval in previous years could be exempted from the voting process, saving both time and resources. Additionally, leveraging online platforms would enable an automated counting system, ensuring that the voting results are accurately recorded and swiftly implemented.

Defending Parents Rights

How about implementing a national "Defense of Parenting Act" that aims to provide clear guidelines regarding the authority of parents or guardians in making decisions related to the physical, medical, and therapeutic aspects of their child's life? This act would ensure that all such choices are solely the responsibility of the parents or guardians, excluding any involvement from the school. In addition to parental rights, it could also include provisions for parent book approval. The inclusion of these measures in the act would strengthen the legal assurance for parents and guardians, affirming their role as the ultimate decision-makers in matters concerning their child's well-being.

Enacting the "Defense of Parenting Act" would not only emphasize the importance of parental rights but also establish a protective measure to prevent schools from overstepping their boundaries and interfering in matters that should be solely within the purview of parents or guardians. By providing a clear framework that defines the rights of parents or guardians and sets appropriate boundaries for educational institutions, this act would ensure that parents and guardians have the final say in their child's upbringing and development.

In addition to protecting parental authority, the "Defense of Parenting Act" would also foster better communication and collaboration between parents or guardians and schools. By clearly outlining the responsibilities of each party, the act would encourage open dialogue and mutual respect, ultimately benefiting the child's educational experience.

Furthermore, implementing this act would alleviate the burden on teachers who may be reluctant to be involved in making significant decisions and attempting to conceal those decisions from parents. It is unfair to ask teachers to mediate such decisions, let alone keep them hidden from the very parents they regularly engage with. By relieving teachers of these administrative responsibilities and eliminating the expectation of secrecy, we can establish a more transparent and collaborative relationship between teachers, parents, and school administration. This would create a harmonious and open educational environment where everyone works together in the best interest of the students.

When it comes to gaining support for a parental rights act, it is crucial to remind politicians and administrators of their role as public servants and the importance of the taxpayers who fund their salaries. The term "public servant" carries a significant meaning, and it is essential to emphasize their duty to the people they serve and the significance of honoring the rights of parents. By doing so, we can build a stronger foundation for the enactment of a parental rights act that safeguards the well-being of families and upholds the core values of our society.

Introducing a parental rights act would not only address the aforementioned issues but also contribute significantly to the overall well-being of families. Such an act would provide a protective framework that safeguards the rights of parents or guardians and reinforces their crucial role in their child's life. It would serve as a constant reminder that decisions pertaining to a child's physical, medical, and therapeutic needs should always be made by those who possess the most intimate knowledge of the child - their parents or guardians.

Freedom of Choice

It is of utmost importance that parents have the freedom to choose alternative options for their children's education in cases where their current schools are not performing well. As parents, we deeply care about the well-being and future success of our children, and it is only fair that we have access to a range of educational choices. These alternatives include vouchers, charter schools, private schools, and even homeschooling. We all strive to provide our children with the best possible opportunities and environments for success in life. It is only natural that we want our kids to be in the most favorable situation to flourish academically and personally. No parent would willingly reject the chance to improve their child's circumstances in order to uphold a rigid belief about their local school.

If you are opposed to the idea of parental choice, I urge you to consider the last statement I made and imagine if your own child was attending a subpar school. Interestingly, when researching individuals who opposed school choice, it was primarily teachers' unions and residents of affluent neighborhoods who voiced their dissent. Strikingly, I never came across any commentator living in an inner-city area arguing that everyone should be compelled to attend under-performing schools that failed to provide a quality education for the local children. Likewise, I never encountered a comment from individuals living below the middle-class threshold suggesting that they preferred their children to remain uneducated.

Why is it that a significant number of affluent pundits oppose school choice? Could it be that they fear the loss of exclusivity that some of these educational options provide? In many cases, they will still possess the financial means to afford superior private schools compared to their lower-income counterparts. At the same time, this may sound like a discourse on class politics; rest assured that it is not. As a proponent of capitalism and an advocate against class warfare, I firmly believe that denying parents the right to enhance their children's education and opportunities is fundamentally unjust. While I acknowledge that the majority of affluent individuals in our society genuinely desire equal opportunities for all children, I find it disheartening that some members of the elite hold a contrary stance on school choice, as if they wouldn't make the decision to relocate their own children if their enrolled school suddenly failed to adequately educate them or became unsafe.

And this is precisely what most parents are requesting—simply the ability to exercise choice for their children. I cannot fathom a compelling reason why a parent should be denied this right. Empowering parents is the most effective way to increase their satisfaction with the education system in our country. If they are dissatisfied with the presence of inappropriate content in the library, for example, they should have the freedom to move their child to a school that aligns with their values. I have witnessed parents fight tooth and nail to secure a spot on a better baseball team for their children, and I am confident that they will go to great lengths to ensure their kids have access to superior educational institutions. This will undoubtedly put underperforming school districts on notice, compelling them to improve their standards and accountability.

A federally mandated policy that prevents states from limiting or restricting parents from exercising all options available to increase their child's chances of academic success is crucial to empowering parents. Such a policy would allow parents to have complete control over their child's education and choose the best educational path for them. States that have already implemented school choice and voucher systems have experienced significant success. The feedback from the population in these states has been overwhelmingly positive. Parents appreciate having the freedom to select schools that align with their values and meet their child's specific needs. They value the ability to explore different educational approaches, such as charter schools, magnet schools, or private schools, that may provide a more tailored and effective learning environment. Parents have seen the positive impact of having options and the ability to make informed decisions about their child's education. By implementing a federally mandated policy, we can ensure that parents in all states have equal access to educational options and can make the best choices for their children. This policy will empower parents to take an active role in their child's education and give them the opportunity to provide the education that best suits their child's individual needs. Ultimately, this will contribute to improving overall academic outcomes and ensuring that every child has the chance to succeed.

At a Lawrence Township Board of Education meeting on

October 19, 2022, lawyer John Comegno said the right of parents "is not to dictate what their children are taught, it is to determine where they attend."

"In public schools, we have a curriculum that is aligned with New Jersey state learning standards," Comegno said.

"But please know... if your students attend these public schools, they're going to be instructed in this curriculum, which is consistent with state learning standards," he continued. "That's not binding. If you choose to have your child attend elsewhere, that's your right. That's your right as a parent."

Exactly. That's your right as a parent; I couldn't have said it better myself.

Kangaroo Courts

During my time playing baseball, I came to a realization that my lack of height and speed would hinder my chances of securing a million-dollar contract. One interesting practice we had on the team was what we called a "kangaroo court." This involved conducting informal hearings amongst teammates to address any infractions or poor efforts within our team. What made this process unique was that it was entirely driven by our peers, with no involvement from team leaders or coaches. The jury, consisting of our fellow players, had the sole responsibility of determining the punishment or outcome.

Building on this concept, I have also contemplated the differences between effective and less effective teachers in my book. From my observations, good teachers are aware of colleagues who may not perform up to par, but they are hesitant to call them out publicly. Why not consider implementing a "kangaroo court" approach within schools? Teachers could form small groups comprising representatives with the most seniority from their school, with each grade level having a voice if it's an elementary school. These groups would conduct hearings to address issues with underperforming teachers. The purpose of these hearings would be to provide teachers with an opportunity to explain themselves and potentially receive a warning or appropriate action, as determined by their fellow educators.

A similar form of informal accountability already exists in some corporations. I have witnessed similar discussions taking place in boardrooms, where team members are expected to explain why their numbers, efforts, or output fall short of expectations. This open dialogue allows the rest of the team to contribute their thoughts and opinions on the provided answers or excuses.

Translating this concept to teachers, while they may not have the authority to enforce consequences themselves, they could issue warnings and recommend appropriate disciplinary actions to the school administration. These disciplinary actions could range from a temporary setback in climbing the leadership ladder to the assignment of additional responsibilities on various committees. Of course, these meetings would be confidential to promote open and honest communication among peers who share the same responsibilities.

Let's consider a scenario as an example: a teacher consistently fails to maintain comprehensive records for Response to Intervention (RTI) meetings, intentionally avoids transferring students to special education to avoid additional workload, and passes students who clearly do not meet grading standards. In such cases, a group of fellow teachers could come together to address this concerning trend. They would highlight the fact that a significant number of students progress to the next grade level without achieving grades that accurately reflect their understanding of the curriculum.

It is important to acknowledge that inadequate record-keeping for RTI meetings can have serious consequences. These meetings play a crucial role in identifying students who require additional support and intervention to address learning gaps. Without detailed records, it becomes challenging to assess the effectiveness of interventions and track students' progress over time. Consequently, students in need of special education services may not receive the timely support necessary for their success.

Furthermore, when teachers choose to pass students who have not met grading standards, it undermines the integrity of the educational system. It sends a message that academic achievement can be compromised and that students can progress without truly mastering the required knowledge and skills.

A collective of like-minded individuals can play a vital role in tackling these challenges. It becomes more challenging to rationalize subpar performance to your peers, who are doing the same job. I firmly believe that if teachers who were not giving their best knew they would be held accountable to their colleagues, there would be fewer problems to address.

In my opinion, if teachers were aware that their peers paid attention to their commitment levels and ability to address underlying problems, few would risk being called out by their colleagues. Currently, teachers who fail to put in the necessary effort or pass students without fulfilling their responsibilities often go unchallenged and unaccountable. Which means there is a lack of accountability.

Let Teachers Teach

In addition to all the previous points, it is essential to prioritize allowing teachers to teach in a way that aligns with their expertise and experience. This approach is crucial if we want to prevent them from leaving the profession and even entice experienced teachers to return. The valuable insight that seasoned educators constantly provide is a testament to the knowledge and skills necessary to instruct their students effectively.

Therefore, it is imperative that we cease imposing new methodologies, curricula, and stringent requirements that limit their ability to adapt their teaching styles to suit the needs of their classes. Instead, we should focus on communicating the desired learning outcomes for each grade level and granting teachers the freedom to impart these lessons in their own unique ways.

When we look at corporations and small businesses, we observe leaders who invest time and money into providing continuous education and training to their staff. They offer classes and expose their employees to new techniques and ideas shared by experts who have achieved remarkable success with these approaches. By adopting a similar approach in the education sector, we can provide teachers with a range of strategies to experiment with, allowing them to integrate new ideas into their existing repertoire. Through this collaborative process, we can share relevant research findings and encourage them to blend these insights with their own tried-and-tested methods.

There may be debate as to whether educational administrators genuinely believe that the constant introduction of new curricula and teaching methods is essential for improving educational outcomes or if they are simply motivated by securing grant funding or spending on programs to satisfy a spending requirement. Nevertheless, we must find a balance. When conversing with teachers, it becomes evident that the overwhelming majority express their frustration with the frequent changes, which were once less frequent occurrences.

At the end of the day, most teachers possess degrees in education, and many have even pursued master's degrees in this field. Their extensive education equips them with knowledge about effective pedagogy, child psychology, and the latest research on how young minds process information, alongside numerous other education-related subjects. Therefore, it is disheartening when educators inform me that the directives they receive from their school districts contradict the principles they learned throughout their extensive training.

As Margaret "Macke" Raymond of Stanford University stated, The flexibility that Charter Schools offer enables educators to explore different approaches and experiment with new ideas, ultimately leading to improved outcomes for students." So why can't public schools see the correlation?

This book consistently emphasizes the importance of experienced teachers' ability to effectively teach and connect with students possessing diverse personalities and varying levels of comprehension. If we strive to enhance teachers' job satisfaction, it is of utmost importance to allow them to apply their expertise. Although this approach may not single-handedly resolve all the issues that contribute to declining teacher morale, it is a significant step in the right direction. Ultimately, embracing this approach will not only benefit teachers but also facilitate improved education for our children.

Give the Teachers Resources

A recent survey conducted by the Grattan Institute, involving 5,442 Australian teachers and school leaders, shed light on a pressing issue in the education sector. The survey, conducted for the comprehensive report titled "Making Time for Great Teaching: A Guide for Principals", highlighted the importance of addressing the lack of teaching materials and resources available to educators.

The findings of the research illustrate the challenges faced by teachers in Australia when it comes to allocating sufficient time for lesson preparation. The excessive amount of time spent searching for suitable resources hampers their ability to deliver high-quality instruction effectively. This predicament emphasizes the need for action to alleviate the burden on teachers.

One of the key recommendations outlined in the report is for school leaders to proactively acquire teaching materials. These materials include worksheets, workbooks, and online resources that can assist teachers in their lesson planning and delivery. By providing educators with the necessary tools, school leaders can enable teachers to focus on what they do best: teaching. This approach mirrors the days of textbooks, where teachers had readily available resources to support their instruction.

Interestingly, the United States faces a similar problem in its education landscape. As discussed in previous chapters, many states grapple with a scarcity of teaching resources. As a result, teachers often have to resort to purchasing their own materials or creating resources from scratch. This additional burden detracts from their main role as educators. By relieving teachers of this task and ensuring they have access to adequate resources, we can restore their focus on teaching.

Beyond the individual benefits to teachers, the proactive provision of teaching resources can also have wider impacts. Adopting the practice of districts providing teaching resources, as was done in the past, can ensure uniformity and synchronicity in the materials used across schools and grade levels. This harmonization facilitates consistency in curriculum delivery and fosters a cohesive learning experience for students.

In conclusion, addressing the inadequacy of teaching resources is crucial for enhancing the teaching profession and improving instructional quality. By equipping educators with the necessary tools, we can alleviate their burden and create a conducive environment for effective teaching and learning.

Accountability Laws

In corporate America, the consequences for CEOs or managers who fail to act in the best interest of the company or maintain positive growth are clear - they are fired.

However, the same cannot be said for the government sector. Historically, government bureaucracies have not been structured to hold individuals accountable in the same way. As a result, many government agencies continue to underperform or fail to produce desirable results.

When it comes to education, the success of our children and the future of our country are directly linked. Unfortunately, the individuals responsible for managing education at the state or district level often hold their positions for years, with little consequence for the performance of the school system under their watch. This presents a problem that can be remedied with a simple change.

I propose that states or the federal government implement an accountability law that mandates districts to maintain or improve the quality of education they provide to their communities. If a district fails to meet this standard for three consecutive years, they should be automatically removed from their positions. Prior to that, a warning should be issued in the second year, putting the district superintendent on notice that a third year of failure will result in their removal.

To further strengthen this law, school board members - the individuals most people vote for but often know little about - should be disqualified from running for re-election if their district fails to produce positive results for three years of their four-year term.

Let's be clear. These individuals are compensated well enough that we should expect them to actively drive positive change rather than merely collect a paycheck and claim they've done all they can. By implementing a law like this, we can expect to see common-sense changes quickly return to the education system. The unintended consequence would be that superintendents would not allow underperforming school administrators to remain in their positions, as their failures could lead to their own job loss. This would eliminate complacency in district offices and foster a sense of urgency to get things done.

Of course, for this law to come into effect, it would need to be voted on and passed at a higher level, as district leaders are unlikely to willingly adopt such changes, considering most of them know each other and have personal relationships. Additionally, if a district loses students to school choice programs because they are unable to provide adequate support and resources to their schools and teachers, that should also count against them.

Tenure

In discussing the improvement of an organization, it is worth considering the idea of eliminating teachers' unions, although it must be acknowledged that achieving this would require significant effort and is unlikely to happen easily. However, a good starting point for reform could be the concept of tenure, which is often heavily advocated for by unions in states where they have collective bargaining agreements or strong union influence. Granting tenure to K-12 teachers is a questionable practice that merits examination.

Currently, tenure ensures that teachers, regardless of their performance after being granted tenure, remain in their positions permanently until they choose to retire. This policy effectively guarantees job security, even for individuals who may not demonstrate continued effectiveness in their roles.

The notion of tenure in the education sector is quite peculiar, as no private companies or corporations, where employee evaluation and accountability are essential practices, have adopted such a system. Implementing policies that prevent annual assessments and the ability to evaluate whether employees contribute positively to their work and the organization as a whole is illogical.

There are unintended consequences associated with tenure, such as the potential for employees to lose their motivation or adopt a complacent mindset rooted in the knowledge that they cannot be terminated. This can result in minimal effort and a decline in job performance. Additionally, in states where tenure is granted to K-12 employees, there have been numerous instances of teachers who required removal from the classroom but were instead placed in "rubber rooms" for years while their cases were litigated and appealed. The financial burden placed on taxpayers in these states due to such incidents is significant, amounting to millions of dollars.

It is imperative that we put an end to this practice and adopt a more effective approach. Eliminating tenure would not only lead to cost savings for the states where this practice persists but also expedite the process of removing underperforming teachers from the payroll, ultimately benefiting the education system as a whole.

Feed the Students Better

In considering the well-being of students, it is crucial to prioritize providing food options that promote healthy brain function and align with the healthy eating habits taught in most health classes. It is imperative to remove foods from school lunchrooms that contribute to increased glycemic load and subsequent crashes or decreased attention. By collaborating with chefs, schools, states, or the federal government, could develop lunch plates that prioritize both health and taste, even if they come at a slightly higher cost. Ensuring that students receive sufficient protein and vegetables, rather than excessive sugar and empty carbohydrates, is essential for their overall development and academic performance.

Multiple studies have conclusively demonstrated the importance of maintaining a nutritious diet for children, especially during their elementary school years. It is essential to discourage elementary school students from opting for snacks instead of consuming real, wholesome food. Some schools resort to selling snacks to generate additional revenue, but this practice creates a conflict of interest as it undermines the goal of promoting healthy eating habits. To address this issue, parents must actively demand that schools allocate more funds towards providing better quality food for their children.

While some districts aim to oversee students' overall health, they perpetuate the problem by serving food that contributes to obesity and other long-term health issues. It is necessary to rectify this disparity, and the onus falls on parents to advocate for improved food options in schools. By implementing a more efficient management structure and reallocating funds from excessively high salaries, the districts will be able to find the necessary resources to cover the additional expenses.

Finally

In this book, I won't dwell on all the points already made, but my hope is that education experiences a new renaissance. It would be worthwhile if this book leads to positive changes, considering the countless hours I invested in researching and putting it together. However, what matters most to me is not whose book or ideas are used to fix education but rather the strength and pride of our education system as a nation. Unfortunately, at present, it is a significant letdown for many.

There will inevitably be those who disagree with specific points or even the entire book, but I assure you that my words and intentions are sincere. Despite my own children having grown up and embarked on their journey to adulthood, I aspire for my grandchildren to receive the best education possible and become well-rounded individuals.

Perhaps our greatest hope lies in our leaders listening to our demands for positive change that leads to tangible improvements. While our country undeniably has its flaws and complex history, it remains the desired destination for countless individuals around the world. Regrettably, this fact seems to go unnoticed by those who disparage the country. Having had the privilege of traveling extensively within the United States and numerous other countries, I can confidently affirm that my children were fortunate to be born here. I used to remind them of this when they still resided at home.

Our country is a true melting pot, and it should continually astound us that it functions on a daily basis without devolving into countless conflicts. This is the beauty observed by those who love it here, as well as those who have found a new homeland that allows them freedom and the opportunity to pursue their goals and aspirations. It is disheartening to realize that the individuals who love our country most are often those who have recently arrived. They know firsthand what life was like in the countries they left behind, giving them a genuine appreciation for how blessed most Americans are, even when we fail to recognize it or take it for granted.

Let us set a goal to transform our education system into something we can be proud of and boast about. Achieving this would be a monumental accomplishment for our children and future generations.

GLOSSARY

Academic Year - The period of formal instruction, which is usually September to May. It may be divided into terms of varying lengths, such as semesters, trimesters, or quarters.

ACT - A set of college admissions tests and the organization that makes them, the American College Testing Program, located in Iowa City, Iowa. Most colleges now accept either the SAT or the ACT for admissions purposes.

Alternative Schools - An alternative school is an educational setting designed to accommodate educational, behavioral, and/or medical needs of children and adolescents that cannot be adequately addressed in a traditional school environment.

Assessment - Another name for a test. An assessment can also be a system for testing and evaluating students, groups of students, schools, or districts. Summative assessments measure how well students have mastered the content standards at the end of a course or school year. However schools also use formative or diagnostic assessments to evaluate how well the student is learning the material throughout the period of instruction.

Autism - A neurodevelopment condition of variable severity with lifelong effects that can be recognized from early childhood, chiefly characterized by difficulties with social interaction and communication and by restricted or repetitive patterns of thought and behavior.

Average Daily Attendance - The total number of days of student attendance divided by the total number of days in the regular school year. A student attending every day would equal one ADA. ADA is not the same as enrollment, which is the number of students enrolled in each school and district. (Enrollment is determined by counting students on a given day in October.) ADA usually is lower than enrollment due to factors such as students moving, dropping out, or staying home due to illness. The state uses a school district's ADA to determine its funding.

Benchmark - A detailed description of a specific level of student achievement expected of students at particular ages, grades, or developmental levels. Benchmarks are often represented by samples of student work. A set of benchmarks can be used as checkpoints to monitor progress in meeting performance goals within and across grade levels.

Charter School - A public school operated independently under a performance agreement with a school district, a county office of education (COE), or the State Board of Education. Charter schools are funded on a per-pupil basis, freed from most state regulations that apply to school districts and COEs, usually able to hire their own teachers and other staff, and subject to closure if they fail to meet their promises for student outcomes. Charter schools were originally authorized in California in 1992 (Senate Bill 1448).

Charter School Lottery - A charter school lottery is a random selection process by which applicants are admitted to a charter school to ensure that all applicants that do not have an enrollment priority have an equal chance of being admitted. A charter school must conduct a lottery if more students apply for admission to the charter school than can be admitted.

Combined Schools - Schools that combine elementary and middle school under one roof or location.

Common Core - The Common Core State Standards, often referred to as "Common Core" are a set of educational standards that describe what students should know and be able to do in English language arts and math in each grade from kindergarten through 12th grade. California is among the more than 40 states that have adopted them in an effort to establish clear, consistent educational standards across state lines.

Credentialing - A process, implemented by the state Commission on Teaching Credentialing (CTC), to certify that teachers are well prepared to enter the classroom. Most candidates must have earned a bachelor's degree in a non-education major, passed the California Basic Educational Skills Test (CBEST), and demonstrated subject-matter competence by either passing approved college courses or the state's subject-matter exam. In addition, they must complete graduate coursework that includes classroom study and student teaching. At the end of this time, the candidate earns a Preliminary Credential, after which time the teacher has five years to earn the Professional Clear Credential by completing additional professional coursework. There are alternative routes to earning a credential, such as internship programs.

Criterion-Referenced Test - A test that measures specific performance or content standards, often along a continuum from total lack of skill to excellence. These tests can also have cut scores that determine whether a test-taker has passed or failed the test or has basic, proficient, or advanced skills. Criterion-referenced tests, unlike norm-referenced assessments, are not primarily created to compare students to each other. The goal is typically to have everyone attain a passing mark.

Critical Race Theory - A set of ideas holding that racial bias is inherent in many parts of western society, especially in its legal and social institutions, on the basis of their having been primarily designed for and implemented by white people.

Curriculum - The courses of study offered by a school or district. California has adopted a set of standards that are intended to guide curriculum and instruction and tests to measure student proficiency on those standards. The state also approves K-8 textbooks that reflect those standards. The ultimate decisions regarding school curriculum, however, are the responsibility of the local school board.

Dropout Rate - The percentage of students that leave the 9-12 instructional system without a high school diploma, GED, or special education certificate of completion and do not remain enrolled after the end of the 4th year. The CDE began using student level data to report a 4-year-cohort dropout rate with the 2009-10 school year.

Early Assessment Program (EAP) - Begun in 2004, the Early Assessment Program (EAP) was developed through a partnership between the California State University (CSU), the California Department of Education, and the California State Board of Education to determine the college readiness of high school students. Students' performance on the state's Smarter Balanced tests can be used by the California State University and the California Community College system to exempt students from college placement tests or let students know that they need additional preparation during their senior year. All students participate in EAP by virtue of completing the Smarter Balanced Summative Assessments for English language arts/literacy and mathematics. Students must authorize the release of their CAASPP (i.e., Smarter Balanced Summative Assessment) results for each assessment to the CSU and CCC systems.

Education Savings Accounts - (ESAs) in K-12 education establish for parents a publicly funded, government-authorized savings account with restricted, but multiple uses for educational purposes. Parents may use the funds to pay for expenses including: school tuition, tutoring, online education programs, therapies for students with special needs, textbooks or other instructional materials, and sometimes, save for college.

EFL - English as a Foreign Language is learning English in a non-English-speaking country. For example, students in China who are learning English are considered EFL students because English is not the country's official language. But if those same students were in the U.S. learning English, they would be regarded as ESL students.

ELL - English Language Learners is commonly used in K-12 environments. However, it has been brought to my attention that some school districts prefer to use the term ESOL (English Speakers of Other Languages) to describe their student population. This could simply be a preference issue.

Equity - The belief that state governments have an obligation to equalize students' access to educational opportunities and thus life chances. During the 1970s and 1980s, many state courts found great disparities in base per-pupil spending between high and low property-wealth districts. They mandated that these funding disparities be eradicated. In placing districts on a level playing field, the courts often invoked equal protection clauses in state constitutions.

ESL - English as a Second Language is learning English in a country where English is dominantly spoken or the official language. For example, students from non-native English-speaking countries who come to the U.S. and Canada for an extended time learn English as a Second Language. They acquire English to communicate in the dominant language spoken in the community where they reside.

ESOL - What is ESOL? The meaning of the initialism ESOL is English to Speakers of Other Languages. It applies to both ESL and EFL contexts. This term was created because some individuals argue that when students are learning English in a native English-speaking country (ESL), these students are not necessarily learning a second language. It could be a student's third or even fourth language. Then, English as a Second Language is limiting and not fully comprehensive in its description.

ESP - English for Special Purposes includes students learning English in the context of a particular field, profession, or topic. For example, when I was teaching legal English in China, I was teaching English in the law context. These students were learning English to study law through an American university where the professors were all native English speakers.

Every Student Succeeds Act (ESSA) - The 2015 reauthorization of the federal Elementary and Secondary Education Act (ESEA), the Every Student Succeeds Act replaces No Child Left Behind (NCLB). Most provisions of ESSA went into effect in 2017-18.

GACE - A framework for statistics education in grades Pre-K–12 published by the American Statistical Association (ASA) in 2007. The foundations for this framework are the Principles and Standards for School Mathematics published by the National Council of Teachers of Mathematics.

Homeschool - To instruct (a pupil, for example) in an educational program outside of established schools, especially in a home.

Inclusion - The practice of placing students with disabilities in regular classrooms. Also known as mainstreaming.

Individualized Education Program (IEP) - A plan developed for a specific student that outlines what that student needs to learn in a specified period of time and what special services need to be provided based on the student's ability. Special Education students have IEPs that sometimes require exemptions from tests or accommodations for testing such as an exam in Braille.

Individuals with Disabilities Education Act (IDEA) - A reauthorization in 1977 of the federal Education For All Handicapped Children Act of 1975. This law guarantees children with exceptional needs a free and appropriate public education and requires that each child's education be determined on an individual basis and designed to meet his or her unique needs in the least restrictive environment. It also establishes procedural rights for parents and children.

National Assessment of Educational Progress (NAEP) - A national test that is given to specific grade levels in specific subjects every other year. A small sample of students representative of the state are tested. NAEP test scores can be compared to national averages.

National Board Certification - A certificate, awarded by the National Board for Professional Teaching Standards, attesting that a teacher possesses the skills and knowledge of accomplished teaching and meets the National Board standards. To earn a certificate, the teacher must complete a rigorous two-part assessment. The candidate must build a portfolio that provides evidence of good teaching practice. Portfolios include videotapes of classroom teaching, lesson plans, student work samples, and self-evaluative essays. In addition, a candidate participates in a day-long evaluation of his or her knowledge of curriculum design, good teaching practice, assessment of student learning, and subject matter. The two-step process takes approximately one academic year, and most candidates spend about 120 hours on assessment activities.

National School Lunch Program - A federal program to provide food-typically lunch and/or breakfast-for students from low-income families. The number of students participating in this free/reduced price meal program is increasingly being used as a way to measure the poverty level of a school or district population. The number of children in this program can affect schools' or districts' eligibility for grants or other funding aimed at helping lower-income families.

No Child Left Behind Act (NCLB) - The 2002 reauthorization of the Elementary and Secondary Education Act (ESEA), which was replaced by the Every Student Succeeds Act in 2015. Originally passed in 1965, ESEA programs provide much of the federal funding for K-12 schools. NCLB's provisions represented a significant change in the federal government's influence in public schools and districts throughout the United States, particularly in terms of assessment, accountability, and teacher quality.

Performance Assessment - A test that requires students to generate a response to a question rather than choose it from a set of possible answers provided for them. Examples of performance assessments (also sometimes referred to as alternative or authentic assessment) include essay questions, portfolios, and demonstrations.

Performance Standards - Standards that describe how well or at what level students should be expected to master the content standards. For example, while content standards may say that all 8th graders should learn Algebra I, performance standards would say what level of mastery of Algebra I is necessary for promotion to the next grade (or for achievement with honors).

PRAXIS - The Praxis test is a set of American teacher certification exams written and administered by the Educational Testing Service.

Primary School - A school usually including the first three grades of elementary school but sometimes also including kindergarten.

Private School - Private, or independent, schools are privately owned and funded without the assistance of local, state or federal governments. Elementary, middle and secondary schools can be private, as can colleges and universities. At private schools, students pay tuition to attend. In contrast, public K-12 schools cost nothing, and public colleges generally offer significantly cheaper tuition than their private counterparts.

Proficiency - Mastery or ability to do something at grade-level. In California, students take California Standards Tests (CSTs) and receive scores that range from "far below basic" to "advanced." The state goal is for all students to score at "proficient" or "advanced."

Retention - The act or policy of holding students back from advancing to the next grade level if they do not meet established performance standards.

Revenues Per Pupil - The total amount of revenues from all sources allocated to K-12 education, divided by the number of students as determined, most often, by average daily attendance (ADA). The formula for revenues per pupil is based on the amount budgeted by the state rather than on what is actually spent by districts and the state to provide services.

RTI - A way to identify and support students who need extra academic or behavioral help to succeed in school. It is a tiered approach because there are various "levels" of support that students move through depending on how much support they need.

SAT - A test administered by the national College Board and widely used throughout the country as a college entrance examination. National and state averages of scores from the SAT I Reasoning Test (formerly called the Scholastic Aptitude Test) are published annually. In California, the University of California system uses an index of SAT I and SAT II (math, English, and a third subject that a student chooses) test scores plus a student's grade point average for admission to its campuses for freshmen. The SAT I is also required for some students seeking admission to the California State University System.

School Board - A locally elected group, usually between three and seven members, who set fiscal, personnel, instructional, and student-related policies. The number of board members relates to the size of the district. A school district governing board also provides direction for the district, hires and fires the district superintendent, and approves the budget and contracts with employee unions. By law, every school district in California is governed by a locally elected school board.

School District - A local education agency directed by an elected local board of education that exists primarily to operate public schools. In California, there are three types of school districts: elementary, high school, and unified. An elementary district is generally kindergarten through eighth grade (K-8); high school is generally grades 9 through 12; unified is kindergarten through 12th grade (K-12).

Scientifically Based Research - Research that involves the application of rigorous, systemic, and objective procedures to obtain reliable and valid knowledge relevant to educational activities and programs.

Special Education - Also known as special-needs education, aided education, alternative provision, exceptional student education, special ed., SDC, or SPED, is the practice of educating students in a way that accommodates their individual differences, disabilities, and special needs.

Standardized Test - A test that is in the same format for all takers. It often relies heavily or exclusively on multiple-choice questions. The testing conditions-including instructions, time limits, and scoring rubrics-are the same for all students, though sometimes accommodations on time limits and instructions are made for disabled students. Reporting of scores to parents, students, or schools is the same. The procedures used for creating the test and analyzing the test results are standardized.

Standards - Degrees or levels of achievement. The "standards movement" began as an informal effort grown out of a concern that American students were not learning enough and that American schools did not have a rigorous curriculum. The U.S. Congress adopted this concept more formally with its 1994 reauthorization of the federal Title I program. See also Content Standards and Performance Standards.

Tax Credits - An amount of money that can be offset against a tax liability.

Tenure - A system of due process and employment guarantee for teachers. After serving a two-year probationary period, teachers are assured continued employment in the school district unless carefully defined procedures for dismissal or layoff are successfully followed.

The Early Intervention Program (EIP) - The Early Intervention Program (EIP) is designed to provide interventions for students who are at risk of not reaching or maintaining their academic grade level based on their performance on state or national assessments or performance measures in English Language Arts/Reading, Mathematics, or both in order to help them meet grade-level expectations within the shortest possible time.

Vouchers - A school voucher is an amount of money provided by the state government to parents for use for private educational programs, such as tuition at private schools. There are two basic ways the state can finance school vouchers, tax credits or Education Savings Accounts (ESAs).

Milton Keynes UK
Ingram Content Group UK Ltd.
UKHW032044180324
439698UK00001B/47